365 MEDITATIONS FOR
MOTHERS OF YOUNG CHILDREN

365 Meditations for Mothers of Young Children

PATRICIA D. BROWN
MINERVA GARZA CARCAÑO
LEANNE H. CIAMPA
HELEN HEMPFLING ENARI
MARGARET ANNE HUFFMAN
IRIS R. JONES-GBOIZO
REBECCA LAIRD
JOAN LANEY
SHERON C. PATTERSON
KATHLEEN F. TURNER
ANNE L. WILCOX
MARY ZIMMER

DIMENSIONS
FOR LIVING

NASHVILLE

365 MEDITATIONS FOR MOTHERS OF YOUNG CHILDREN

95 96 97 98 99 00 01 02—10 9 8 7 6

This book is printed on acid-free recycled paper.

Library of Congress Cataloging-in-Publication Data

365 meditations for mothers of young children / Patricia D. Brown . . .[et. al.].
    p. c m.
    ISBN 0-687-01246-5 (alk. paper)
    1. Mothers—Prayer-books and devotions—English. 2. Devotional calendars.
I. Brown, Patricia D., 1953-   . II. Title: Three hundred sixty-five meditations for mothers of young children.
BV4847.A15   1993
242'.2—dc20   92-44072
                                                                              CIP

Scripture quotations, unless otherwise noted, are from the New Revised Standard Version Bible, copyright © 1989, by the Division of Christian Education of the National Council of the Churches of Christ in the United States of America. Used by permission.

Those marked NIV are taken from the Holy Bible: New International Version. Copyright © 1973, 1978, 1984 by the International Bible Society. Used by permission of Zondervan Bible Publishers.

Those marked KJV are from the King James Version of the Bible.

MANUFACTURED IN THE UNITED STATES OF AMERICA

CONTENTS

FOREWORD

THIS UNIQUE COLLECTION OF DAILY MEDITATIONS is written especially for you: a mother of young children. Twelve Christian women who also are mothers have contributed one month's worth of meditations each to offer encouragement, reassurance, comfort, inspiration, and hope for the joys and trials of motherhood. As you make your way through the year with these women of faith, you will be enriched by a variety of experiences and perspectives that illustrate how motherhood influences, changes, and enriches a woman's daily life and spiritual journey.

The meditations in this book follow no set pattern. Some writers begin with suggested Scripture readings; some end each meditation with a prayer; others use prose alone; one writer uses dialogue. But in their various styles, these writers share common themes: the evidences of a deepened spiritual journey; the sense of connection with creation, with the lives of biblical women of faith, and with Christian tradition; the joys, blessings, and insights that children provide; the responsibilities and challenges of parenting; the assurances of faith for a mother's concerns; the emotional and physical demands of mothering; the necessity of spending time alone with God; and others.

The contributors themselves represent a variety of life-styles and family situations. Among them are new mothers, experienced mothers, biological mothers, adoptive mothers, and one grandmother; mothers who work primarily inside the home and mothers who work primarily outside the home; mothers who are married and mothers who are or have been single parents.

It is our hope that the discipline of daily meditation and the thoughts that will be triggered by these pages will make every day more meaningful for you.

About the Writers

Patricia D. Brown is an active speaker and workshop leader across the country and serves in an official capacity in an agency of her denomination. At the age of twenty-five, she was widowed with a three-year-old-son, Christian, who is currently attending school in Pennsylvania. Today Patricia makes her home on Staten Island with her husband, Dale, and their five-year-old son, Stephen.

Minerva Garza Carcaño is a minister in cooperative mission in Albuquerque, New Mexico. She and her husband, Thomas, are the parents of one-year-old Sofía Teresa, who graced their lives when they were older than most new parents. In addition to contributing to *365 More Meditations for Women*, she is a frequent contributor to several periodicals.

Leanne H. Ciampa is the author of *Friends and Followers in the Bible*, volumes I and II, and the co-writer and producer of the video resource *Creative Sermons for Children*. She is an associate pastor in Middleton, Ohio, where she lives with her sons, Julian, age four, and Britton, age two.

Helen Hempfling Enari is a part-time social worker for child protective services and part-time associate pastor in Clarkston, Washington. In addition to writing, she has participated in community theater and has traveled throughout the United States, Europe, and the South Pacific. Helen and her husband, who is from Western Samoa, are the parents of five-year-old Allison, three-year-old Samuel, and seven-month-old Jonathan.

Margaret Anne Huffman is the author of *Second Wind: Meditations and Prayers for Women* and a feature writer for *The Shelbyville (Ind.) News* and other periodicals. Margaret Anne is also a community speaker, a pastor's wife, a mother of three, and a grandmother. She lives in Shelbyville, Indiana.

Iris R. Jones-Gboizo is a free-lance writer, a full-time student, and a single mother of a six-year-old son, Anatole. When she can find time in her busy schedule, Iris enjoys storytelling, creative writing, music, and arts and crafts. She resides in Washington, D.C.

Rebecca Laird is a freelance editor and writer who specializes in spirituality and social justice. She is the author of *Portraits of People in Places Not Like Home* and *Robinson Rabbit, What Do You Hear?;* the co-author of *No Hiding Place;* a regular contributor to various periodicals including *Herald of Holiness;* and a licensed minister. Rebecca and her husband, Michael Christensen, live in Summit, New Jersey with their daughters, Rachel, age three, and Megan, six months.

Joan Laney is a full-time mother of four children: Ruth, age eight; Hudson, age seven; David, age five; and Will, seven months. She has been an English teacher, a grants writer, and a retreat hostess. For seven years Joan has worked with her pastor husband, Billy Vaughan, in various ministries of a small inner-city church, including food and clothing ministries. Currently she is taking pre-nursing courses to prepare for nursing school. Joan and her family live in Memphis.

Sheron C. Patterson is a pastor in Dallas, Texas, the author of *Ministry with Black Single Adults,* and an active speaker and workshop leader. She has been a professional journalist and the host of a local television program. Sheron also established a church-based adoption ministry in the Dallas/Fort Worth area. She and her husband, Robert, live in Dallas with their four-year-old son, Robert, Jr.

Kathleen F. Turner is a freelance writer and former fiction editor who lives in Fort Wayne, Indiana. In addition to her involvement in prison ministry, Kathleen and her husband, Darrell, provide a puppet ministry for children. She is the mother of two daughters: Dawn, age six, and Heather, age three.

Anne L. Wilcox is former Bible study columnist for *Today's Christian Woman;* the author of two books, including *A Woman's Workshop on Ruth;* and a contributor to *365 More Meditations for Women.* She and her husband, Brian, are basking in the quiet interlude between the preschool and teenage years as they parent their eleven-year-old daughter, Jaime. Anne also assists in teaching literature, math, and language arts courses at an elementary school in their hometown of Seattle, which allows her the privilege of enjoying one hundred other children each day.

Mary Zimmer is a Christian education professor and a writer and retreat leader on biblical women and spirituality. For eleven years she worked as a social worker with mothers of young children. Mary and her husband, Steve, live in Louisville, Kentucky, with their two sons, Jacob, age eighteen, and Michael, age thirteen.

JANUARY

The Blessing of Children

MINERVA GARZA CARCAÑO

JANUARY 1   Read Psalm 40:1-3.

Before my daughter was born I suffered two miscarriages. They were both difficult experiences, but during the second miscarriage God touched my life in a transforming way.

It was Christmas Eve, a day of life and hope, but Thomas and I were again facing death; dying was our hope of a child, our dreams of a family, our desire to pass on our humble legacies.

It was a cold day. The hospital was dark and empty. It seemed as if patients and staff had all gone home. We felt alone and abandoned. We knew exactly what was happening to us and that there was nothing that we could do about it except pray.

Eventually I was left alone in a sterile and unfriendly operating room, and I prayed even more telling God that I could not go further without his help. Then I heard a voice. I did not recognize the voice, but the person to whom the voice belonged seemed to know me. As she came within my range of vision, I realized that it was a Christian friend whom I knew. She was to be the nurse assisting through the surgical procedure that I would have to undergo. She took my hand and told me how much she appreciated me. I felt comforted as my body gave in to the anesthesia.

As I came through the procedure, I heard another voice; and again though I did not recognize the voice, the person spoke to me with familiarity. She was telling me that she was changing my gown so that I would feel more comfortable. As I began to see more clearly, I recognized her. She was another Christian friend, whose children I had come to know well through church. She shared with me how much her children loved me. Then she told me that she and the other friend who had been with me earlier had not been scheduled to work that day, but early that morning they had both been called to come into work.

My prayers had begun very early that morning. Some would say, "What a coincidence that these friends would be there for you." But I say that God is faithfully present in our lives and responds to our prayers when we call out to him. With the psalmist I will praise God!

Dear God, I am so thankful for your faithful and loving presence in my life. As I face the challenges of motherhood that lie ahead, I am encouraged and strengthened by the knowledge that you hear my every prayer.

JANUARY 2   Read Isaiah 49:8-15.

Nursing my baby daughter was one of the most incredible experiences of my life. A few hours after she was born, a nurse brought her to me and asked me if I was ready to nurse her. In a daze I remember thinking, "How am I going to do this?" I need not have worried, because though I did not know what I was doing, she did. Immediately she began sucking at my breast. Her crying made the milk flow from my breasts. I had no control of them. When for some reason I did not nurse her, my breasts would ache from their fullness. There was not a single moment when my breasts would allow me to forget my child.

Like a woman's body responds to her suckling child, so God responds to his people. The relationship is intimate and so interrelated that there is not a moment when God is not aware of the needs of his children. Our cries make God's mercy flow. Our needs make God's spirit ache. Even more faithful than a mother, God never forgets his children. God gives his children protection, guidance, comfort, compassion, favor, salvation, freedom, and food and water for their bodies and their souls. God does not forget.

O God, I am grateful that sometimes your self-revelation comes to us in the image of a woman. Today I celebrate your presence and praise you for also revealing yourself through me.

JANUARY 3   Read Psalm 104.

The day that Thomas and I brought our firstborn home was a somewhat scary day. We were "old folks" in comparison to most new parents—I was thirty-seven and Thomas was forty— and we were setting out on a new venture. What would we do with this tiny bundle of person in our hands? Would we know when to feed her and how to take care of her? Would we know when she was ill and know what to do? How would we help her to grow? Would we know how to discipline her? What would we teach her? We were nervous.

To make matters worse, Sofía Teresa just cried and cried and cried as we attempted to sign all the papers that the hospital needed for our dismissal. She did not want to be nursed. She did not want to be carried, but neither did she want to be put in her bassinet. The attendant who pushed my wheelchair out of the hospital suggested I stick a finger in her mouth to stop her crying. Sofía Teresa was getting on her nerves, too! But then something happened—something that made me aware of the fact that whatever I might be able to teach this child, this gift of God, there would be many things that she would teach as well.

Though Sofía Teresa had been crying for what seemed a solid hour, the minute we stepped outside the hospital she immediately stopped crying. I had just covered her with a light blanket and was watching her take a deep breath, her eyes opening wide as she felt the breeze on her cheek. Not only did she stop crying, but she also became very still. Only her eyes moved as we passed under the trees at the entrance to the hospital. She seemed aware of the fact that she was coming into contact with something new and wonderful. As the sun hit her brow she squinted her eyes, and I thought that I saw her trying to open them ever so slightly as she became accustomed to the sunlight.

Watching her made me aware of that beautiful day. I realized as I followed her movements and expressions that she was indeed seeing God's creation for the very first time in her life. Birds were chirping. Could she hear the birds? I wondered. People were coming and going. Could she sense their presence? Could she smell the fresh air? It was an amazing experience to observe her encounter with God's handiwork.

Even more amazing was, through her help, to have my old eyes see God's creation in a new way. I learned a significant lesson from my then three-day-old daughter. God's creation is marvelous and wonderful, filled with beauty and grand surprises, if only we'll stop to see it and hear it and feel it. The psalmist must have had this freshness of spirit when he wrote Psalm 104.

Our children have so much to teach us about God's creation. During this day may we be their attentive students, seeing life through their eyes and allowing our spirits to be renewed by their witness.

Dear God, for our children who help us to know you in new ways, we give you thanks.

JANUARY 4   Read Genesis 18:1-15; 21:1-7.

"Oh, yes, you did laugh," said God to Sarah. It wasn't enough that three traveling strangers had come saying that Sarah, at the age of ninety, was to give birth. Now here was God scaring Sarah to death by confirming that what the strangers had said was not only true, but also from God, and that God had been listening in when Sarah had laughed at the message.

What an interesting conversation Sarah and God must have had that afternoon. I can hear trembling in Sarah's voice as she gulps and finally confesses to the Lord, "I did laugh, Lord, but please try to look at it from my side. Don't you think it's pretty funny to think of two old weathered codgers like Abe and me experiencing the pleasures of childbearing? It is a bit ridiculous. What are the neighbors going to think?"

God must have seen Sarah's side, because he forgave her for laughing at the message he'd sent her, and he did for Sarah as he had promised. But something else occurred. God affirmed Sarah's laughter. Upon Isaac's birth, Sarah proclaimed, "God has brought laughter to me; everyone who hears will laugh with me."

Sarah's laughter gives us the opportunity to catch a glimpse of the very special relationship she had with God. How wonderful to think that from that day forward Sarah and God laughed together. Isaac must have time and time again heard about how God had made his mother laugh. It must have made him feel very special.

I believe that the God whom we share in common with Sarah also laughs with us. We may need to get in touch with this aspect of our relationship with God, but Sarah confirms that it is a real possibility. Knowing that God laughs with us somehow makes life's struggles more bearable. What a marvelous witness it would be for our own children to know that we, like Sarah, laugh with God. It might make their burdens lighter and their lives more special.

Laugh with us, O Lord, and embrace us with your warmth.

JANUARY 5   Read Proverbs 20:11.

One day I could not find ten-month-old Sofía Teresa. She and I were alone at home, and suddenly I realized how quiet it was. In a panic I began to search for her, remembering that I'd left her crawling on the den floor as I'd gone into the kitchen. I called her name as I frantically looked for her—but nothing.

After a few long minutes, I found her. She was sitting behind a couch being more still than I'd ever seen her before. In her lap she was holding a book that she'd pulled off one of our bookshelves. She'd managed to tear a couple of pages out of it, and she was clutching them in her chubby little hand. She had a startled reaction as she realized I was standing right over her.

At that moment I didn't know whether to scold her or laugh at her apparent effort to hide. I caught myself before I could choose between these two responses. Instead, I knelt next to her and gently took the book and torn sheets from her hand, telling her at the same time, "No, no, no." She'd heard the word *no* many times before, and she even knew the appropriate shake of the head that goes with it. Even at ten months she was learning that tearing pages out of books is an unacceptable act.

At a year of age Sofía Teresa still gets into trouble because of the books on the bookshelves, but on occasion she demonstrates some level of awareness of what is right and what is wrong.

Teaching our children what is "right and wrong" is every parent's responsibility. But even more important is the responsibility of teaching our children what is pure and right in God's sight. How true are the words of Proverbs: "Even children make themselves known by their acts, by whether what they do is pure and right." What an awesome responsibility. May God enable us to fulfill it.

God of purity and right, help us to be righteous in our acts so that our children may be known for their righteousness.

JANUARY 6   Read Matthew 2:1-12.

Today is Epiphany, the day that Christians around the world commemorate and celebrate the visit of the wise men to worship the infant Jesus. Different traditions have arisen around this special day. In the Mexican tradition of my heritage, Epiphany, rather than Christmas Day, is when gifts are given following the example of the wise men who came bearing gifts for baby Jesus. Whatever our traditions may be, we all can remember and celebrate the incredible story of the birth of the Christ Child and the star that illumined the path of those who searched for him. How can we celebrate the story with our children?

With infants and toddlers, we can celebrate the story by offering them our gifts of love. Of course, we give our love to our children every day, but today we can savor our gifts with tender hearts as we give thanks to God for his unconditional gift of love to us: Jesus.

With preschoolers, we can celebrate the story by offering them our gifts of love as well as by beginning to share the details and meaning of the story.

Most children are fascinated by light. Consider lighting a candle in a semi-dark room to represent the star of Epiphany. Explain how just as the candle helps them see their way around the room, so also the star helped the three wise men see their way to where baby Jesus was.

The three wise men will also need to be interpreted in modern-day terms. One way of doing this is to suggest that the wise men were like scientists searching for the answers to the world's problems. The gifts that they carried with them were for Jesus, whom they knew was the one who would save the world and bring peace. They wanted to thank him for coming into the world. The wise men brought gifts that represented those things which were held in highest esteem in their day. Ask your children what gifts they would give to Jesus if he had been born today and they were the wise people visiting him. Finally, talk to them about how Jesus' birth has changed our world.

Star of Bethlehem, shine for us today and lead us to Jesus the Christ. May we share our gifts of love with our children today and every day.

JANUARY 7   Read I Samuel 1:1-11*a*.

I confess that I am unable to comprehend Hannah's thoughts when she asked God for a child while in the same breath promised that she would then give the child back to God. The child, she vowed, would be a nazirite, one set aside and consecrated to the service of the Lord. Did Hannah have a profound need to fulfill her maternal instincts? Perhaps the heavy-handed treatment she was receiving at the hands of her husband's other wife, because of Hannah's barrenness, was becoming unbearable. Or then again, she may have wanted a child to please her husband, whose love toward her was unwavering. All these thoughts and others may have been in Hannah's thoughts and prayers, but how could she promise to surrender that same hoped-for child?

It is impossible for us to fully know Hannah's soul as she came before God with her petition, yet we may learn from her example. Hannah reminds us that we and our children, and *their* children, all come from the Lord, creations of divine hands. Hannah's example also reminds us that our children are not ours, but the Lord's. Can we receive these reminders with glad hearts and thankful spirits?

On this day I am filled with gratitude as I contemplate my daughter. How truly blessed I am that God allowed me to be the vessel in which he worked to give her shape and life. Gratitude is often in my thinking as I am touched by her, but possessiveness also creeps in on occasion. All too frequently I act as if she is a child growing and being formed only through my care and guidance, and therefore mine and mine alone. My sister Hannah brings truth to light: We have the responsibility of leading our children to the Lord as Hannah took Samuel to the house of the Lord in order that he might serve him. It is a responsibility that springs from the fact that each one of us is made *by* God our Creator and *for* him, for God is the one who gives us life and, in life, perfect care and guidance.

We give you thanks, loving Creator, for the blessing of children whom you place in our care and who thus bring joy to our hearts. Forgive us when we assume that they are ours alone. Help us to be faithful and responsible mothers in guiding our children to know and serve you.

JANUARY 8   Read Genesis 21:14-20.

As a pastor, I have seen a great deal of suffering. The human suffering that I have found most difficult to bear has been that of children, and that of their parents as they watch their children afflicted by suffering, pain, and sometimes even death. A mother sitting anxiously as her five-year-old child undergoes open-heart surgery. Young parents holding each other as their doctor tells them that their days-old baby will probably not live. A father who has just received word that his youngest daughter has been killed in an automobile accident. These experiences have caused me the most anguish and left me feeling wordless and even useless.

God's manifestation in the life of Hagar and her son Ishmael helps me to better address this very real aspect of life and, I hope, to be of comfort to others. All mothers can find comfort and hope in this beautiful story.

Hagar cannot bear to see her son suffering from the heat and thirst of the vast desert that surrounds them like a burial hole, so she lays him under the shade of a bush and goes and sits at a distance from him. There is no hope in their predicament, and Hagar does not feel that she has the emotional fortitude to watch her child die. Ishmael crys out, and Hagar begins to mourn him.

Unbeknownst to Hagar, God hears Ishmael's cry, and word comes to Hagar through the lips of an angel of God that she can come close to her dying child and hold him fast for God will give him water to drink and save him. As Hagar opens her eyes she beholds a well of water from which she takes and gives drink to her child, pondering the words of the angel that from Ishmael God would bring forth a great nation.

Hagar and Ishmael's life story is incredible and unique, but through it runs a common thread that joins all mothers and their children. It is the thread of God's mercy toward children. God heard the cry of Ishmael. God hears the cry of every child. Recall the words of Jesus: "Let the little children come to me. . . . For it is to such as these that the kingdom of heaven belongs" (Matthew 19:14). Each child is different, but to each God sends waters of refreshment and healing; and whether they live or die, each drinks of the waters that spring forth for eternal life. It is God who gives us the fortitude to hold our children close in moments of suffering, for they shall live.

Merciful God, continue to hear the cry of our children. Give to them the waters of healing and eternal life, and to us give a spirit of courage and confidence as we trust in your presence and in your will.

JANUARY 9 Read Proverbs 13:1.

One of my sisters-in-law corrects her child by calling a time-out. When her child has misbehaved, she is given a time during which she must quietly consider what she has done. After this quiet period, she is invited to talk about what she did wrong and how she is going to rectify it. My niece is an intelligent child, but I credit her time-outs with giving her a depth of maturity beyond her young years.

As time goes by, I believe that my niece is becoming aware of the reason for the discipline in her life. Though I do not think that she enjoys it any better now than she did the first time it occurred, with each time-out she grows.

Proverbs speaks of wise children who love discipline. I don't know a single child who fits this description, but I do know of one child who is growing in her understanding of discipline and becoming wiser for it. Discipline was not her choosing, but a wise and patient mother has guided her well.

God, give us the patience and creative wisdom to lift up daughters and sons who love discipline, that they might be called wise children before you.

JANUARY 10 Read Matthew 6:33.

I grew up next door to my maternal grandparents, and as a child I did everything that I could to spend as much time at their house as possible. There was good reason for this. My grandparents' home was always bustling with activity: constant visits from aunts, uncles, and cousins; interesting conversations; and always plenty of food, regardless of the hour of day. There would often be new relatives to meet from just down

21

the road to as far as remote villages in Mexico. I was amazed at how large our family was, and how wealthy my grandparents were to host such splendid meals for those who came to visit.

It was not until some years later that I discovered that all those aunts, uncles, and cousins were not all relatives in the strict sense of the word. I also came to know that by the standards of the community we lived in, my grandparents and our entire family were poor. Many of the persons whom I had grown up considering relatives were actually persons whom my grandfather had met while he and his sons worked in the fields, persons whom he'd encountered along dusty country roads, or persons he'd heard about from others. They were persons who had had some need in their lives when my grandfather had met them, and to whom my grandfather had extended a helping hand, welcomed into his home, and shared his family's food. As I now recall, the meals that I'd participated in were actually simple meals of beans, fried potatoes, tortillas, and other such foods. They were nothing close to fine meals, but in their spirit and in their joy they were true banquets served up lovingly by my grandmother.

One day, as I was attempting to comprehend why my grandparents would open up their home in such a way to sometimes absolute strangers, and why they would give their food away to them, I heard my grandmother say, "Dios no permite que hagamos menos"—God requires no less of us.

Through these blessed grandparents of mine I first came to know the meaning of seeking first the kingdom of God and his righteousness. All other things did come as promised. Today I thank God for my grandparents.

Dear God, thank you for the gift of grandparents and the beautiful ways they bless our children's lives. Through the years may our children come to understand and appreciate those blessings seen and unseen.

JANUARY 11   Read Luke 7:11-17.

Motherhood can be such a joy. It can also be such a tremendous task. I have but one small child and a caring and helpful husband, yet there are days when I am overwhelmed by them and tasks of my role as a mother. I constantly pray for friends who have four and five and more children—and less ideal circumstances. I don't know how they do it!

Sometimes the responsibilities of motherhood are so great that they evoke in me a deep sense of loneliness. My child is satisfied only if I hold her. My husband is convinced that only I am fully able to address the needs of the child we love in common. My neighbors brag about my superwoman capacities and forget to ask how I'm doing. In my loneliness, I long for someone to care for me.

Oh, in good time my husband recognizes the symptoms of maternal exhaustion and comes to my rescue. Our child remembers the joy of her father's companionship and goes off to play with him. My neighbors tell me that I need a day off and they offer to care for my daughter. I am indeed fortunate. More fortunate are all who trust in the Lord and his care, for his is a care that is with us even before others are able to respond. This was the experience of the widow of Nain.

The widow of Nain thought that her loneliness and her need for support would be the state of her existence till death. She was a widow in the midst of burying her only child. She had no one to care for, but also there was no one to care for her. She cried bitterly for her dead son, and, as is the case when a loved one dies, she probably shed some tears for herself. But in the midst of her loneliness and pain she was comforted as compassionate Jesus came near and brought her son back to life. More important, Jesus let her know that she would never be alone, for he was with her.

This same loving and compassionate Lord is also with us. Let us not be overwhelmed by the tasks that motherhood presents us. Let us not be consumed by our loneliness and need for care. Rather, let us remember that Jesus is caring for us and find strength in that word.

As we care for others, care for us, O loving Jesus.

JANUARY 12 Read Genesis 1:26-27.

Earlier in my ministry I served a congregation that had a five-year-old girl who always participated in church programs and activities with great attentiveness. At Sunday morning worship she would come and sit in the middle of the front pew and participate actively and with joy. After the worship hour she'd run to stand right next to me as I greeted people at the door.

One day when I visited her home, the little girl met me at the door. Her beautiful brown eyes opened wide when she saw me. She gave me one of her warm smiles and, without saying a word, ran off. Watching her as I stood at the front screen door of the home, I saw her hurry down the hallway to the back of the house. And then came the most honorific welcome I've ever received. As she ran down the hallway she called out in announcement to her mother: "Mommy, Mommy, come quick; God is here!"

The child's mother explained that she and her husband had instructed the child by telling her that Sunday was the day to visit God and that church was the place of the visit. Since I was the one who seemed to be "running the show" at the church, she had apparently assumed that the church was my home and, therefore, I must be God! After that it was hard trying to convince her otherwise.

Of course, none of us is God, but God is in each of us. This is the clear message of Genesis 1:26-27. It is a lesson that was given to me as a gift from a five-year-old child. There is such innocence in children, but also such wisdom. May God give us innocent wisdom as we look upon one another.

Dear God, as we interact with other persons today, help us to remember that you are to be found within them and to act accordingly.

JANUARY 13   **Read Matthew 5:9.**

A new friend recently told me and another friend about a time in her childhood when she had participated in a Sunday school exercise to see who could quote the most Bible verses from memory. She says that she stood up, confident that she could quote Matthew 5:9. Her rendition of it, however, was slightly different. Proudly she stated: "Blessed are the shoemakers, for they shall be called children of God."

We laughed at her story, but it occurs to me that she might have uncovered an important understanding of what it means to be peacemakers. If a shoemaker makes shoes for those who are without shoes, is he or she not a peacemaker?

So often we have difficulty with the concept of peacemaking because we have a hard time defining it. Perhaps it would help us to think of persons and actions that denote peacemaking.

"Blessed are the bakers who bake bread for the hungry,
   and the builders who build homes for the homeless."
"Blessed are the teachers who teach what is right and just,
   and the preachers who denounce all that is wrong."
"Blessed are the fortunate who share their abundance with
   others, and the friends who welcome a stranger.
   They shall all be called children of God."

Peacemaking is an important way of life that we must pass on to our children. Talking about shoemakers may be a good way to start.

God, help us to be peacemakers in our families, our communities, and our world so that our children may learn to be peacemakers as well.

JANUARY 14 Read Mark 7:24-30.

The Syrophoenician woman was a woman of amazing spiritual insight, faith, and courage. All of her life she had been told that Gentiles and Jews did not relate, at least not in any positive manner. Jews thought that they alone knew God. She wondered about that, but even then she had been taught that only men had the mental capacity to reach any meaningful understanding on the matter. Still she wondered.

She'd also heard of one named Jesus who seemed to have the spirit of God within him and who performed miracles that only one who was indeed God could do. Could he possibly heal her sickly daughter? Something in her spirit told her that he could if he would.

Kneeling at Jesus' feet she begged him to heal her daughter. But why should Jesus spend his energies on healing a daughter from outside the circle of the Chosen People? The Israelites, the children of God, were to be cared for first. The woman was not to be dismissed easily, however. Her child was ill, and if Jesus was truly the incarnation of God, then he could care for all the Israelites and still have enough to care for her daughter, just as even dogs sitting under a children's table are able to eat from what is left.

What an insightful statement for a Gentile and a woman of her day to make. She was right! In response to her faith, Jesus healed her daughter.

How does our own faith fare in comparison to that of our sister the Syrophoenician? Are we too easily persuaded by those around us that we are unworthy or incapable of approaching Jesus for healing and wholeness for our lives and those of our children? How might we follow in the steps of the Syrophoenician woman?

Dear Jesus, we know firsthand the depth of love and concern this woman had for her child. As you touched the life of our sister, touch our lives on this day. May your Spirit give us insight, faith, and courage so that we may care wisely for ourselves and our children.

JANUARY 15   Read Mark 12:41-44.

How foolish of the widow to have deposited all of her money into the temple treasury! What person in her right mind would give away all that she had to live on? According to this world's economy, she had invested her money poorly! But according to God's economy, she had multiplied her funds. What a strange inversion of things.

The widow is credited with having a pure heart because she gave her all to the support of God's house, but it must also be said that she had a trusting heart. Her spirit, as seen through the eyes of Jesus, is one of complete confidence. She knew that even though she was giving all that she had, she would be sustained. Hers was the acceptable gift.

What have we been giving the Lord lately? Have they been abundant gifts yet empty ones, because with them we have failed to give him our total confidence? How can we surrender our all to him so that we can be found to be right and faithful before him?

As mothers, we sacrificially give ourselves and our resources to our children. Although it is neither healthy nor wise for us to give our children *all* that we have to give, we are called to give abundantly to our children, trusting that God will sustain us. When we give in this spirit, ours is an acceptable gift.

Dear God, help us to trust in you as we seek to meet the needs of our children.

JANUARY 16   Read I Kings 22:51-53.

My maternal grandmother had a Spanish saying that all too often cut to the core in explaining the wayward ways of a son or daughter. Loosely translated, the saying was: "The splinter is only like the stick it came from."

Though we all know parents whose children grow up to become just the opposite of them, the more common experience is that children grow up to be very much like their parents, for better or worse. The older I get the more I appreciate the compliment that more and more I look and act like my mother. When I tell her this, she blushes and reminds me of what, according to her, are her bad qualities. She hopes that I have not incorporated these qualities into my character and way of being.

Ahaziah was a poor and sinful king of Israel. There was reason for this. He was every bit the son of his father and mother. As they had done evil in the sight of the Lord and caused Israel to sin, as they had served Baal and worshiped him, as they had provoked the Lord, the God of Israel, to anger, so did Ahaziah. It was what he had been taught and what he had learned. He was a splinter-image of his parents.

What are we teaching our children? While they are certainly their own persons, we are the primary teachers in their lives. God permit that someday they may demonstrate through their living that what they have learned from us is goodness.

O God, forgive us when we are a poor example for our children. Strengthen us that we might live your goodness for their sake.

JANUARY 17 Read Job 1:20-21.

Can anyone be more important in a child's life than his or her mother? As mothers, we would undoubtedly answer "No," no one is more important to a child than his or her mother. Job disagrees with us. Even more important than us is the Lord, from whom our children came and to whom they return.

I spend time with my child, attempting to develop a relationship between her and me that I hope will be loving, affirming, challenging, joyous, and special. This is an important part of mothering. I am sure that you do the same. But just as it is important that we take time to develop such a relationship with our children, it is also important that we guide them in building a strong and solid relationship with God, their Creator.

Our children's first and last relationship is not with us but with God. Their relationship with God will be the one constant in their lives. As they grow, they will determine whether they will be close or distant in this relationship, but God has promised that he will always be present for them. At some moments, God's presence in their lives may be one of judgment. At other moments it may be one of mercy. Always the divine presence will be grace-filled.

As much as I may work on my relationship with my daughter, Sofía Teresa, I recognize that I am but a finite and imperfect being. God, and God alone, will always be there for her in the most perfect of ways. For this reason, I want her to know God throughout her life.

God, from whom we come and to whom we return, you alone are always with us. In birth and in death you accompany us. In your mercy and in your love, reveal yourself to our children. Care for them and receive them in your own good time.

JANUARY 18   Read Mark 14:3-9.

I am amazed at how early children learn about what is in style. What is fashionable dictates the likes and dislikes of even kindergarteners. My four-year-old niece, Christine Rebecca, can rattle off a number of the latest popular fashion labels. Television and other children reinforce a generational message of what is most acceptable in dress, toys, cars, and a number of other material possessions. The values of our children are being formed by what they see and hear around them; and the word seems to be that the more we can possess and the more expensive those possessions are, the better. Many times even we join our children in losing perspective on what is of real value.

Such was the case of those who gathered at the house of Simon the leper when, to their dismay, they watched the woman pour an entire jar of expensive oil of nard on Jesus' head. They counted every last penny that the oil might have brought on the market. They claimed interest in the poor, suggesting that they might have been able to make a significant gift to the less fortunate through the sale of the oil.

Considering the character of most of the persons who followed Jesus with a critical eye, they were not persons who had much genuine concern for others. What they did concern themselves with was preserving those things that they considered to be of material worth. So they became angry and grumbled at what to them were the foolish and wasteful actions of the woman who anointed Jesus. They were blinded by the material object before them, so much so that they were unable to see that which was of most value before them—Jesus himself. They scolded the woman for what she had done while Jesus praised her.

Only the woman was able to recognize that what was of most value in life was her relationship with Jesus. Using her possessions to demonstrate her love for him was the wisest use of what she had. For her good service to Jesus, she gained for herself a place in history.

What are our values on this day, and what are we doing to help shape Christian values in the lives of our children? Do we show them how to give to others in love, to serve their church out of commitment, to sacrifice for their community out of concern for its well-being? Are we teaching them that what is of highest value is to love God and others? It is these values that bring blessings for a lifetime and beyond.

Dear God, help us to compare our values to what scripture teaches us, so that we may be better examples for our children.

JANUARY 19   Read John 20:1-18.

"Sir, if you have carried him away, tell me where you have laid him, and I will take him away" (John 20:15*b*). Mary Magdalene had a strength of faith that went beyond her temporal and physical capacities. Peter and John had been to the empty tomb at Mary's encouragement, but seeing nothing and not understanding the meaning of what was before them, they had gone home. Mary alone had remained at the tomb. She refused to let Jesus go.

When Mary encountered Jesus, believing him to be the gardener, she begged him to tell her if he had taken Jesus. With her own arms she would carry Jesus away, if only he would tell her where he had laid Jesus. How true is the old proverb, "Love feels no load."

Mary persevered. She continued to serve her Master even after his death. In her perseverance Mary was blessed, for Jesus called out her name and made her the first witness of his Resurrection.

Mary Magdalene is such a wonderful role model for us. There are many "diversions" and responsibilities in a mother's life, but we must persevere in our personal Christian walk—we must remember to seek Jesus first. Mary's faith, perseverance, and devotion to the Lord are worthy of our attention and our following.

Lord, help us to be strong in faith, to persevere, and above all to serve you.

JANUARY 20   Read Matthew 9:20-22.

My mother suffered from an extremely painful and chronic ulcer on one of her ankles for almost twenty years. After four skin grafts, she was beginning to lose hope that she would ever be well. One day the ulcer became so large and so painful that she thought surely she would lose her leg. She felt so poorly that she called one of my sisters and asked her to take her to a doctor.

On the way to the doctor, as she struggled to keep her courage, a thought crossed her mind. "Pray for yourself" was the thought. In those moments she began to try to remember when she had last prayed for herself. My mother is a woman with a strong, disciplined prayer life, but she could not remember when she had last prayed for herself. Her prayers had been filled with concern and thanksgiving for her children, her family, her church, and others, but it had been a long time since she had prayed for herself. But on that afternoon, she reached out to Jesus in prayer for herself.

The doctor showed great concern for her leg. He gave her some medication, but he told my sister that he could not assure her that he could save my mother's leg. My mother, on the other hand, felt deep in her soul that the Lord had heard her prayer. Like the woman who touched the fringe of Jesus' cloak, reaching out to Jesus in prayer for herself, my mother found healing for her body.

So often we mothers think of others before thinking of ourselves. It is good to be caring and loving of others, but our well-being is important too. Jesus welcomes our reaching out to him for our own sake. On this day, let us reach out to him for ourselves and hear his loving words: "Take heart, daughter; your faith has made you well."

Lord, you know my need even before I speak it, but I find release when I share the burdens of my heart with you. When I become preoccupied with the needs of others, remind me to bring my own needs to you in prayer.

JANUARY 21   Read Matthew 5:14-16.

The community where I live celebrates an annual hot-air balloon fiesta. During a two-week period, the sky is filled with the most beautiful balloons: bright-colored ones that look like Easter eggs; animal-shaped ones like pigs, cows, and even parrots; and even people-shaped balloons. Delight fills the air!

One morning during this period I was driving to work through my neighborhood, and I noticed that children who should have been headed for school were riding their bicycles in erratic ways. I noticed that they were all looking up, so I looked up as well. Right above us was one of those gorgeous hot-air balloons, slowly descending into a nearby field. The children who were focused on the balloon were trying to follow it, and they were having a great time doing it.

As I drove on to work, I thought to myself, "If only our children would follow Jesus with that same enthusiasm." I began to consider how I demonstrate my enthusiasm for Jesus. Do the children in my life see my enthusiasm? And what about my own daughter? As she grows, will she be able to see and even "feel" my excitement in knowing Jesus?

Enthusiasm is contagious. Our children will want to know more about Jesus if they sense our own enthusiasm for following him.

Lord, help us to let our lights shine for our children and for others by sharing our enthusiasm for you.

JANUARY 22   **Read Philippians 4:10-13.**

The home in which I was reared was one of those which contributed to the poverty statistics. My parents worked hard enough, but having little to no formal education made it difficult for them to obtain jobs that paid much. My father was a butcher and later a machine operator, and my mother took in sewing for others. Some summers my mother and the older children in our family worked in the cotton and tomato fields. Life was hard, but my mother always made it easier for us through her unwavering faith.

We might very well have lived in a state of constant insecurity had it not been for the fact that my mother lived the faith of the apostle Paul—she and her family could do all things in him who strengthened them. Looking back on all that we were able to overcome as a family, I have to say that we've come this far because of God's providential care; and what kept our eyes on God was my mother's faith. Had it not been for her, we might have lost sight of God and many a time been overwhelmed by the desperateness of the situations we faced.

My home is now wealthy in comparison to the home in which I was reared. Interestingly enough, though I now have more than I need and my family lives in comfort, crises still arise. I've come to realize that insecurity can afflict the haves as well as the have-nots. The lesson that this has taught me is that my mother's gift of faith is the best gift a mother can give her family. I pray that as my own family grows, I might follow in her footsteps by being a pillar of faith and a blessing for my home.

In all circumstances, Lord, may we stand firm in our faith and commitment to you. Make us a blessing of faith for our families and all those around us.

JANUARY 23 Read Romans 6:1-11.

When my father died, one of the most difficult things I had to do was explain to the grandchildren in my family what had happened to their grandfather and what it meant. The grandchildren were then nine, five, four, and two years of age. It was a tough assignment given to me by my mother, who thought that a minister would know how to do it.

Well, I sat down with them and began by telling them that grandfather was gone. I didn't have to go much further. As much as we had tried to protect them from the details of my father's accident, they knew all the basic facts and then some. They also knew some of the faith explanations of where he now was. They knew that their grandfather wasn't coming back; that he was in heaven with the angels; that he'd be there waiting for the rest of us; and that someday, if they were good, they would get to see him again.

I pushed the litany of responses a bit further and asked them if they knew who else grandfather was now with. One of the children quickly responded, "Jesus. Grandfather is with Jesus." They all nodded in agreement, except for four-year-old Joey who seemed frustrated with the entire conversation. So I turned to him and said, "Joey, do you know that grandfather's with Jesus?" Then Joey said something that I will always remember. He said with sorrow and confusion on his small round face: "Aunt, I know that grandfather's in heaven. I know that he's with Jesus. All I want to know is if he's all right." All I could do was take him in my arms and assure him that yes, grandfather was all right.

According to Romans, as persons of faith we have the assurance that in death things will be all right; they will be all right because of the risen Christ in whom we have placed our trust. However, the assurance is dependent on how we live our lives. Shall we go on sinning so that grace may increase? "By no means," says Paul. We have died to sin, so let us say no to sin that we might have the blessing of life.

What an important responsibility we have to teach our children that Jesus assures us that everything will be all right—in this life and the next—if only we will trust in him. In our unsure and sometimes frightening world, this is an assurance that every child needs.

Lord, help us to assure our children of your everlasting love and to help them understand the importance of living lives of grace and holiness.

JANUARY 24   Read I Timothy 5:1-2.

One of the greatest blessings in my life has been a large extended family. Even though I live hundreds of miles from my blood family, I am never without family because of the family of Christian sisters and brothers who surround me and embrace me with love and support. These sisters and brothers have counseled me, called me to accountability, comforted me in moments of pain, and celebrated my victories with me. They have taught me about life and made my life more meaningful. For each one of them I give God thanks.

Paul speaks to Timothy about how Christians are to live with one another. Older men are to be treated as one would treat one's father. Older women are to receive the respect one would give one's mother. Younger men and women are to be treated as brothers and sisters. These relationships are to be pure in their intention. To be as family is the goal.

In a world where community is under constant attack and families are finding it ever more difficult to stay together, the hope and vision of a community of faith made strong through its commitment to be family is a welcome prospect. Throughout the generations of the Christian community, efforts have been made to be family and lives have been made better for it.

What mothers and fathers, sisters and brothers from the community of faith have made a difference in your life and the lives of your children? Who in your community of faith might be a father, brother, sister, grandmother, or grandfather for you or your children? Who in your community of faith might need you to be a mother or sister for them on this day?

For the Christian family we give you thanks, O God. Help us to truly be as family so that we might strengthen one another for faithful living.

JANUARY 25

Read Genesis 25:27.

As my husband, Thomas, and I consider having a second child, we have long conversations about how we will nurture that child. We know that we will love that child, but how will we know if we are giving that child the attention it needs, for we will then have two children? How does one create special moments for each child that are very much his or her own? If we are blessed with another child, how will we help our children to love and respect each other, especially in light of the fact that each will have his or her own gifts and graces, weaknesses and strengths? The more my husband and I talk about this, the more I remember Rebekah.

Rebekah received the blessing of children in a way that I do not long for—she conceived and had twins! She had such a miserable pregnancy that she cried out for death itself. The twins struggled in her womb, and, at her wit's end, Rebekah decided to inquire of the Lord as to what was happening within her. It was at this point that she became aware of the fact that she was pregnant with twins. The Lord also told Rebekah of the differences between the two sons she was to birth, and of how those differences would help them to grow and develop for purposes unique to each of them. At birth, Rebekah's sons, Esau and Jacob, were different in appearance. In manhood, Esau became known as a man of the field and Jacob a tent-dweller. Each had his own knowledge and skills.

As I remember the story of Rebekah and her sons, it strikes me that if we parents would seek God's wisdom in understanding our children, who they are and their unique characteristics and abilities, we might better nurture them into being all that they are meant to be. We might then better guide them in celebrating their own and each other's contributions to family, church, and community. This seems to be the most loving thing to do, and the best way to give our children good guidance whether we are blessed with one, or two, or many.

Lord, help us to know our children as you know them. Through loving nurturing, help us also to affirm and celebrate with them who you have created them to be.

JANUARY 26   Read Luke 13:10-17.

Unfortunately, so many of us women, like the woman from Luke's passage, find ourselves bent over, crippled, and ailing. I am not speaking of a physical impairment, but rather a spiritual and emotional affliction that keeps our vision at ground level. It is a destructive and terrible illness in our society called sexism—the discrimination against the feminine gender in the human race for the sole reason that we are women.

I see it everywhere. The woman who is abandoned by her husband and then scoffed at because she takes on the job that supposedly should have gone to a man. The woman who breaks ground by assuming a position of power never before held by a woman and then is weighted down by unreasonable expectations while both men and women gather around to see her fail. The woman who is treated like a fool by her doctor, her mechanic, her banker, and sometimes even her preacher, because they think that she "doesn't know any better." Sexism! It is the age-old cry of the leader of the synagogue who could not stand to see a woman healed and made well.

Some may argue that the leader of the synagogue was simply protesting the fact that Jesus healed the woman on the Sabbath, when no work was to be done. But he was the leader of the synagogue, and this woman had been coming to the synagogue bent over and hurting for eighteen years. Why had he not done anything for her before? Not even on a workday had he attempted to help her. He cared more about his animals, considering them important enough to break the Sabbath law in order to take care of their needs. In his callousness and sexism, the leader of the synagogue was losing touch with his humanity as much as the bent-over woman was being dehumanized by her illness and the treatment that her gender brought her.

As a woman who has chosen a traditionally male-dominated career, I daily struggle against sexism. It is a burden and a worry to me. But what is beginning to worry me more these days is not so much how sexism affects me, but how it will affect my child, her cousins, her friends, and all the children of the world.

Shall we continue to allow more than half of the world's population to live bent over? Do we dare allow yet another generation to live under such a sin? Or shall we live lives that with Jesus proclaim, "Woman, you are set free from your ailment" (Luke 13:12)? Wellness for our world must mean wellness for all.

O Lord of our salvation, set our world free from the sin of sexism so that our children may become all you would have them to become and live together in harmony.

JANUARY 27   Read Mark 5:21-24, 35-43.

Not all synagogue leaders in Jesus' day were calloused and uncaring of the feminine sex. There was one synagogue leader who begged for the life of a young girl. His name was Jairus, and the young girl was his daughter. She was close to death when Jairus went to Jesus, knelt at his feet, and begged him to lay his hands on her so that she could be made well and live.

I am moved by Jairus' humbling of himself before Jesus and the multitude of people around them for the sake of his daughter. But is this not what any caring parent would do? The one who truly moves me is Jesus. While receiving the adoration of a great crowd, he chose to go to the bedside of one small, dying girl.

Jesus had much more to gain by remaining with the crowd. Leaders of synagogues were not his best supporters. Acts of mercy toward young girls in his day were not considered by most to be the best use of his time. But there he was in Jairus' home, holding out his healing hand to this dying daughter and then worrying about getting her something to eat.

The good news for us and our children is that Jesus will leave adoring crowds, enter unwelcoming homes, and cut through the world's prejudice to give life to us—even to the "least of these." How comforting it is to know that we and our children are in Jesus' constant care.

For healing, wholeness, and life, we give you thanks, O Jesus our Savior.

JANUARY 28   Read I John 4:11-13.

When I was a kid, I was skinny and lanky, and I had an uncle who ribbed me constantly about my appearance. "You're the strangest-looking kid I know," he would say. "Look at those arms and those long, skinny legs. . . . You look just like a mosquito!" I would look at myself in the mirror, and sure enough I did resemble a mosquito.

One morning my grandmother caught me looking at myself in the mirror with disgust and asked me if something was wrong. I told her that I hated the way that I looked and that my uncle was right—I looked just like a mosquito. She gently came over and asked me if I knew who had made me. "God," I responded, a bit perturbed that she would want to give me a Bible lesson at a moment when my entire future development was in question. She continued, "God made you, and inside you God put beauty and love. You worry about the outside, but if you look inside you will see God's beauty and love. Look in the mirror again, and don't look away until you see that beauty and love. Look way deep down inside of you."

I sat in front of that mirror for a while and contemplated her words, and then an assurance filled me. I thought at that time that it was my grandmother's wisdom and care. I now know that it was God's affirming Spirit at work in my life. I had come face to face with God's love within me.

How are your children feeling about themselves these days? Perhaps its time to remind them that God made them with beauty and love.

Lord, help us to show our children how beautifully you have made them—inside and out.

JANUARY 29   Read II John 1-6.

It is assumed that the apostle John wrote this epistle at an elderly age. It is written to a woman who was well known among the churches. Apparently many had been recipients of her hospitality and had either seen or heard of her fidelity to the Lord. To have a letter written to her by a distinguished member of the church and to be a woman well known and respected in her community would have been honor enough. But these are not her crowning glory. John writes to congratulate her for her children who were walking in the truth. He commends her for successfully instructing her children to live the commandment of loving one another and encourages her to continue instructing all her children.

Children can bring either glory or shame to their parents. Much of it has to do with how they are instructed to live. We mothers have an important role to play in the formation of our children. We can spend long hours becoming known as faithful and hospitable women, but nothing will measure the depth of our testimony like our children. How we instruct them through word and example will reveal who we truly are. My prayer for you is that your children might bring glory to your name, and honor to the cause of Christ.

Lord, let us not be so concerned for how others see us that we forget that our children need our guidance in knowing and living your truth.

JANUARY 30 Read Matthew 18:1-5.

Some years ago I had the opportunity to visit El Salvador with a group of Christians who were concerned about what was occurring in that country at that time. While there we spoke with many persons, but the ones who spoke to us with greatest clarity were the children.

One afternoon we visited an internal refugee camp, a camp filled with rural folk who had been left homeless because of civil war. At this camp, as in the other camps that we visited, we found ourselves surrounded by children. One child of the hundreds that we met will always stand out in my mind.

She was a timid girl of about seven years of age. She sat on the ground outside the shanty that provided shelter for her and her family. She had with her a box of colored pencils and several sheets of paper. She was drawing. Her mother told us that since their town had been destroyed in the civil conflict, the child hardly spoke but preferred to spend her time drawing.

One of the other women in our group knelt by the little girl and attempted to engage her in conversation. The effort was futile. She did not speak to us, but she did allow us to see her drawings. She had drawn pictures of airplanes and helicopters dropping bombs, and people big and small on the ground with blood oozing from their bodies. And in one of the hands of each of the persons she had drawn she had colored a flower. That child did not utter a word to us, but on that afternoon she led us to an even deeper understanding of the preciousness of life and the evils that threaten it. In her own way, that child was protesting the killing of her people. Unless the human race changes and becomes like children, we may never enter the kingdom of heaven.

Children have a way of communicating great truths. If we will open our eyes, ears, hearts, and minds, our children may lead us to an even deeper understanding of God's gift of life.

O God, give us the heart of a child that we may find life everlasting.

JANUARY 31   Read Judges 5:1-7.

So often when we think of mothering, our thoughts are of small children and lullabyes. Some of us may think of car pools and daycare. Others of us may think of the jobs of being breadwinners and perhaps sole supporters of families. Usually we tend to think of mothering in the context of our immediate families. The prophetess and judge Deborah, however, gives us another model.

In her wisdom, Deborah arose to be a mother for all of Israel. When Deborah's people found themselves under the tyranny of captivity, it was she who laid out the battle plan, even choosing and commissioning and accompanying the troops into battle. Through Deborah, God brought salvation to his people.

I believe there are women among us today who are being called by God not only to be mothers within our own family circles, but also to be spiritual mothers in our communities of faith and wise and courageous mothers for a hurting world—mothers in the footsteps of those such as Deborah, Joan of Arc, Susan Anthony, Rosa Parks, Harriet Tubman, or Mother Teresa. Women who have, through their womanhood, talents, and love, mothered society for the better. Might God be calling you to enlarge your vision of the realm where your gifts of mothering may be needed?

God of all wisdom, help us to discern your call for our lives. In all things, enable us to be mothers of hope and healing.

FEBRUARY

Feed My Sheep

JOAN LANEY

FEBRUARY 1   Read John 21:15-22.

This text was written for mothers! When Jesus asks Simon Peter if he loves him and Peter answers yes, Jesus tells him to "feed my lambs," "tend my sheep," and "feed my sheep." Tending to the flock means making sure the sheep have food, keeping them from harm, healing their cuts and scrapes, keeping them all together, herding them from pasture to pen. That sounds a good bit like motherhood to me!

All of these are little actions. Jesus isn't asking for heroics. But, strangely enough, Jesus predicts that those actions will lead Peter to a cross. Feeding Jesus' sheep will change the world and threaten the principalities and powers. Though a humble task, it is life-changing for Peter—and for us.

When Peter asks about John, Peter wants to make sure that his companions are in for the same fate that he is. Jesus responds by deflecting the question. He's not going to allow the comparisons. He simply reminds Peter to follow him.

Like Peter, I often wonder why I have been given this vocation of raising children while others have been called in other ways. Jesus says to me through this text, "That is no concern of yours. You are to tend the flock I have given you."

May we embrace our vocation as Christian mothers—to feed Jesus' sheep—wholeheartedly.

FEBRUARY 2   Read II Kings 5:1-15.

This is the story of great men affected by a little girl, a little slave girl who wished healing for her master and set into motion that very healing. We don't even known her name— all we know is that she was an Israelite who had been captured by the Arameans and had become a slave to Naaman's wife. There's a lot of untold tragedy in her story. She is far away from her family, her friends, her country, her religion. She is a slave, so she has no rights or freedoms. But this child has great dignity. She is so eager for her master's healing that she tells his wife about the powers of her people's prophet. In their desperation, they listen to her. Eventually, Naaman is healed.

Madeleine L'Engle, a Christian writer, is convinced that there is such a thing as a "butterfly effect." The flutter of a butterfly's wings on earth causes physical changes that ripple to the outermost edge of our galaxy. She contends that no action is too small to cause long-reaching results. Certainly this story from II Kings bears witness to a butterfly effect in that the unnamed child's action cures her master of leprosy and causes him to confess Yahweh as the one true God.

There's so much about motherhood that seems trivial— there are so many little details to attend to. The day-to-day routine with all its petty irritations seems so insignificant in the long run. But remember the butterfly effect: we may be changing the course of history far more than we will ever know!

FEBRUARY 3 Read Luke 10:38-42.

Martha must have been a mother: one of those organized, always-in-charge mothers who lists things she needs to do, who always has a contingency plan and does not settle for anything less than a spotless home! Martha is the type of mother who listens to the children with one ear and thinks of how she can do a million other things at the same time; she's distracted by her many tasks, the text says.

Jesus doesn't buy into Martha's sense of justice. He says, "Martha, Martha, you are worried and distracted by many things; there is need of only one thing. Mary has chosen the better part, which will not be taken away from her" (Luke 10:41-42). All the busyness in the world will not amount to much; it is perishable; it will vanish. Mary's willingness to stop her activity, sit at Jesus' feet, and listen is much more important in the long run.

How do we as mothers appropriate this for our lives? All of us, no matter how busy, would be more than happy to set aside our agendas if Jesus were to show up at our door. But we have to make time in our lives for silence, for letting go, for focusing on God's grace. It is hard to do. The pay-off isn't instant or tangible. Doing "nothing" seems unproductive when there are toys to put away, outgrown shoes to replace, and pediatrician visits to make.

Nonetheless, if we order our lives according to the gospel, we will make time, just a little time, for the One who loves us and calls us by name.

FEBRUARY 4 Read Matthew 15:21-28.

I would like to meet this woman. I can imagine her—an outsider, rather disheveled from following after Jesus, not inclined to be polite or mannerly, downright embarrassing in her insistence on being noticed by Jesus. But what a woman! Even Jesus' silence doesn't deter her! He turns her down twice after ignoring her, and still she persists. Her final retort is so humble and witty that Jesus relents. She converts him. And all for love of her daughter.

In an article entitled "Prayer and the Powers," Walter Wink describes intercession as "spiritual defiance of what is in the name of what God has promised." This woman knew that Jesus promised wholeness. She refused to let either the reality of her daughter's illness or the reluctance of Jesus silence her plea for healing. She was spiritually defiant. And it worked!

As mothers, we are called to be no less persistent, no less steadfast than this woman. In the face of God's silence, we are to beg for mercy for our children. Our intercessions may have to be downright pushy. We may have to remind God, as this woman reminded Jesus, to attend to us and be with us. But our foremother in the faith, this unnamed Canaanite woman, has shown us how to do that with humility and grace.

FEBRUARY 5 Read Luke 5:17-26.

I'm intrigued by this story because the paralytic doesn't have a lot to do with his own healing—his friends do. Because of their faith, his sins are forgiven and he is cured of his paralysis.

The story connects sin and paralysis. Unfaced pain and wrong freeze a spirit, immobilize it, paralyze it. We have a choice in any situation to work to change it or just to passively accept it. Maybe in the case of the paralytic, sin means his resignation to the paralysis.

Or perhaps he's resentful. He sees his lot as unfair. In the book *Cry Pain, Cry Hope*, Elizabeth O'Connor urges us to thank God for bad things. That helps transform our own bitterness into a wider acceptance of God's ways.

The friends of the paralytic, on the other hand, go to a lot of trouble to "intercede" for him. They don't let any obstacles stand in their way: they simply do what they have to do to get the paralytic close to Jesus.

As a mother, oftentimes I am like the paralytic's friends. I see my children's needs—or the needs of others—and I am willing to be inconvenienced to meet those needs. At other times, however, I am like the paralytic, needing a community of friends to urge me to heal, even to drag me to the place where I'm willing to be healed. Regardless of which role I am playing, it is essential for me to have a community of faith that prods me, supports me, allows me to share my gifts, and takes me into the presence of my Lord.

FEBRUARY 6   Read I Kings 17:8-16.

It is a time of famine, and a widow is gathering sticks when Elijah asks her for water and bread. Her response is one of despair. She and her son are at the end of their supply of food and are going to die of hunger. And Elijah says to her, "Do not be afraid" (I Kings 17:13).

So often I feel like the widow. I have so little to give after dealing with my children, after negotiating their fights and trying to meet their seemingly constant needs. I say to God, "There's nothing left."

God, through Elijah, asks the woman to do the impossible: to make Elijah a small cake from her almost nonexistent resources before she feeds herself and her son. Her leap of faith in doing so leads to her needs being met throughout the famine. As she gives, she is given to.

God says to us, "Do not be afraid." And then God promises that our resources will not give out when we continue to use them for others. Our energy for our children may flag and we may fail, but God's grace will provide for us as we allow it to.

FEBRUARY 7   Read Luke 12:32.

This is such a tender verse, showing gentleness and grace, that I often overlook it when reading the Scriptures. Jesus is talking to his disciples about the life-style of the community of faith: that we are not to be anxious about food or clothing. And then he says these words, "Do not be afraid, little flock, for it is your Father's good pleasure to give you the kingdom" (Luke 12:32).

Since becoming a mother, I am so much more aware of the role of fear in my life: fear about the fragility of life, fear about my children's future, fear of cancer and AIDS and accidents—the list is endless. And here is Jesus saying with infinite understanding, "Do not be afraid."

I am also continually aware of how much being a follower of Christ sets me and my family against the mainstream of our culture. Hence, "little flock" sounds comforting to me. Jesus knows there is not going to be a huge crowd following him to the cross. He knows the community he is forming will be small.

And then, in verse 32, the promise after the reality of our fear and our paltriness: "It is your Father's good pleasure to give you the kingdom." If I were to name what I most want for my children, it would be for them to experience the kingdom of God. And Jesus is telling us that we have been chosen for the abundant life. Fearful and faithless though we be, God has promised us the kingdom. What more could we ask?

FEBRUARY 8   Read Luke 17:11-19.

The lepers are the outcasts of society. They stand safely apart from Jesus, crying for mercy. Jesus immediately responds to them. As they follow his instructions to go to the priests, they are cured. Strangely, only one bothers to turn back to thank Jesus. The others are much more intent on doing what Jesus has told them to do.

What's wrong with the nine lepers doing what they've been told? In their singlemindedness, they forget or ignore the source of their healing. They can't let themselves be interrupted from the task at hand even long enough to say a simple thanks. Perhaps they feel that they have deserved the healing.

Of course, that's why I identify with the nine lepers! As a mother, I tend to be so task-driven, so eager to fulfill the letter of the law (have a clean house, a nice yard, well-behaved children, a somewhat organized life) that I forget to turn back and thank the source of all good gifts.

On the other hand, the Samaritan, the outsider, suspends his agenda, throws himself at Jesus' feet, and is made whole. I think that his spirit as well as his body is made whole, which is what happens when we stop being so driven (even if we are driven for a good reason) and acknowledge the One who heals us.

My prayer is to live with daily thanksgiving to the One who makes my healing possible.

FEBRUARY 9   Read Luke 5:1-11.

Simon must have been a bit perturbed at Jesus for telling him to go back out into deep water for a catch. He'd been out all night and was washing out his nets, presumably getting ready to go home and get some sleep.

As a mother, I often feel like Simon—a whiney Simon saying to Jesus, "I've been working so hard to no avail. I try to be the best mother I can be, but I get discouraged when I do not see tangible results." And Jesus says, "Let down your nets anyway." Do this act of utter faith even though you are exhausted and discouraged. Jesus calls us to lay down our expectations and our hard work (sometimes even our common sense) joyously and trustingly and to let go in faith.

Look what happens! Simon's nets are so full that they begin to split. He must call his partners to come help haul in the fish. This one act of faith becomes a community event. The text says that all of his companions are amazed at the catch. When we are willing to follow God's call, our actions have ripples that affect those around us—our children, our family and friends, and even strangers.

To their amazement, Jesus replies, "Do not be afraid" (Luke 5:10). I think he says this to us too. Don't be afraid to let go in faith, to travel that extra mile, to ignore your better judgment. Don't hesitate to call upon God when you're at the end of your patience and energy. If at that very moment you "let down your nets," abundance will await you.

FEBRUARY 10   Read Exodus 3:1-6.

God tells Moses to take off his shoes because he is standing on holy ground. And there, in the wilderness, God reveals his name to Moses as the God of all history. No wonder Moses hides his face!

I think God tells us daily to take off our shoes because we too are treading on holy ground. Every moment, especially those shared with our children, is a holy moment, if we only have eyes to see. They don't often feel holy as we live them, but in retrospect they make a pattern that is beautiful.

I never realized this until I walked my oldest child to kindergarten. It hit me that five years had flown by and from that point on she would be gone almost as much as she would be home. Suddenly the moments we had shared were holy moments in which we both had been formed, she as a child and I as the parent. As I looked back over the years I could see God present in particular moments: her birth, her baptism, family celebrations of Easter and Christmas. But underlying all our time together was grace. God had been present in the ordinariness of our lives as well as the highlights.

We are called to take off our shoes, to attend to the time we share with our children. It is holy time, time to savor, time to watch for glimpses of a God who is not too great to be seen in the eyes of our children.

FEBRUARY 11 Read Matthew 10:29-31.

What an incredible God! This God even accompanies a tiny sparrow when it falls. And instead of manipulating us like puppets, this God walks with us through the valleys of our journey. This God stands with us at the bedside of a sick child, grieves with us when we suffer loss, and celebrates with us when we gather in joy and thanksgiving.

Several years ago, some dear friends were in a terrible auto accident. The parents were rushed to a county hospital, but one of their daughters was taken to a children's hospital in the city because her injuries were so extensive. Since her parents could not be with her in the hospital, friends took turns sitting by her bed day after day.

One night after she had been told that her spinal cord was irreparably damaged, she began to move her hands in "sign language." A few minutes later she sang in a tremulous voice, "Father, I adore you, lay my life before you, how I love you." At that moment my heart was filled with a mother's love, as if she were my own child. And I felt God with us in that hospital room. This little sparrow had fallen, and God undoubtedly was right beside her, watching over her. Through God's loving presence, God was promising to stay with her. It was a holy moment.

We mothers worry about the safety and well-being of our children, as well as all of God's children. But when worry overtakes us, we need only remember Jesus' promise: "So do not be afraid; you [and your children] are of more value than many sparrows" (Matthew 10:31).

FEBRUARY 12　　　　　　　Read Luke 7:11-17.

This is a story of a grieving mother who has lost her only son. She is also a widow, the most unprotected, vulnerable person in her society. Jesus' heart goes out to her. Without her even asking, he raises her son from the dead.

As mothers, we'll likely experience all facets of this story: the grief, the powerlessness in the face of suffering, and sometimes the awe when healing surprises us. Central to our experience will be our relationship to the Christ. Will we see a grieving Christ walking with us in our suffering, his heart full of compassion? Will we stop our procession through life for his healing touch? Will we acknowledge the love and care bestowed upon us without our having asked?

I give thanks for a God who is with me in my joy and in my sorrow.

FEBRUARY 13　　　　　　　Read John 11:17-44.

This story begins with a reproof. When Jesus finally makes his way to the home of Lazarus, Martha runs to meet him, crying, "Lord, if you had been here, my brother would not have died" (John 11:21). "If you only" is often our cry to God. If you had only done this, Lord, my child would not have suffered. If you had only done that, Lord, I would have known how to help my child. You would solve our problems and free us from pain.

But what happens? Jesus goes to the grave and orders the onlookers to do some of the work. He tells them to remove the stone. He wants their participation in this resurrection. He wants them to get moving. He doesn't seem to mind the utter ridiculousness of his request—the stench of the dead body and the size of the stone.

And even when Lazarus comes forth from the grave, the gathered community has more work to do! Jesus instructs them to unbind his funeral cloths. God needs our help in the healing. There is no magic, only the gathered community of Christ doing the work Christ has taught us to do.

As we face times of great hardship and pain in our families— particularly when the pain directly touches the lives of our children—we are to call upon God to be with us. Then God calls upon us to participate in the answering of the prayer.

FEBRUARY 14   Read Ephesians 3:14-21.

This is a gorgeous prayer, a prayer of overflowing love from Paul to the church in Ephesus. It covers everything, asking nothing less than wholeness and shalom for the people Paul loves so dearly.

Amidst the prayer is a reminder that God is able to do "abundantly far more than all we can ask or imagine" (Ephesians 3:20). What amazing words! What a wonderful promise! This God, who loves us so dearly, gives to us so abundantly that we can't even fathom it.

On this Valentine's Day, the day of love, we can pray this prayer as a gift for our children. In fact, we can pray this prayer for our children every day. For it is a prayer that our children, as they grow and are "rooted and grounded in love" (3:17), will come to know and understand the depth of God's love for us and the extent of God's power in our lives.

FEBRUARY 15   Read Isaiah 40:28-31.

Any mother of young children, living in a state of perpetual exhaustion, would be comforted by these words. The problem is the word *wait* in verse 31: "Those who wait for the LORD shall renew their strength." I feel like asking God why we have to wait so much! Why can't we have instantaneous strength, vigor, and energy?

When I was chasing two toddlers and caring for an infant I used to pray, "Lord, give me patience RIGHT NOW." I felt very close to desperate all the time! Having to wait made me realize that any semblance of patience or strength I had was sheer gift. I was not in control; I could not summon those gifts by an act of will.

It is that very powerlessness that makes motherhood so difficult and so life-changing. We are forced to rely on God to get through each day. I suspect that as we shed the illusion of being in control, we become healthier human beings.

So I will learn to wait on the Lord, trusting in that day when I will run without fainting from exhaustion.

FEBRUARY 16   Read I Samuel 1:1-19.

I like this story of Hannah because she is willing to bring her distress before God. She pours her heart out to God so intensely that the priest, Eli, thinks she is drunk!

Once Hannah has prayed passionately to God, she is willing to let go and trust. "Her countenance was sad no longer," the text says in verse 18. How remarkable! One of our vocations as mothers is to bring our heartache and concern to God, laying our burdens at God's feet and then letting them go. I tend to prefer to explain to God how to fix things, and I'm not very good at letting go. But Hannah has a lesson to teach us: We of faith must let God do the work.

In Richard Foster's book *The Celebration of Discipline*, he discusses ways to incorporate spiritual disciplines into our daily lives. One prayer posture he mentions has given me an image of what Hannah did: when my heart is burdened, I come before God and I turn my palms up in supplication, naming each concern and lifting it to God. Then I follow that naming by turning my palms down, as I let go of the very troubles that I named. It is a symbolic way to remember that I'm not in control.

This has worked wonderfully amidst the crying of the children, the constant messes, the minor crises, the sense that I never accomplish anything: palms up as I raise each petty irritation to God; palms down as I let go, trusting that God will take care of it all.

FEBRUARY 17   Read John 5:2-9.

Crippled for thirty-eight years, this man is asked by Jesus in verse 6, "Do you want to be made well?" Strangely, the man doesn't protest, "Of *course* I want to be healed," but rather whines, "I have no one to put me in the pool." He seems almost ambivalent!

I identify with this crippled man. Though I often see areas of my life that need healing, I'm not always sure I want to be healed. That may mean changing old patterns. Like the crippled man, it is sometimes easier to lie there and feel sorry for myself than to summon up the energy to move toward the healing waters.

Amazingly, despite the man's ambivalence, Jesus heals him. Jesus doesn't worry about whether or not the man deserves the healing. Neither does he insist that the man be appropriately thankful. (He isn't.) Jesus simply sees his need and responds with words of healing.

This text is a graceful guide for one such as me, called to both receive and give life. As a woman, I hope that my children see me as a human being prepared to seek healing when healing is offered. As a mother, I pray that I will reach out to my children without demanding appropriate thankfulness.

FEBRUARY 18   Read Matthew 25:1-13.

In this story of the wise and foolish bridesmaids, these bridesmaids go to the wedding with their lamps, a clue to us that they are expecting to wait at least until nightfall. Five bring additional oil in case the wait is much longer than that. They are ready for the contingency.

Now, any parent of young children learns through bitter experience to be prepared for every contingency—a leaky diaper, a sick child, a broken something-or-other. This story reminds us that as Christians and as mothers we have to be prepared for a delay. It's going to be a long wait until we see the fruits of our labor, until we see how our hours with the children count, until we see if prayers for loved ones are answered. In our society, where efficiency is highly valued, we rarely have to wait a long time, unless we are standing in a food line or waiting in a public health clinic or waiting for a bus. We Americans are used to quick and easy solutions to our problems.

On a trip to Nicaragua several years ago I realized that waiting is a natural part of life in other parts of the world. A typical day for a Nicaraguan woman included a long walk to get water, a wait to get the fire started, and a wait for a bus to get food. Delay was a fact of life, so these women were prepared. They sang, they visited, they sewed—all while they waited.

There are many accounts of waiting in the Bible. Perhaps waiting is not an inconvenience or an afterthought but, for us Christian mothers, part of the divine picture.

FEBRUARY 19   Read Psalm 84:1-7.

I've always been captivated by the image in verse 6: "As they go through the valley of Baca [tears] they make it a place of springs."

We've all known people who have done this, people who have transformed their suffering into salvation. We've also known people whose suffering has turned them bitter. Apparently we have a choice, no matter how heavy our burden. We don't have to believe that God wills us to suffer, but we can believe that God will redeem our pain and accompany us on our journey.

Our choices will affect our children and teach them how to deal with pain. That's the scary part. We do not act in a vacuum. I've watched my mother deal with crises she never would have imagined she'd face. She has chosen to learn from each one, and she's used her new-found knowledge to change. She's been able to do that by turning to God for strength and by trusting in God's goodness.

I pray for the gift to transform my valley of tears into a place of springs, so that my children may also learn how to allow God to redeem their pain.

FEBRUARY 20   Read Isaiah 55:8-11.

Before I had children, this text bothered me. I wanted God's ways to be *my* ways! I could think of a number of solutions to the world's problems—and to mine—that would avoid a lot of needless suffering. Sometimes I even fussed at God for not "following my instructions" or answering my prayers as I thought they should be.

Isaiah makes it clear that God's ways will accomplish what God intends. We will not understand them necessarily, but we can trust them. This is the lesson I've learned from my children: God's ways are better than my ways. I would have my children never suffer pain, never grieve, and never experience yearnings. But how would they learn compassion or depth or tenderness? How would they ever learn to celebrate? Isaiah puts it metaphorically in verses 10 and 11:

For as the rain and the snow
    come down from heaven,
    and do not return there until
        they have watered the
        earth,
making it bring forth and sprout,
    giving seed to the sower and
        bread to the eater,
so shall my word be that goes
    out from my mouth;
    it shall not return to me
        empty,
but it shall accomplish that
    which I purpose,
    and succeed in the thing for
        which I sent it.

Thank goodness God's ways are not my ways!

FEBRUARY 21   Read Isaiah 65:19-22*a*.

What marvelous promises we have in these verses! No infant mortality, no untimely deaths, no misfortune awaiting our children. However, the promises of healing and wholeness come hand in hand with a vision of simplicity. All will live in houses they have built and eat fruit that they have planted. There will be no more exploitation and no more greed. Children will be able to work for their living. What a radical idea today!

I often tremble in fear at the thought of my children's future. It seems so precarious. But this promise was given to Isaiah long before we came along. And this promise has a command in it: we must live as citizens of the new world even before we have evidence that the new world is here! We are commanded to be good stewards of our resources by only taking what land and food we need, by not exploiting others, and by delighting in our work. As we do so, our children will be blessed.

That sounds grandiose for those of us with small children who don't feel as though we have much power or influence. But we can choose actions that demonstrate hope in this new world. We can be less wasteful. We can recycle. We can car-pool. We can plant gardens and teach our children reverence for the earth. We can try to be aware of the ways our life-styles affect the life-styles of those in other countries.

I doubt that God is depending on our actions to help bring about this new world. Nothing we do, in one sense, will ever be enough. But God's grace has a marvelous way of transforming our efforts into a realization of this promise. Our task is to do what we can when we can, and to trust.

FEBRUARY 22   Read Isaiah 65:22b-23.

The promise in these verses is that we mothers do not labor in vain. Our endless days of dressing children, feeding children, wiping dirty faces, piling in and out of the car, doing laundry, picking up, and worrying that we are doing it all right—this is not labor in vain.

The Sunday school class I teach—with children stepping on my guitar, wiggling during the Bible story, jumping up and down, giggling—this is not labor in vain.

The after-school program at our church with twenty-five neighborhood children, most from single-parent homes—all hungry for attention, love, food, and safety—this is not labor in vain.

Our children are not born for calamity, says this text, but are blessings from God. As I trust this promise, claim it, and make it my own, I will not feel so defeated by the endless demands. They are part of the blessing. They are molding me into a more sensitive and patient person.

We are called to remember, when swallowed up by the details of our lives, that our work with our children is not in vain and that God is with us, blessing us amidst the chaos.

FEBRUARY 23　　　　　Read II Kings 4:1-7.

When this widow comes to Elisha to appeal for his help, he first asks her what her resources are. She replies, "Your servant has nothing in the house, except a jar of oil" (II Kings 4:2*b*). With that jar of oil Elisha is able to provide her with enough to redeem her boys from slavery and to live on.

When we come to God for help, we first need to look at what we have rather than what we don't have. God can use whatever small gift is ours to offer. Similarly, when we want to help our children, we need to remember to look at their resources before we step in and provide everything for them. This is not easy to do. As mothers we instinctively want to provide for our children's every need. But empowerment is different from paternalism. Elisha empowers this widow to take control of her life; he doesn't take care of the situation for her.

It's also important to note that the community is involved in helping the widow. Her neighbors provide the jars for the oil. We all need one another for times like this. The support given by others empowers the widow.

As mothers with often limited resources, especially resources of time and energy, we desperately need one another to sustain us when we figuratively have "nothing in the house." The good news is that, like the widow, we do not have to be victims. We can look at the resources at hand, call the community together to help, and trust God. We will then be empowered to change our lives.

FEBRUARY 24　　　　　Read Proverbs 3:5-6.

I had to memorize these verses as a child, but they never meant much to me until I became a parent. It seems as if I am continually learning and relearning that I am not in control—even of my children—and that my understanding is very limited.

The part of the text that speaks most to me is the line "do not rely on your own insight" (Proverbs 3:5*b*). It is easy as a parent to think that my judgment of a given situation is accurate, yet I find very often that my judgment has been wrong. Instead of jumping to conclusions, I need to prayerfully consider other ways of looking at a problem. Trusting God with the problem is a way of giving up control, not relying solely on my own insight.

We are admonished to acknowledge God in all our ways. There is always something I'm not willing to give up to God, something that I want as my own. Usually it has to do with the children. It is very difficult for me to think that God might have a better understanding of their needs than I do! At the same time, my experience of parenting has been the most humbling and eye-opening experience of my life. I marvel that I and my children have survived the lessons I've learned.

I have found this verse helpful when I feel powerless or out of control. As I recite it to myself over and over, I thank the fifth-grade teacher who drilled it into our heads, for it comforts and sustains me in those times.

FEBRUARY 25   Read Ephesians 5:20.

This verse tells us that we are to be thankful every day for everything. So often we fail to see the blessings around us.

A child down the street from us is the four-year-old son of an unwed teenager; he is living with his grandparents. His name is Kevin. Kevin's mother was addicted to drugs when he was born, so he is a very slow learner and struggles to speak.

Kevin likes to appear at our door at all hours to play with my five-year-old, David. Since Kevin has not played with many children, we've had to teach him how to take turns with toys, how to work out problems instead of fighting, and how to put toys back where they belong. For a while I felt as if I had another youngster to raise, and I would grown inwardly when Kevin rang the doorbell.

It was one of those mornings when I was dragging, not feeling that I could face the morning, much less my own children, when David taught me a lesson. At breakfast my husband asked the children to name a blessing that they were thankful for. Without a moment's hesitation, David said, "Kevin is my blessing."

Oh, to see with the eyes of a child! David had gospel eyes. He saw all the things in Kevin I had overlooked—his sense of humor, his bright eyes, his persistence. I felt very humbled. My inward groaning changed from, "Lord, help Kevin change" to "Lord, help me change."

May the Lord help each of us to see with the eyes of love and to be thankful.

FEBRUARY 26   Read Psalm 131.

Since becoming a mother, I have learned to appreciate this simple psalm. So much of motherhood is submitting ourselves to the demands of others, always being on call for the children. So much of motherhood is not being in control when we would so love to be in control. So much of motherhood is tending to trivial matters.

The psalm likens us to a weaned child clinging to its mother. We certainly know what that means! It means that God loves us as unconditionally as we love our children. It means that this all-powerful God holds us as tenderly as we would hold our children. We need that tenderness. We need that love. When I'm the most discouraged, I imagine God telling me that all will be well, like a mother comforting me.

FEBRUARY 27   Read Isaiah 46:3-4.

In these verses in Isaiah we see such a passionate God, half fussing, half reassuring. "Listen to me," this God orders almost in anger, "you've been a load on me since before your birth! But I will carry you until you are old."

This God sounds like an outdone mother dealing with an insecure, worrisome child. "Of course I love you," the mother says, wondering how the child could question that love. "I will love you forever, no matter what."

The image of God carrying us when we are white-haired is so tender, so comforting. God's love spans our lifetime. God's grace holds us up from birth to death. As we watch our children grow up and ourselves gray a bit around the edges, we are reminded that God accompanies us as passionately and as lovingly as we do our children. God wants for us no less than the wholeness we want for our children.

FEBRUARY 28   Read Hebrews 10:23.

I've always found reassurance and hope in the line "he who has promised is faithful" (Hebrews 10:23*b*). The Bible promises so much: new life, wholeness, a new creation. Our world seems so far from the vision of shalom. How could God make such rash promises?

We are called to be a hoping people, to confess our hope. As we approach a new millennium and as our children grow up to be tomorrow's leaders, we must continue to work out of hope for a better world. All the material goods we accumulate will not touch their lives as much as our being good stewards of our resources. If they see us recycle or conserve energy and if they see us deal fairly and lovingly with people of all races, classes, and backgrounds, they will learn respect of the earth and of others that will help transform earth and bring about God's promise of shalom. They need to see in our hopeful actions a conviction that everything we do makes a difference.

Years ago Dorothy Day wrote: "One of the greatest evils of the day is a sense of futility. Young people say, 'What good can one person do? What is the sense of our small effort?' They cannot see that we must lay one brick at a time, take one step at a time; we can be responsible for only one action of the present moment. But we can beg for an increase of love in our hearts that will vitalize and transform all our individual actions and know that God will take them and multiply them as Jesus multiplied the loaves and fishes."

MARCH

God's Children

REBECCA LAIRD

MARCH 1   **Read Acts 17:28a.**

hen the pastor quoted Acts 17:28 and said, "Now that's a womb image if I ever heard one," something in my spiritual growth quickened. You see, I was sitting uncomfortably in the back row of the church trying to listen while my two-year-old daughter drew noisily on the Sunday bulletin. Her ceaseless activity and the bulk of my seven-months pregnant belly made it difficult for me to hear or concentrate on the pastor's words.

The pastor went on to explain that we are "insiders" with God whether we know it or not. It's as if all of our lives are contained within the womb—the essence and sphere of God.

I thought of the growing child within me. This child doesn't consciously know I exist. My body is but the watery world that nourishes and provides space to grow. All this child needs to survive is mysteriously pumped and piped without even asking. When the baby kicks, flips, and explores, I feel every movement. For a time my body provides this baby with protective care so that he or she can go about the business of becoming strong and fully formed.

Like a womb, God is the one who nourishes me when I am not aware of my needs, the one who protectively holds my life and willingly accepts my "kicks" so that I may grow into maturity as a fully formed human being.

MARCH 2   Read Acts 17:29.

My daughter doesn't like to be very far away from me. When she first learned to talk, we lived in a long and narrow Victorian house. Her room and toys were at the front; the kitchen, laundry, and my desk and phone were at the back. Many times a day I'd hear her high-pitched toddler voice ask, "Mama, where you?" as her footsteps sounded on the hardwood hallway. She would look room by room until she found me, and she would hug me as if we'd been separated for hours. She wanted to be near me and would search until she found me.

When the apostle Paul used the words, "We are God's offspring," he was preaching in Athens to a bunch of philosophers who had asked him to explain the strange new ideas he was "babbling" about God.

Paul was distressed about the idols he saw all over Athens. He wanted to make it plain that the God he spoke of was not made of "gold, or silver, or stone, an image formed by the art and imagination of mortals." He wanted these people to know that God was the Creator, our intimate Maker—the One to whom we are closely related.

The God Paul describes is never far away from us. The image Paul used is of parent and young child, two who are rarely separated for long. What a comfort it is to know that when we "search for God and perhaps grope" (17:27), we will find God.

MARCH 3   Read I John 3:2.

As I grew up, people who had known my mother when she was young said, "You look just like your mother!" Others, who knew my father, said I resembled him. My parents look nothing like each other, but people could tell that I indeed belonged to them.

People have said the same thing to my daughter, who has a mixture of my physical characteristics and her father's.

But then there is my nephew, who doesn't resemble anyone on either side of the family. Members of the extended family often wonder if, as he grows, we'll see some resemblance to at least a relative or two. We don't yet know who among us this young boy will eventually look like, if any; but regardless of physical similarity, we know that he is a cherished member of the family.

Just as we know that my nephew is our own, so also we can know that we are God's children. Sometimes we look and act as God would. Then other times people must wonder where we came from! But we have the assurance that someday we will stand face to face with God and see that we are closely related to, indeed made in the very likeness of, God. God willingly claims us as beloved family members.

MARCH 4   Read Isaiah 49:15.

It would be impossible for a nursing mother to forget about her child. If by some miracle an infant were to sleep quietly through a feeding, thus allowing the mother to pay attention to other matters, the heaviness of her full to overflowing breasts would cause enough discomfort to remind her of the child. There is a physical interconnectedness between a nursing mother and her baby.

How marvelous it is to think that there is a similar, undeniable bond between God and us. Isaiah promises that it is easier for a nursing mother to forget her child than it is for God to forget us. Every few hours a nursing mother comes close, skin to skin, with her child. Can it be that throughout the day God is as available for intimate, nourishing contact with us if we but cry out and acknowledge our great need for comfort and care?

MARCH 5   Read Exodus 2:5-10.

Only three stories in the entire Bible talk directly about mothers and daughters. Almost all of the mother and child stories focus on famous sons. And even the first mother/daughter story is but a smaller tale within the larger epic about Moses. Yet in the account of Moses in the bulrushes, it is Miriam, Moses' older sister, who watches closely over her baby brother and shows great cunning and courage in approaching the Egyptian princess to offer to find a nursemaid for the baby. Miriam then seeks her mother, Jochebed, who must have been overjoyed that the child she hid in order to save his life has been returned to her care.

How many times throughout human history have mothers and daughters worked side by side using their wits and fierce love to further the aims of good with little recognition? Had Jochebed lived long enough to hear the word of Micah 6:4 recited, how proud she would have been to listen as Moses, Aaron, and Miriam were honored by God as the ones sent to redeem the Israelites. Miriam and her brothers were all precious and necessary in God's sight to bring freedom to their enslaved people.

Even in our modern times it is not uncommon for a man's accomplishments to be publicly honored more readily than a woman's. But God is no respecter of persons or gender. God has created us all: Miriam and Moses, sisters and brothers—each to do our part to bring about good and wholeness in the world.

MARCH 6   Read Matthew 14:8.

What an awesome responsibility mothers have to their children. The gruesome and callous story of Herodias and Salome shows how a vengeful woman encouraged her daughter to participate in having John the Baptist beheaded. The old cliché "like mother like daughter" seems to have proven true in this case.

Cultural stereotypes promote the idea that giving birth miraculously endows a woman with kindness, compassion, and goodness. But we all know better. I can witness that I quickly was made more aware of my weaknesses and impatience *after* I brought my daughter home from the hospital than I was before. Godliness and generosity are not prerequisites of giving birth; they are characteristics that God hones and whittles into our characters over time. Motherhood provides a rigorous training ground where we can daily practice and model the disciplines of love, honesty, and compassion before our children.

MARCH 7   Read Ephesians 5:19.

When the opportunity arose for me to accompany my husband overseas for a couple of weeks, my parents eagerly agreed to care for our daughter in our absence.

Our daughter handled the separation well, and when we were resettled at home, she asked us to sing songs with her. The problem was that we couldn't tell what she was singing.

We tried all of the songs we had taught her, but she didn't want to sing those. We sat together in the living room, baffled by the words she was singing. Then it dawned on us: Her grandfather had been teaching her choruses we both had learned long ago in Sunday school. We opened up our storehouses of memory, and the words and actions to "Deep and Wide," "Into My Heart," and "This Little Light of Mine" quickly returned.

I retrieved a cassette tape I had stored away that had many of these songs on it. That night I played it for her after the light was turned out and she was settling in for the night. From down the hall I heard her shout, "Yes, Sir!" A few moments passed and she said it again. I tip-toed to her door, and in the semi-darkness, I saw her saluting as she sang along to "I'm in the Lord's Army."

Night after night she drifted off to sleep to the time-tested songs of the church. Her delight reminded me that passing on our spiritual heritage is a joy.

MARCH 8 Read Luke 1:38.

By the time Mary, the future mother of Jesus, got around to saying, "Let it be with me according to your word," she already had expressed fear and essentially had said "get real" to the angel who came to bring her some pretty incredible news.

Who of us didn't first feel a mixture of apprehension, fear, and excitement upon first hearing the news of being pregnant? How much more anxiety and dread there must have been for Mary and the millions like her who were unmarried, pregnant, and very young.

Mary was skeptical. The angel's promise sounded too good to be true. She asked how it could be so, since she had no husband. Mary was practical and quite aware of the facts of life. She was convinced only after the angel told her about the late-in-life pregnancy of Elizabeth, her beloved kinswoman. Mary needed to know there was another woman, a sister of sorts, who was experiencing similar things before she fully accepted the role God had ordained for her.

After Mary knew she was not alone, she chose to say yes to the difficult life of bearing a child destined to proclaim in word and deed the saving love of God. She needed support, and so do we.

The strength and solidarity found in friendships with other expectant or experienced mothers make it easier for us to say yes to the challenges of motherhood.

MARCH 9   Read Luke 2:48.

While at an amusement park crowded with children, I heard a mother holler as she pointed her finger, "I found Mark! He's in the castle!" Hearing her, the boy's father marched resolutely over to the boy, grabbed him firmly by the shoulders, and said, "Why did you go off by yourself? I told you to stay where your mother and I could see you!" The child shrugged and tried to explain the allure the castle had for him.

Every parent has felt that awful surge of panic when a child has scurried out of sight. Imagine what you would feel if your child explained his or her absence the way Jesus did when he stayed too long at the Temple. How would you respond if your son or daughter said innocently, "Did you not know that I must be in my Father's house?" I probably would have retorted angrily, "No, I did not know that. All I know is that I told you to stay near us."

It's hard for all parents to understand the impulses of children. May we be attuned to the possibility that some of the inner pulls and desires of our children are well-intentioned and not just meant to frustrate us.

MARCH 10   Read Luke 2:51.

Twice in the second chapter of Luke the Gospel records that Mary, Jesus' mother, "pondered" or "treasured" the unusual words said about or by her son. It's almost as if Mary placed these unusual bits of Jesus' life into an inner storehouse where piece by piece she began to put together the puzzle of who this son of hers truly was. As Mary reflected upon her son's life, she was able to see him as more than her firstborn. She came to understand that this child was God's beloved gift who was brought to the world for a purpose far beyond that of being her son.

How wise Mary was. By taking the time to reflect upon the wonder of her son's life, she was able to later let him go to become God's messenger. She was able to move beyond being his mother to become a true disciple who learned from him.

Could it be that our children, likewise, have a purpose in the world and lessons to teach us if we will but ponder the wonder of their developing lives?

MARCH 11   Read Matthew 7:1-2.

With relief, I claimed a seat behind another mother and toddler on an airplane. I knew the chances of her being understanding were good if my daughter found it hard to sit for the duration of the flight. But to my pleasure, my daughter played happily and sang in a quiet, cheery voice as we flew home.

But that other mother's child was a terror. He pulled her hair, reached over the seat back, dropped ice cubes on my head, and then threw his bottle backward as if it were a missile aimed at obliterating my daughter from the planet. I was lucky to deflect it before it hit her square in the face.

PLEASE DONATE TO THE MINNESOTA
WORLD WAR II VETERANS MEMORIAL.
CALL 1-888-LOTTERY FOR DETAILS.
THANK YOU!

006071159646090

POWERBALL $1.00

** MAR30/02 SAT **

19 31 34 35 45   POWERBALL 05 Q6

33003/00068

0890 7021 7277 76

Important: Tickets are bearer instruments unclaimed. All tickets, transactions, and winners are subject to the rules of the Minnesota State Lottery. Void if torn, altered, illegible, or incomplete. Not responsible for lost or stolen tickets. If sending this ticket in by mail, please fill in the following information. Thank You.

George R. Andersen
Director
Minnesota State Lottery

SOCIAL SECURITY #_____

SIGNATURE_____

NAME_____

ADDRESS _____

CITY _____ STATE _____ ZIP _____

PO

143081810

Important: Tickets are bearer instruments unclaimed. All tickets, transactions, and winners are subject to the rules of the Minnesota State Lottery. Void if torn, altered, illegible, or incomplete. Not responsible for lost or stolen tickets. If sending this ticket in by mail, please fill in the following information. Thank You.

George R. Andersen
Director
Minnesota State Lottery

SOCIAL SECURITY #_____

SIGNATURE

Without realizing it, I had begun to judge the other mother. Couldn't she control her child? Where were his toys or books to keep him occupied? Why did she let him holler like that?

I thought these things while the bottle the boy had thrown lay underneath my seat behind my reach. Then the plane lurched and the bottle rolled forward where I could pick it up. I hesitated, and that surprised me. Then I realized how harsh my thoughts were toward this mother. It was clear she needed all the help she could get, and I had spent more time judging her than offering a simple helping gesture.

I quickly retrieved the bottle and handed it over the seat. The boy quieted down for a few minutes, and the mother sighed with relief. How soon I had forgotten my own hopes that she would be understanding of my child's behavior.

One of the easiest snares of motherhood is to compare our children's behavior with that of others and to judge our effectiveness as parents accordingly. When we let our children learn and develop at their own pace, we offer them the gift of grace—unmerited love. Unconditional love is not earned by good behavior, nor does it compare or judge. Growing up is difficult. Our children will thrive most readily when they know we love them through the tantrums and squeals of life.

MARCH 12   Read I Corinthians 13:4a.

Love is patient.

My husband watched me standing in the hallway as our two-year-old said, "Stand there. I go first. I carry my Lambie myself."

I obeyed my little commandant's orders and waited as she wrapped a blanket around her most precious toy, a limp, tattered stuffed lamb.

I had been trying for ten minutes to get my daughter to her training potty. I couldn't get on with the day until this major feat was accomplished.

As she attempted to fold the blanket around the toy for the umpteenth time, my husband said, "Toddlers teach you patience, don't they?"

What a true statement! Toddlers cannot be hurried. Eventually she tucked Lambie in to her satisfaction and carried it down the hall. Then she dutifully did her duty.

All morning long I thought about my husband's comment. Without conscious effort I had attained a new level of patience simply by learning to love and care for my daughter. Patience is the ability to wait without complaint, and it's not an easy virtue to learn. Whereas I once would have felt I was wasting time coaxing the child for ten minutes, I now knew that I was teaching her the tools of self-sufficiency while she taught me the virtue of patience.

MARCH 13   Read I Corinthians 13:4*b*.

Love is kind.

Family life is a daily testing ground for living kindly. Just yesterday afternoon after returning from the park, my daughter took off her shoes and left a pile of sand on the floor. I whisked her off for a nap while my husband sat down only inches from the pile of sand.

When I returned some time later, the sand remained. I stifled the urge to sarcastically say, "Do you think that if you ignore that pile of sand some cleaning genie will come and magically whisk it all away?" My second thought was just to be "nice" and clean up the sand myself, but I knew that would leave me harboring resentment. The kind response called for honesty. I asked, "Will you please clean up that sand as soon as you can?"

He agreed and did. Kindness is a fruit of the Spirit; niceness isn't. Kindness takes extra effort and honesty, but then virtuous living always does.

MARCH 14   Read I Corinthians 13:4c-6.

Love is not envious or boastful or arrogant or rude. It does not insist on its own way; it is not irritable or resentful; it does not rejoice in wrongdoing, but rejoices in the truth.

One Mother's Day I heard a speech about two mothers. One was an inner-city mother who carefully raised her child in a neglected neighborhood, only to witness him killed in a senseless drive-by shooting. The other mother was the speaker's own—a single mother who had raised him in rural America, struggling to make money enough and time to hold their family together. This mother, unlike the first, was now revelling in success as she watched her son achieve recognition and prominence in his career.

The point was clear: Both mothers were exemplary. Something beyond the love of the mothers was needed to create a society where each child could thrive and grow up to make a difference.

The speaker declared that the qualities of "a mother's love" have largely disappeared from our society. National leaders who are supposed to serve the people have forgotten what nurture and care demand. Businesses often seem most interested in beating their competitors than working toward a kinder and more just world.

The speaker's point rang true. Love that rejoices and emphasizes the truth and does not wallow in wrongdoing or envy will help make the world a place where all children can thrive. The qualities of a good mother's love are needed in all sectors of society. A mother's love is not something to keep only at home.

MARCH 15   Read I Corinthians 13:7.

[Love] bears all things.

Many words are used to describe love, most of them lofty sounding and often idealistic. Yet how does love act? In answering this question for myself, I thought of my own mother, whose birthday is today.

When I read the phrase "love bears all things," I recall the very real act of love it took to bear me into being. When my mother was five months pregnant with me, she began to hemorrhage and was ordered to bed by her doctor. Somehow she managed to care for my brother and get enough extra rest to hold on for two more months until I came racing into the world—a four-pound preemie who needed constant care.

Thirty years later, when I discovered that I was pregnant with my second child and my first was not yet two years old, I reeled with despair. I couldn't imagine how I would cope. I was just starting to feel the freedom that comes when a toddler can feed herself and communicate her basic needs.

When I told my mother, she reminded me that when she became pregnant with me, my brother was only nine months old—not walking, not talking—in every way an infant.

I gained new respect for my mother and for what she did in choosing to bear me, give birth to me, care for me, and bestow upon me a quality of love that I can recall in my bones and pass on through my body.

MARCH 16   Read I Corinthians 13:7.

[Love] believes all things.

When I went to bed on March 15, 1990, I did so full of the knowledge that March 16 was the due date for my first child.

Earlier that day I had felt my first contraction. Now, hours later, the contractions had subsided. I lay there for a while, rubbing my very large stomach. Soon this part of me would be a baby. What would he or she be like? Would this baby be like a friend or a stranger to me?

I drifted off to sleep, and at 2:00 A.M. my bag of waters broke. A few minutes later my husband and I began walking the two blocks to the hospital, carrying a small bag of essential items. I laboriously made my way up the hill, stopping a couple of times to rest and savor the stillness of the warm night.

The doctor checked and verified that I was on my final approach to motherhood. But there was a problem: the labor rooms were full. No room. We would have to go to the medical center across the city.

In an hour or so I was settled in the hospital. In between telephoning updates to family and friends, my husband watched the dawn break and the slow approach of barges entering the bay visible outside the window. I, on the other hand, walked the hallways until I no longer could. For a day and a half I waited and grew weak. I was ready. Where was that baby?

I waited; I worried; and in those laborious hours, I held fast to the belief that God would see me through.

<hr>

MARCH 17

Read I Corinthians 13:7.

[Love] hopes all things.

At 4:22 A.M. on March 17, 1990, thirty-five hours after my first contractions, an eight-pound, one-ounce baby girl with black hair took her first breath and let out a loud, lively squall. Rachel had arrived. Instantly, ready or not, I was a mother.

That night after all visitors had gone, I determined to keep Rachel in the rolling crib near my bed. This would be my trial run. She awoke at 1:00 A.M., then again at 3:00 A.M. I buzzed the nurse and asked her to watch Rachel. She was just twenty-four hours old, and I wasn't getting any sleep!

I slept soundly for a couple of hours until the nurse came in early to tell me I could go home at noon. What? They were going to let me take this little person home already? Didn't they know I'd never done this before?

When my husband arrived, the nursery supervisor handed us a set of papers and pointed us toward the elevator. I kept thinking that someone was going to stop me and say, "Hey, where are you going with that baby?" I was sure they could tell this was my first time at the helm as a parent.

When we went outside into the brisk air, questions overtook me. Was she warm enough? What if she got sick? What if we crashed on the way home? Once we were all buckled in, I looked back at our tiny passenger. She blinked her alert, bright eyes as if to say "Let's go home." Her trust in us restored our hope. We ventured forth to become a family.

MARCH 18

Read I Corinthians 13:7.

[Love] endures all things.

For me, the initial days of motherhood were exhilarating, but the nights were frustrating. Why would this baby awake crying? She was fed, dry, warm. What did this little creature want? Some nights I would just have to pull myself out of bed and rock her. Over and over I played soothing lullabies—more for me than for the baby. I learned to sit quietly and be present to Rachel. She seemed to want, most of all, to be close to me. Late in the night, when I wanted nothing more than sleep, I endured the cold, pushed away my fatigue, and held my arms in her favorite position—sometimes until they felt numb.

I had an occasional moment of bliss, feeling bonded to my baby—but mostly I endured, kept on going with an act of the will and a deep desire to get this child back to sleep.

In the dark, the realization swept over me that I was the most essential person in my daughter's life. Her father was very important to her, but I was essential. Without me, at this early stage, she would struggle to survive.

My endurance was essential to her sustenance. After a few weeks, I began to trust Rachel to tell me what she needed and wanted. She was certainly trying. It was up to me be patient with us both as I learned her language.

MARCH 19   Read Matthew 2:11*a*.

I was almost thirty when I became a mother. As the initial weeks passed, I marveled at my daughter's development. Her every action became a momentous occasion, but life itself was mundane.

For years I had jumped out of bed and rushed off to work. Now I awoke very early only to face a day of diapers, laundry, messy feedings, and little conversation. When one house-bound day followed another, I got depressed. Some days I felt isolated and alone. In my head I knew these days wouldn't last long; I wanted to fully cherish these fleeting days of infancy, but my mind wandered.

In an attempt to keep my mind active and my spirit alive, I signed up for an evening spirituality course. During one of the sessions, a slide of a woman and small child was projected on the wall. The picture had the quality of a portrait of Mary with the infant Jesus. The image moved me deep inside.

This madonna was listening to the unspoken needs of the little one attentively, with her whole heart. Aha, my spirit said. This is what this season of my life is about. As Rachel's mother, I must stay put to surround her with love, presence, and nurture. In an environment of attentive, protective presence, she could put her energy into the important work of sleep, play, and being alive.

MARCH 20   Read Ephesians 5:1*a*.

When Rachel was about ten months old, I received a letter from a friend. During an extended period of illness, my friend was struggling with her sense of importance to God. She felt ready to serve but unable. Unless she could do something for God, she felt worthless. I understood all too well that trap of thinking one had to achieve, produce, and behave to be loved. As I prayed for guidance on how to respond to my friend, God brought a scene from the breakfast table to my memory.

That morning, Rachel had awakened with a runny nose. Her eyes were bleary and she was cranky. When I made a silly noise trying to encourage her to eat a little breakfast, she tried with all her might to smile at me. That smile offered through her suffering meant the world to me. I love Rachel when she is sick, when she is cranky, when she is fun to be around and when she is not. That morning I learned how unconditionally she loves me too. Even in her suffering she wanted to smile at Mommy.

I relayed the story of Rachel's smile to my friend. Rachel showed me how God loves us all. God loves us through runny noses and cranky attitudes. God, like a loving parent, knows us and loves us even when we have little to offer in return. Our desire to smile at God through our troubles is received with pleasure by the One who loves us completely.

MARCH 21   Read Luke 17:5.

One Sunday evening while our daughter took a late nap, my husband went alone to a party. The day was turning cold so I turned on the heat; hot air billowed up from the ancient metal floor vents.

One-year-old Rachel woke up, and we sang her favorite song, "Clap Your Hands, All Ye People." I loved to watch her little hands clap and her face light up with pride as she made off-key but exuberant attempts to sing. Soon Rachel crawled off my lap and started down the hall. She was just beyond my sight when I heard her scream. "Rachel, no!" I cried out, knowing she must have put her hands on the hot furnace register. But I was too late. Her hands were already seared by the hot metal. I grabbed her and heard my own wailing, "I'm sorry. I'm sorry. Mommy forgot. I'm sorry!" I ran cold water over her red, criss-crossed hands. Rachel wailed all the way up the hill to the hospital. The nurses put me in a waiting room, and I paced.

Why hadn't I remembered the furnace? As a rule, I only turned it on when Rachel slept. I knew it was a hazard. What was wrong with me? I felt like a horrible mother.

The doctor came in and assured me Rachel would survive. She would heal—children were resilient. That I could believe, but was *I* resilient?

In a couple of weeks Rachel's hands healed, as did my confidence. Even with bandaged hands she crawled over to me and lifted her arms to be held. She still loved me.

That emergency taught me how important my faith is as I do my best to be a good mother. I can plan, organize, ask for help, and still there will be unexpected pain and needs. As Rachel's mother, the most I can do is love her fully, do my best, and beseech God to surround her with love, presence, and compassion when I am unable to be there for her.

MARCH 22   Read Romans 12:1*b*.

As my daughter neared her second birthday, I was offered a responsible and lucrative job in a distant state. I had two weeks to decide. While I deliberated, my body began to send me signals of being pregnant. I thought I must be imagining things—this couldn't be happening now! Another baby certainly was not in my plans, but sure enough, child number two was on its way.

I felt forced to sacrifice several more years of my life to caring for another infant. I raged against the timing and especially against the lack of control I had over my life. I turned down the job and became depressed. What kind of cruel trick was God playing on me?

As the weeks wore on, I struggled to accept my situation. I looked at my daughter and took courage in knowing every sacrifice made for her was well worth it. I could feel that way about another child, couldn't I?

As my stomach grew I began to let go of my desire to control my life. I accepted the little person forming inside me with fondness. About halfway through my pregnancy, I reread the biblical call, "Present your bodies as a living sacrifice." The verb *present* seemed emblazoned in light. I *did* have a choice after all. No one, no situation, no circumstance could force me to become a living sacrifice. Only I could choose to present my life to God and trust I would be transformed and renewed as I lived through the uenxpected turns and twists of my life.

MARCH 23 Read Psalm 32:8.

One afternoon when I went to pick up my daughter from day care, I bent down to say hello to one of the other toddlers in the class. He said, "Mary too rough." I repeated his words, trying to puzzle out their meaning, and the teacher heard me. "Oh yes," she motioned me over. "He's trying to tell you that Mary played too rough with Rachel today and tore out a clump of her hair. We've all had a talk about the kind of play that is too rough."

Rachel soon ran up and started telling me about the day. She had forgotten the earlier altercation. Just then Mary's mother arrived and was updated on the day. Her countenance sagged and her shoulders slumped. She sought me out to apologize for Mary's behavior. I tried to encourage her: "You aren't responsible for every one of Mary's actions. She's just being a toddler, learning to know her strength and boundaries."

That mother left that day looking so defeated. I, too, have felt that way before. Yet raising good children is not about feeling proud about perfect behavior or feeling destroyed by their inevitable battles. Training children in the way they should go requires many trial runs. As long as we keep our eyes on these little ones and gently coach them as they learn to master new skills and develop relationships, they will learn. They really will!

MARCH 24   Read Psalm 32:6.

One morning while my parents were visiting, we were halfway through breakfast when Rachel said, "Mommy, we no pray." She was right. We'd forgotten to say grace. So we stopped eating, held hands, and I asked Rachel to pray after me.

"Dear God," I started and she repeated the words. Then I said, "Bless the food." She parroted, then continued on her own. "Bless Papa, Grandma, and Mommy." We then followed her lead. "And keep Daddy safe on his trip." She remembered her father had left on an airplane the night before. "Amen," I concluded, and the adults resumed eating. But Rachel left her hands outstretched. "Bless my friends," she continued. We all looked at her and smiled at her persistence. We joined her again as a litany of friends from day care followed: "Bless Mary, Jenny, Justin. . . ."

While we adults had consented to pray to fulfill our morning table ritual, the smallest among us had the heart and determination to include all those for whom she cared. God, no doubt, was delighted to heed the requests of this little godly one who was learning to regularly bring her cares and joys to God in prayer.

MARCH 25   **Read Proverbs 1:8.**

My father's instruction can be boiled down to two often repeated phrases: "Givers are winners" and "It's not what the facts are; it's how they are perceived." I took these adages to heart and lived by them as unchallenged rules until giving too much wore me out, and I realized that some "facts" mattered regardless of how anyone else perceived them.

During a difficult time in adulthood, I dreamed about an incident in my adolescence when two friends and I were wrongly accused of drinking while on an out-of-town band trip. Our entire high school band was sent home early, and many friends and their parents were furious with us. So was my father. But my mother simply asked me what happened. I told her the truth, and she believed me and stood by my story. My dream reminded me of the balance my mother's quiet teaching offered in my life. Through that incident and others, she taught me by example to stand firm in what I knew to be the truth no matter what other people thought.

I'm beginning to see the different and yet equally important roles my husband and I play in our children's learning processes. Whereas my husband shows Rachel how to climb back up a tree after falling off a low limb, I encourage her to try it on her own while assuring her that getting up the tree isn't a measure of her ultimate worth. Together we trust that both our daughters will learn to strive hard and believe in their worth even when they may fall short.

I am thankful that God graciously gives us more than one person in our lives to balance out and expand our knowledge of life.

MARCH 26   Read Proverbs 22:6.

I once heard a one-point sermon on childrearing: The father must be the spiritual head and final authority on family decisions. As the pastor hammered home his views, I thought of the single moms and other nontraditional families in the church. The pastor implied that any family that didn't have a father filling a strictly prescribed role would result in pagan children. He obviously believed that there was only one right way to raise children.

More recently in another church, when I looked at my Sunday bulletin and saw that the day's sermon was on childrearing, I groaned. But this pastor's first point was different: There is no one foolproof way to raise children to ensure they will always follow the path we desire. The godly way to parent is to be godly people. I could say "Amen" to that! Then he said we are called to always accept our children, even if we don't approve of their choices. The third point was the best: Even though it's hard to believe, God loves our children more than we do. When we can't get through to our children, God will find a way.

I left church determined to be a godly woman who passes on the sound principles and spiritual practices I've learned. I vowed to try to accept my children unconditionally. I felt reassured that I could parent with confidence, knowing that God remains a faithful member of my family, who also teaches, loves, and guides my children.

MARCH 27   Read I Thessalonians 2:7b.

When pregnant with my second child, I talked often to my daughter about the baby inside my tummy. Soon Rachel took a pronounced interest in her life-sized doll. She began bringing her doll to the breakfast table. She designated one of her outgrown blankets as the "baby's blankie" and insisted that it go everywhere the doll did. One day as we left home she declared we were "two mommies going to the store"! She loved being like me.

Sometimes the doll was dragged roughly around by its red hair or abandoned for some other toy. But one night as she put the baby in its cradle she said, "Gentle with the baby," and gave the rubbery face a tender goodnight kiss. Her actions warmed my heart. The times I've been impatient and cross linger in my memory, but Rachel reminded me of the many other times when my gentleness and tenderness got through.

It's humbling to be reminded that our children learn most by watching and imitating us. Our actions do speak more loudly than our words. May we all pray today for an extra measure of gentleness and wisdom, so that we can be proud of the ways our children imitate our care.

MARCH 28   Read Ecclesiastes 3:1-2a.

The periods of pregnancy and early motherhood provide incredible open doors to people's lives. Tiny babies are wonderful conversation starters. Several older women in corner stores or coffee shops have stopped me to tell me about their great-grandchildren. Other young mothers have claimed the bench beside me at the park, and we've talked about our families and compared our children's development. But not everyone has a happy story to tell.

When my hairdresser cut my hair just before my daughter was born, she sadly told me of the surgery that left her unable to bear children. When a friend came to congratulate me on hearing I was expecting our second child, I rolled my eyes and said, "Not exactly perfect timing, but I'm getting used to the idea!" She grabbed my arm and begged me, "Oh, don't say that. We've been trying for so long to get pregnant. I'd love to say I was expecting."

Childbearing and rearing touch us at our deepest feelings. How important it is to walk and talk gently and compassionately with one another.

MARCH 29   Read I Thessalonians 2:8.

Most people come to faith because others have shared the varied texture of their lives with them. Living what we believe is the "proof" of faith. The heroes of the faith for me are those who have let me see both their pain and their hope. How much more, then, must we honestly share our lives with our children, these little souls who have been placed into our care for a while?

It's easy for me to laugh when my children are around. It's harder for me to cry, but sometimes I do. I am committed to living a whole life—joys and tears—with them. How else will they learn that faith is not just a matter to be discussed in church but a daily way of living?

MARCH 30   Read Ecclesiastes 3:4a.

The late months of pregnancy are a time for laughter and enjoyment. Think of it; when else can you eat six times a day without anyone wondering if you have an eating disorder? When else can you buy six boxes of baby wipes, three jars of dill pickles, and a gallon of butter-brickle ice cream and blame it all on "nesting instinct"? Best of all, when else can you take naps in the afternoon without anyone thinking you're lazy?

One day just before my second child was born, I saw a former co-worker who exclaimed, "You look like you are going to have twins. You look like a balloon that could burst open any second!" I laughed and said, "Just call me the human Hindenburg." Later that afternoon a neighbor pulled out of her driveway and stopped me as I stood on the sidewalk. "You sure are huge!" she said. "You're sticking straight out. Last time you must have carried lower." I turned sideways to give her a better look at my distended profile, and she drove away laughing.

I went inside with conflicting feelings. I didn't like being reminded of my largeness. But then I stood in front of our full-length mirror. My belly was incredible. I resembled a female Buddha from my neck to my knees. I, too, began to laugh. There was no denying my femaleness or my fruitfulness. My husband came in and said with a smile, "Your body is amazing."

Yes, the female body is amazing and even awesome in the late stages of pregnancy. God designed the female form to stretch beyond belief while filling up with more life than seems possible. What more can we do than rejoice in God's sense of humor? We can honor God by joining in the amazement of new life with joy.

MARCH 31   Read Psalm 139:13.

God's work is mysterious. While pregnancy is one of the more public events in a woman's life (even strangers who see a protruding stomach often want to comment or touch), the actual "baby making" remains an invisible wonder. We may be able to trace fetal development from cell division to delivery, but the definite answers to why and when life begins are beyond our ken.

Isn't it just like God to give us visible signs, like big bellies, to prepare us for miracles? Even with the foreknowledge of great things to come, often we are still taken by surprise when new life pushes, squalling and struggling, into the world before our very eyes. What a mysterious, miraculous work of God, indeed!

APRIL

God's Promises

IRIS R. JONES-GBOIZO

APRIL 1   **Read Genesis 2:18-22.**

In an act of love, God, the Creator, made woman from the rib of man. And why did God do it? Because God said, "It is not good that the man should be alone" (Genesis 2:18*a*). But why did God choose the rib of man? Perhaps God chose to make woman from the man's rib because she was meant to be very close to him. Perhaps God wanted to express that we need each other to live.

God had a purpose for the man and the woman. Their job was to tend the garden and watch over all the animals God had made. God meant for the man and the woman to share in that responsibility. And, as with the animals, God commanded that they "be fruitful and multiply."

I'm glad that God made me, and I'm glad that there is work for me to do. I thank God that I am a woman and a mother, for God has blessed me with a fine son. Although I have been divorced for several years, with God's help I have made it through the difficult times. A single parent's life is not easy, but God has never failed to provide for me and my son. I just take my problems to the Lord in prayer.

Over the years, Jesus has been a confidant, an advisor, a teacher, and a constant companion. He is as near to me as I need him to be, and I need him to be very, very close. The thing that keeps me going is knowing how much God loves me. I couldn't make it if I thought for a moment that God didn't care. Even through the hard times, God loves us all.

God made woman for man because God cared. I once read that God used Adam's rib to make Eve because woman was meant to be dearly loved. I like that reason best of all. Today I will act like a woman who is very dearly loved.

APRIL 2   Read Genesis 3:16*a*; Romans 8:37.

Labor. What an appropriate word for the process of having a baby. It's work, that's for sure, but it is also joy. Even under difficult circumstances, there is joy in bringing a new life into the world.

My marriage was not going well even before I found out that I was pregnant. Although things did not get better between my husband and me, I knew that the child growing inside me was a miracle in the making. I prayed that I would have a healthy baby, and I tried to have a positive attitude.

Throughout my pregnancy, and especially my delivery, there was always someone who offered a word of encouragement or who took hold of my hand. I know Jesus was with me; he never left my side.

God's promise is true: We are overcomers through Christ.

APRIL 3   Read Genesis 21:6.

At age thirty-six, my girlfriend just had a baby boy. More and more women are having children later in life these days, but my friend was still a little embarrassed about being pregnant. You see, she remarried a few years ago, and she thought people would think she was silly to have another child at her age. But no one was laughing.

Her husband was "pregnant" right along with her. One Sunday morning he looked positively grim. I asked him what was wrong, and he could hardly get the words out: "I can't wait until the baby comes. I don't think I can take much more of this." I smiled reassuringly. When I asked if they planned to have more children, he quickly replied, "No, no more. This is it!" After their son was born, I've never seen a happier family.

Isaac's name means laughter, or someone who laughs. I guess it was funny to think of Abraham and Sarah having a child. They were very old. But others laughed with Sarah, not at her. Isaac was the child God had promised them. He would be the child through whom the nation of Israel, God's chosen people, would come. Indeed, Abraham and Sarah had the last laugh.

No one laughed at my friends. They are an example that marriage can be good, even the second time around, and that nothings's too difficult for God.

APRIL 4   Read Genesis 21:8-21.

Hagar was the first surrogate mother we know about. But her son, Ishmael, did not become Abraham's heir. When Sarah finally had Isaac, Hagar and Ishmael were sent away. Reluctantly, Abraham packed bread and water for Hagar and sent her off. But God promised Abraham that Hagar and Ishmael would be provided for, and God kept his word.

I'll never forget when my son caught the chicken pox. His case was complicated by a skin infection, which caused him to develop large pockets of pus all over his body. It was awful to look at and hard to care for. He couldn't stand to be touched, and he refused to let anyone else care for him. For a whole week he suffered unbearable pain.

After a week of this, I was exhausted. I was worn down to the point that I began to cry. I felt helpless, and I cried to the Lord to help my son. Then I fell asleep. God must have heard my prayer because when I woke up, things had changed. Each day my son was better than the day before. He could eat, he watched TV, and he was even interested in playing games.

God had stepped in and turned an unbearable situation into a bearable one. For Hagar, it was life-sustaining water, seemingly coming from nowhere. It was like that for me and my son, too, but our well was on the inside, renewing our strength. God had not left us—not even for a minute. Praise the Lord!

APRIL 5   Read Genesis 25:21-23.

We don't really know why it took Isaac twenty years before he prayed that Rebekah would have a child. Yet it certainly took no time before his prayer was answered. Because she was experiencing such distress, Rebekah inquired of the Lord as to her condition. Imagine her surprise at knowing she would have twins.

It must have been rough for Rebekah. Rabbis have described what was going on inside Rebekah this way: Whenever Rebekah walked past a house where the Torah was studied, Jacob would become active, and whenever she walked past a place where idols were worshiped, Esau would become active. And the rest of the time, Jacob and Esau fought each other. Poor Rebekah!

I don't have twins, but I do have a very active little boy. He skips, hops, and jumps from one place to the next. He's a ball of energy in motion. Even in the womb, he was very active.

But through all my ups and downs as a single parent, I have managed to keep both my sanity and my sense of humor. It is said that God never gives us more than we can handle, and I believe it.

I'm sure God's words comforted Rebekah. Jesus' words also comfort me. Though he never promised to spare us of trials and tribulations, he promised always to be with us. And that's good enough for me.

APRIL 6   Read Exodus 2:1-10.

The things a mother won't do for her child! How carefully this plan was devised and orchestrated. Moses' mother planned with her daughter, Miriam, to place Moses in a basket at the water's edge, close to where Pharaoh's daughter would be bathing. Miriam asked Pharaoh's daughter if she should get a nurse for the crying baby, and then she ran home to get her mother. It was masterful!

Moses was born to lead the people of Israel out of slavery in Egypt and to deliver them into the hands of Joshua—that was his purpose. Because of his purpose, and because of his mother's courage, God made a way for Moses' mother to hide him as long as she could. And when she could no longer hide him, God arranged for Pharaoh's daughter to find him and raise him as an Egyptian.

When Pharaoh's daughter found Moses, he began to cry. As the scripture tells us, she "took pity on him" (Exodus 2:6). Because Pharaoh's daughter believed that the child was hungry, it was easy for Miriam to step forward and offer to get a nurse for Moses. Who says God doesn't make a way!

As a mother, it is comforting to know that God is never far away. Although God sits high, God also looks low. God is always watching.

APRIL 7 — Read Ruth 1:16.

Change does not come easily. We still have not become the color-blind society we so desperately need to be in order to live together as one human family. But love knows no color barriers.

When I was growing up, people were just people to my family. Nobody ever made any distinction about race or ethnicity. No one group of people was considered to be better than another. As I got older, however, I found out that there is an ugly idea, known as racism, that dictates that races should not mix.

To me, we are all God's children, regardless of the color of our skin. Now that I have my own child, I am teaching my son about God's unconditional love for all races. The challenge is trying to explain why some people mistreat others whose skin color is different from their own, and trying to help him understand why love and forgiveness are the right responses to racial prejudice.

In the book of Ruth, no issues are raised about her ethnicity—not once. Neither is she denied or discriminated against. Could God be trying to tell us something?

When we sow seeds of hatred, we reap a crop of injustice, violence, and oppression. But when we sow seeds of love, something beautiful happens, and the world becomes a better, safer place. This is the message we must pass on to our children: never to let anyone cause us to stop loving or forgiving. God forgives us, and we ought to forgive one another. For Christians, there is no other way to live.

While God could have made us all the same color, I believe that it is our diversity that makes us beautiful in God's sight. Perhaps the book of Ruth is included in the Bible to reinforce this principle. Perhaps we, the mothers of the world, are the ones who can best teach our children how to live together in love.

APRIL 8   Read I Kings 3:16-28.

It takes more than childbirth to make a woman a mother. In the case of the two women who came before King Solomon, only one of them could be the child's mother. Solomon's judgment was swift and clean: Divide the child between them. Case closed.

But wait a minute! As the king brought the sword closer, the Bible tells us that the child's mother showed compassion for her son. She would rather give up her son than allow him to be killed. Yet the other woman was content to see the child die. How could anyone care so little for a child?

God asks us the same question today. We are all God's children. As a mother cares for her child, God cares about us and does not want to see any of us hurt. God's love is deeper and wider and higher and stronger than anything we could ever imagine. I think Solomon understood this. He said, "Give the first woman the living boy; do not kill him. She is his mother" (I Kings 3:27).

Just as God is attentive to us and to our needs, so also we must be attentive to our children. And we must not stop there, because all God's children want to be cared for and affirmed. We are all precious in the sight of God.

APRIL 9   Read II Kings 4:8-16.

Elisha was the prophet who succeeded Elijah in the political life of Israel. Much is known about Elisha's political involvements, but he also was very much involved in the lives of the common people. In this account, Elisha is rewarding a wealthy Shunammite woman for opening her home to him and his servant.

We are not told that the Shunammite woman wanted to have a child, or whether she was barren. But when Elisha told her that she would have a child the following year, she seemed to be taken by surprise.

I knew that I would be a mother about five years before I met my son's father. At the time, however, I tried to deny it, just as the Shunammite woman did. Nevertheless, the Lord set his plan in motion.

First, God gave me a song. The melody went round and round in my head. Then a musician friend of mine asked me to put words to the tune; he wrote the musical score. It turned out to be a lullaby. To make it more interesting, some of the words the Lord gave me were in French. Years later I realized that the song was written for my French–West African son, Anatole.

God's ways are mysterious. The Shunammite woman found out, as I continue to learn, that nothing is beyond the power of God.

APRIL 10   Read II Kings 4:18-37.

In the story of Elisha and the Shunammite woman, she utters these words in the midst of her crisis: "It is well" (II Kings 4:26 KJV). Not only does she say this to her husband, but she also says it to Gehazi as she arrives at Mt. Carmel. But how could it be well? She had lost her son. A mother can imagine no greater loss.

This story reminds me of H. G. Spafford's hymn, "It Is Well with My Soul." Spafford wrote the words to this hymn just after the death of his four daughters. The luxury liner on which his wife and daughters were traveling was rammed by a British sailing vessel, causing the loss of 226 lives. He had not been traveling with them at the time.

Spafford is said to have penned the words as his ship sailed over the spot where his children had been lost. He wrote,

"Whatever my lot, thou hast taught me to say, 'It is well, it is well with my soul!'"

Elisha revived the Shunammite woman's son, but Spafford's daughters were not returned to him. Yet even in his grief, the Lord was with him—comforting him and assuring him of his presence. There are many things that happen in life that we cannot understand. But Spafford gave us words to encourage our hearts.

When life's trials overtake us, we need to run to God. God will see us through.

APRIL 11 Read Esther 4:15-16.

In Old Testament times, fasting was a common practice by which people humbled themselves before God. Esther instructed Mordecai to "gather all the Jews" to fast for three days. She knew that she could be killed if King Artaxerxes was offended by her unannounced visit. By fasting, she was preparing for her death.

Esther must have struggled as she considered Mordecai's request that she plead for the lives of her people before the king. Despite her great beauty, it was her piety that would save her people and herself. Her self sacrifice moved God to act on behalf of the people of Israel. The king honored Esther's request, and the Israelites were spared. Esther's story reminds us that God hears the prayers of those who humble themselves before him.

We mothers also know the meaning of self-sacrifice. We love our children so much that we are willing to "do without" or risk our own safety to ensure our children's well-being. Although our sacrifices may differ, the love we have for our children is universal.

Of course, the greatest example of sacrificial love is Jesus' death upon the cross. Jesus offered himself as the atoning sacrifice for our sins. As we prepare our hearts for Easter, may we

consider Jesus' atoning act of love for us and surrender ourselves to his will. Jesus gave his life, and Esther offered hers.
But our acts of self-sacrifice are not punishable by death. What
do we have to lose?

APRIL 12   Read Proverbs 4:23.

Parental advice. We all need it, but often we fail to accept it.
When I encounter this passage of scripture, I envision King
David speaking to his son, Solomon. What care, diligence, and
patience David takes as he instructs his son!

Solomon, now king, is retelling the story of how his father
taught him. And yet Solomon seems to miss the important
piece of advice: Guard your heart. Solomon's negligence eventually led him to idol worship and his own ruin.

We guard our hearts when we pray that God will help us to
hide his word in our hearts. There are many creative ways to
memorize scripture, but the more difficult task is to be obedi-
ent. Although we fall short, we are to keep trying.

Why should we guard our hearts? Because when we don't,
we often are led astray. Instead of being alert, we grow dull
and begin to forget God's word. And often we get into trouble. Yet when we discipline ourselves to spend time with God's
word, something wonderful happens. Not only do the fruits of
the Spirit begin to manifest themselves in our hearts, but our
attitude changes, too.

As mothers, we are called to give our children guidance and
advice, but perhaps there is no better wisdom we can share
than this: Keep God's word in your heart.

APRIL 13   Read Proverbs 11:16a.

What does it mean to be a gracious woman and a gracious
mother?

A gracious mother is a woman of God. She diligently studies God's word and teaches her children God's word. God's grace flows through her because the Holy Spirit dwells within her. The Holy Spirit, our Comforter, instructs her and guides her in her spiritual journey. A gracious mother draws upon divine intelligence through prayer to find wisdom and strength for her many responsibilities. And for this virtue, she is honored and respected.

As I mature in faith, I have discovered that being gracious is not an overnight process. Just as our children grow and learn daily, so also we are perfected daily. And sometimes we are perfected through our suffering.

It is in our suffering that we grow spiritually. During the difficult times, in particular, we are in need of God's word; and we are nourished and renewed by God's word.

Paul's words in Romans 5:3-4 encourage us: "We also boast in our sufferings, knowing that suffering produces endurance, and endurance produces character, and character produces hope." With God's help, through and by the power of the Holy Spirit, we are perfected one day at a time.

May the Lord teach us how to take one day at a time, graciously.

APRIL 14   Read Proverbs 14:1; I Peter 2:4-8.

One Sunday when I was a little girl, the leader of devotions drew two houses on the chalkboard. One house was off balance—its foundation was incomplete—and several important parts of the house were missing. The other house was well balanced—its foundation was sure—and all parts of the house were in place. When our teacher asked us which house we would prefer to live in, we all chose the stable, complete house.

Children are natural builders. Not only did we understand the need for a firm foundation, but we also knew what major building materials would be required to complete the unfinished house.

Then our teacher read I Peter 2:4-8. We learned that we are called to build a spiritual house, a house that is complete and has a firm foundation. Our teacher told us that in order to build this house, we need a chief Cornerstone, who is Christ Jesus. Once we accept Jesus as Lord and Savior, with God's help we become living stones—strong, durable, and able to stand. Then she explained that as we build our spiritual house, we need to check the foundation and the building materials to be sure we are building a house that will stand. Her words marked a turning point in my life and have stayed with me to this day.

Likewise, the words of Proverbs 14:1 have come to have great meaning in my life. The wise woman builds her (spiritual) house, and the wise mother also helps her children become wise builders. Although our children's (spiritual) house will not begin to take recognizable shape for some time, we can help them choose strong building materials and begin laying firm foundations.

What kinds of builders are you helping your children to become?

APRIL 15   Read Proverbs 31:10-28.

The Bible speaks of wifehood and motherhood as blessings. One Bible dictionary defines blessings as finding favor with God. Proverbs 31:10 calls such a woman a virtuous woman (KJV). She possesses character, strength, and ability. She is faithful (v. 11); she is a partner to her husband, and she doesn't mind working (v. 13); she knows where to find a bargain (v. 14); she is compassionate and generous (v. 20); she is wise and kind (v. 26); she knows how to keep a house, and she also keeps herself busy (v. 27); and she is loved and appreciated by her husband and children (v. 28).

My grandmother is just such a woman. She is loved by her children and respected by all who know her. And she was the apple of my grandfather's eye.

We all know virtuous women. Most of us strive for these qualities ourselves. But it is easy to become discouraged when we do not receive or we fail to recognize encouraging words and gestures of appreciation.

Young children express their love and appreciation in many ways—a contented cooing sound, a smile, a touch, a simple "I love you, Mommy." But often we fail to see or hear the thankful, affirming messages within these simple expressions. So if you know a virtuous woman, why not give her a call today and thank her for her example? You just might make her day.

APRIL 16   Read Isaiah 49:13-15.

It was very early in the morning. My son had been up and down all night. He was about to lose his first tooth.

When my son expressed his fears, I tried to console him by telling him that losing a tooth is natural, but not necessarily painless. And when he expressed his anxiety about whether losing the tooth would cause more pain, I assured him that once the tooth was out, the pain would cease and a new tooth eventually would replace it. With that, he settled down and went to sleep.

Perhaps my son's fear was not unlike the anxiety Israel felt. In pain, Zion lamented: "The LORD has forsaken me, my Lord has forgotten me" (Isaiah 49:14). Just as I comforted my son, so also God, like a loving parent, consoled Israel. God would not forget his chosen people.

God who made us has compassion for all his children. His constant care and compassion are like that of a mother for her child.

God would not forget Israel, and God will not forget us. These are comforting words, indeed, to us and to our children.

APRIL 17   Read Jeremiah 31:3b.

A Christian radio program for women begins each broadcast with this verse from Jeremiah. Even though I no longer listen to the program regularly, this verse has stuck with me.

As I look back over the past year, I realize the power of these words. I didn't know it then, but I was being drawn away from worldly cares and toward my Savior's everlasting love and faithfulness. God's faithfulness continues to draw me closer with each passing day.

Everlasting love and faithfulness. These are two things a good mother knows and understands. A mother expresses her everlasting love as she comforts, guides, protects, and consoles her child each day. And a mother's faithfulness is constant. Whenever her child needs her, she is ever ready to be there for that child.

Jesus loves us with an everlasting love and a constant faithfulness. Every day he tells us of his love. He comforts us, guides us, protects us, and consoles us; and he is always just a prayer away.

Perhaps this verse is a good beginning not only for a radio program but also for a mother's day.

APRIL 18   Read Micah 6:8.

Since you became a mother, have you spent much time thinking of yourself as a *child*?

We are the children of God. We are God's own special possessions. We have been given dominion over the earth, and God expects us to be good stewards of what he has given us.

Everyone is struggling for his or her rights. But what about God's rights? Does God have a say? What does the Lord require of us?

God wants us to serve him. God doesn't want our leftovers. God wants you and me—mind, body, heart, and soul. God wants our availability. Sometimes that frightens us. We fear what God might ask us to do.

The first time I asked God what he wanted me to do, I spent the next three months as a volunteer at an emergency women's shelter. It was a new and sometimes frightening experience for me, but I grew as a result of it.

We must learn to trust God more—to think of ourselves as children of God. God knows us better than we know ourselves. Jesus loves us and wants to bless us. And Jesus wants us to be a blessing to others, especially to our children.

Listen to God's call. What is the Lord asking you to do?

APRIL 19   Read Matthew 15:21-28.

She was not a Jew, but she had heard the stories about Jesus. When she addressed him, she called him Lord and Son of David. The disciples must have given her a hard time. Perhaps they grumbled, "How dare she ask the Master to listen to her feeble request!" But in spite of all the odds, she made her request known.

She humbled herself before Jesus, and he healed her daughter. Her confidence in Jesus was such that she would have gladly accepted a crumb of his favor. She knew that even a drop of Jesus' favor would restore her daughter. Her compassion for her child was so great that she sought Jesus' help despite the discouraging words.

I imagine that Elizabeth Codner penned the words to "Even Me" for just such an occasion: "Lord, I hear of show'rs of blessings . . . Let some drops now fall on me!"

As mothers, we have many concerns and prayers for our children. The beautiful promise of this story is that if we will humble ourselves, Jesus will hear our prayers and answer them.

APRIL 20   Read Mark 16:9-11.

Courage and commitment. These are two qualities that every mother requires.

We need courage to discipline our children, and to know when not to discipline them; courage to be consistent with our children; courage to give our children the independence they need to grow and mature; courage to watch our children venture into a dangerous world; and courage to teach our children to be different—to be followers of Christ in a world that does not call Christ "Savior."

We also need commitment—commitment to sustain us through the difficult times and the times when we are tempted to believe that our efforts do not make a difference.

Courage and commitment are also two qualities that every follower of Christ requires. Mary Magdalene was such a follower.

The disciples did not believe Mary when she told them that she had seen the risen Lord. They must have felt that Jesus should have appeared to them first. Why did Jesus appear to Mary Magdalene first?

When Jesus was arrested, the disciples fled in fear. Yet during the whole ordeal, the women moved about quite freely. Perhaps Jesus appeared to Mary Magdalene to reward her courage and commitment to serving him.

Unlike the disciples, who were expecting to rule and reign with Jesus, Mary Magdalene wanted only to know Jesus and serve him as Lord. Her love was of a pure heart, and perfect love casts out fear. There was nothing and no one who could stop her from serving Jesus.

As we strive to become better mothers and better followers of Christ, let us consider our level of courage and commitment.

APRIL 21   Read Luke 1:26-55.

All parents want the very best for their children. We want them to be doctors or lawyers or successful in whatever careers they may choose. We want them to be well-educated and to have all the things in life we may never have had. We don't want life to be the struggle for them that it may have been (or may be) for us.

In the Magnificat (Luke 1:46-55), Mary praises God for what God has done, for what God is doing, and for what God will do in the future. Her son will be great. The angel Gabriel has announced it (Luke 1:26-38). Jesus will be king!

Indeed, Jesus was not an ordinary child. At the age of twelve, Jesus was already going about his Father's business (Luke 2:49). By the time Jesus began his ministry, he was hard at work fulfilling the Old Testament Scriptures. And although the end seemed near as he hung on the cross (Luke 23:38), Christ was raised from the dead and ascended into heaven, where he is King of kings and Lord of lords. And Christ will come again.

Our children are not our own. They come through us, but they do not belong to us. They have their own minds and their own parts to play in God's kingdom. Just like us, they must decide whether to take up their cross. As parents, we have the responsibility to point the way. What a wonderful opportunity we have to teach our children about this man called Jesus.

APRIL 22   Read Luke 2:22-38.

Anna was devoted to God. She showed her love by serving in the temple. Scripture tells us that she fasted and prayed. She was an example of one who never wearies of well-doing. Whether you consider her to have been eighty-four years old or to have served in the temple for eighty-four years, Anna was very old.

Sometimes we have the notion that we outgrow our need to learn about Jesus and to serve God. We focus so much of our energy on teaching our children about God that we often neglect our own spiritual growth. Of course, teaching our children about God and helping them to grow in faith is very important; but we forget that our children often learn best by example—that the best teachers are those who practice the discipline themselves.

Sometimes we even begin to look forward to "spiritual retirement." But there is no such thing. We are expected to serve God in whatever capacity we can until the day we die. And for many of us, that will be a long, long time.

I'm not sure why Simeon was ready to die after seeing Jesus, but Anna made it her business to get the word out. Anna was one of the first evangelists of her time. Jerusalem should have been hungry for this news. Their redemption was at hand. Their long-awaited Messiah had come.

Although we have not seen Jesus face to face, we feel his presence inside us and all around us. And that's news worth spreading—to our children as well as to our friends, our relatives, our co-workers, and others. God is not willing for anyone to be lost. Tell someone today!

APRIL 23   Read Luke 10:38-42.

Choices. We make them every day. Some choices we make consciously; others we make without even realizing it.

In this Scripture passage we meet two sisters, Martha and Mary. They were the sisters of Lazarus, whom Jesus raised from the dead. These sisters did not travel with Jesus and his disciples, but they always opened their home to Jesus when he passed their way.

Martha was an excellent hostess, paying close attention to every detail in order to make Jesus' stay a pleasant one. And Mary usually assisted her. Ordinarily, Martha was very organized, but this visit caught her off guard. In fact, Martha seemed unusually preoccupied, whereas Mary was content to sit at the feet of Jesus.

What made this visit different? Perhaps there were rumors circulating about Jesus' many confrontations with the scribes and Pharisees. Perhaps Mary sensed that Jesus would not be among them much longer. Whatever the reason, Mary seated herself with the disciples. She wanted to hear the Master more closely this time. Jesus commended Mary for her choice, even though it meant that Martha was left to manage the affairs of the house alone.

Too often we mothers of young children choose—whether intentionally or unintentionally—to be like Martha rather than Mary. Although taking care of our children and household responsibilities is very important, Jesus invites us to also choose to spend quality time with him. Through prayer, fasting, meditation, and studying God's Word we can have a fuller, richer walk with the Lord.

It's often difficult to find time to be alone with God in prayer and study, but even a few minutes of private time—in one sitting or scattered throughout the day—can nourish the soul. Just as we would never think of denying our children the nourishment they need to grow, so also we must not neglect our own spiritual nourishment.

APRIL 24   Read John 4:1-15.

The sixth of Jesus' seven last words was, "I am thirsty" (John 19:28). The Bible tells us that Jesus uttered these words when all his work was finished.

It is interesting that Jesus never said he was thirsty until he hung on the cross. Even when Jesus met the Samaritan woman at the well in Sychar, he didn't say he was thirsty but only asked her for a drink. Jesus' work was not yet done. He knew what was in the woman's heart, and he offered her living water.

"I am thirsty" are words we mothers hear quite often. Young children do not hesitate to make their needs known—especially their need for liquid refreshment! Our children teach us an important lesson.

Many of us walk around carrying great burdens that are well hidden from others. But Jesus stands ready to bear our burdens if we will let him. He offers us the free gift of salvation and then equips us with the Holy Spirit, our inner spring of living water.

We cannot hide our problems from Jesus, no matter how large or small they may be. Jesus is our burden bearer. Cast your cares upon him, for he cares for you.

APRIL 25 Read John 12:1-8.

Mary's single act of love and devotion will always be remembered. Although her gift provoked much criticism, we know that she gave freely, without holding anything back.

Perhaps you have have heard the story of the widow who had nothing to put in the offering plate. When it was passed to her, she placed it on the floor and stepped into it. She gave her whole self to the Lord. Like Mary, she wanted to show her gratitude for what Christ had done in her life.

When I became a mother, I questioned my ability to give. "Do I really have what it takes to be a good mother?" I asked myself. Then one day I thought of the widow and of Mary's act of love. "I'll just give my love," I thought, "my very self." As time has progressed, I've found myself in situations and roles that I'd never dreamed of. But always I bring my love, my joy, and my gratitude to every task of "mothering." And I have found motherhood to be one of the most exciting adventures I've ever had.

So often we pull back, and we don't give God our all. When we are confronted with new challenges, we question our ability. Change does not come without risk. Yet Jesus' assurance that he will always be with us and provide for our needs far outweighs the risk. God is faithful. Every day with Jesus *is* sweeter than the day before.

APRIL 26 Read Acts 16:14-15.

God knows our hearts better than we do. God planned that Lydia would meet Paul and receive his words about Jesus. All Lydia had to do was to accept the will of God and receive Jesus as Lord and Savior.

Once Lydia accepted Christ, she was baptized. Later everyone in her household was baptized. Lydia was indeed blessed, and she became a blessing to her whole family. But she didn't stop there. She opened her home to Paul, Silas, and Timothy and became a blesing to them as well. That's what Jesus wants for all his children—that we would be a blessing to one another.

It's so easy to name the ways our children are blessings to us, but how are we blessings to our children? One way to know how we bless our children's lives is to think of how our mothers or grandmothers or other loved ones have blessed us. Sometimes it is only by looking back that we are able to see into the present. By considering how we bless our children, we gain a humble understanding of how greatly our Lord blesses us, his children.

Jesus loves us and calls us to draw near him. If we will surrender our will to him, as Lydia did, then he will come into our lives and use us to bless others.

APRIL 27   Read Philippians 3:10.

Paul is talking about commitment in this verse. To know Christ and to become like Christ require commitment. This is the goal toward which Paul was striving, and it is our goal as well.

My son likes to play and pretend. He especially likes watching videos about Jesus. At his young age, he thinks of Jesus as a "super hero" who is fun to imitate. But to us, imitating Christ is not an act; it's hard work—and serious work. Imitating Christ requires that we get to know him. And that takes time.

Getting to know Christ takes a lifetime, yet so many of us never even try. Some say they're waiting until they have more time. There's always some excuse. But we can know Christ only if we diligently seek him.

Going to church on Sunday and doing nothing the rest of the week does little for our spiritual lives. We also do our children a disservice when we train them to be "Sunday-morning Christians" and nothing more. Our children look to us as examples, and they see the depth of our commitment to Christ.

Commitment requires effort and sacrifice. Every mother knows that! But just as the joys and blessings of motherhood outweigh the sacrifices, so also the rewards of a committed, disciplined relationship with Christ fill our every need.

APRIL 28   Read II Timothy 1:5.

There is much to be said for good home training. Timothy's mother and grandmother, who were devout Jewish women, trained him in the Torah. Then, through the missionary efforts of Paul, Timothy accepted Christ as a young man and went on to become an effective leader of the church.

As a mother, I am thankful for God's saving grace. My son recently answered what may prove to be the first of many "calls" God will make in his life. Even though he is still small, he has inclined his ears to God. Who knows how God will use my son. So I continue to train him in the Word of God.

But perhaps the best way to train our children is by our own example. By reading the Scriptures, praying, loving one another in word and deed, and worshiping regularly, we show our children how to live the life that Jesus modeled for us. God will do the rest.

APRIL 29   Read II Timothy 4:8.

My son and I went out for pizza several weeks ago. While we were waiting, we watched the waitress prepare for a child's birthday party. At the head of the table sat a paper crown for the child to wear. My son turned to me and said, "Can I have a crown, too?"

A crown is highly valued and something to strive for. The Bible makes mention of several spiritual crowns: an incorruptible crown (I Corinthians 9:25); the crown of life (James 1:12); and a crown of glory (I Peter 5:4). This verse from II Timothy speaks of a crown of righteousness.

It is not easy to obtain a crown. It takes discipline, endurance, grace under pressure, and love. We cultivate these qualities by reading and studying God's Word each day. Spending time in silent prayer and meditation, reading devotional materials, and reflecting on the Scriptures are ways we mothers can gain the strength we need to make it through our sometimes hectic days.

John writes Jesus' words to us in Revelation 3:11: "I am coming soon; hold fast to what you have, so that no one may seize your crown." Christ will reward our faithfulness.

APRIL 30   Read Hebrews 12:1.

In this Scripture passage, Paul's words urge us to consider the lives of the patriarchs and matriarchs of the Christian faith. They obeyed God and trusted in God's promises.

As children of God, we are children of the promise, too. We seek God's kingdom and await the day when Jesus will come to take us home. But until he comes, we must live a life of faith, with perseverance. We may not be all that we should be, but we thank God that we're not what we once were. Each day we grow in grace.

To me, the people of the Bible are family—sisters and brothers in the faith. Their lives serve as models of what to do—and not to do. I read and reread their stories and gain fresh insight, words of comfort, and renewed strength.

We have examined the lives of a number of these sisters of faith, many of whom were also mothers. Some of their stories are more familiar than others, yet the theme is the same for all: Keep the faith—God's promises never fail.

When my spirit is disturbed, I think of Mary Magdalene and regain my peace and sense of purpose. I always smile as I remember Mary, the sister of Lazarus, who was pleased just to sit at Jesus' feet. And when I've done all that I can do, I think of Hagar and take comfort in knowing that God is watching over me and my son.

God is able, and God's promises never fail. Praise be to God.

MAY

May Days

MARGARET ANNE HUFFMAN

MAY 1

*S*unrise and I reached the yard together to gather flowers for May baskets on this first day of legitimate spring here in the Midwest. Violets, late daffodils, early lily of the valley.

March is a madcap month, and April pouts in droopy, teary moods, showering us at will. May, however, greets us in giddy delight, inviting us to grab her days like streamers on a May Pole.

I grab the first one today as a grandmother, a granddaughter having arrived since last summer's blossomings, and as a mother of a grown and scattered trio. I tie it as a ribbon for my hair as I ponder a month's thoughts about past, present, and future motherings, for it is a continuing role.

Venture now into spring, inviting God into our backyards where children are waiting to lead our winter-weary spirits into an adventure of rediscovery. Play, rest, sharing, curiosity, tears, giggles, hugs. Let us meet them halfway, for childhood is a journey best shared.

Lord, spring is an opportune time for pondering the ordinary days of mothering, days that only later will we understand are really extraordinary. Be with us as we savor these May days in the rhythm of your seasons, times known so well by mothers, for we are linked to their blending. Bless our May memories, our May hopes, and our seedling dreams.

MAY 2

We hurried across the parking lot to the mini merry-go-round. In a flurry of indecision, the kids fretted over which painted pony to mount for a gallop through fields of fertile imagination.

Eventually they realized the merry-go-round could move only with quarter-fed steam. But by then, they were at least open to discussing choices: a quarter for a brief mechanical ride or a pack of gum; a dollar for stickers or saved dollars for a ball. Those imaginary rides took us around the first circuit of choosing where I learned to say, "Yes."

We so often teach by only saying, "No." Yet there are two parts to the advice. "I have set before you life and death. . . . Choose life" (Deuteronomy 30:19). How can we know for sure which is which? How can we compare and choose if we always think, "No"?

It is good to practice how to decide, how to choose, while minds are young and agile enough to leap aboard painted ponies for whirlwind rides, quarter-fed or not. Making little choices is a dress rehearsal for the choices that come with adolescence, college, marriage, and careers. The stakes are higher then, the cost more than a quarter wasted.

Lord, we are our children's first guides in decision making; keep our hands, minds, and hearts steady while they ponder.

MAY 3

Traveling on Christmas Day seemed wonderful in October. By December 23, however, I was past even "Bah, humbug!"

Nonetheless, the camel train made it to our hastily assembled manger, and the gifts beat the kids to the tree by a minute.

If you don't intend a child to play with a toy, why give it to him? I have since asked myself.

I don't know what I thought my five-year-old son, a joyous, budding artist, would do with his new easel and paints, but when I saw the full jar of holiday red paint trickling down the easel, onto the carpet, and across his good shoes, I lost it. I wince in memory, for he'd only thought to enjoy his gift—from me.

It was weeks before he touched the easel, no matter how sincerely I apologized or how humbly I coaxed, and then it was to use crayons; the paints dried in their jars.

Today, a silvery moon shines over a midnight barn, illuminating not only a spring sky but also the talented, confident brush strokes of the artist who sent me an early Mother's Day painting from his living-room studio 2,500 miles and twenty years away. I must remember to ask if he remembers the Christmas disgrace. Yes or no, I feel forgiven.

Lord, sometimes children aren't the only ones who need to grow up. May our children, like you, continue to give us second and even third chances.

MAY 4

Moms are supposed to know something about everything: why babies cry at 4:00 A.M.; where birds go in the rain;

whether all snowflakes really are different; why all people really *are* different; where babies come from, and why we need more babies, especially new brothers/sisters, anyhow; where God sleeps; and why we're the only family in the world without a video game machine.

Yet with my first child, I didn't even know if I could provide basic nourishment! With a hungry child at the breast, I received my first introduction to the possibility that as a mother, I might not have all the answers.

It's been bluff and bargain since then, for moms work with, at best, speculation; at worst, wild guesses when questions bombard us.

An answer that always worked for me? "I don't know, but I'll go ask Grandma."

Everyone knows that if you have a question, you go ask Mom.

Thank you, Lord, for the ability to think on our feet, while half asleep and completely in the dark. Thank you, too, for the sparks of knowledge, of insight, of genuine wisdom that surprise even us as we speak, for they come not from within but from you, a God who understands the need to welcome curious children's questions.

MAY 5

"But Mommy, my heart isn't big enough," my littlest child cried, sketching a Valentine heart in the air. "I don't have any-more room to love anybody else," she wailed, her sobs echos of the ones I kept swallowing as I thought about the step-father she was about to get.

I pledged that her heart wasn't going to be asked to stretch beyond itself. Consoled but unconvinced, she moped behind me into the store.

On sudden impulse, I bought a bag of balloons. Using all my air and the final ounce of emotional energy I had left from sin-gle parenting, I huffed and puffed into a rainbow-hued balloon.

Soon I was to remarry, bringing three children to sit at the table with a gentle, caring, childless man. Instant family, and my feelings were as mixed as the colors on the slowly growing balloon.

I stopped when it was a small blob. "More, Mommy, blow it more," she urged, her small face mirroring my concentration.

Obediently, I blew again. "More, Mommy."

"Are hearts like balloons?" I wondered aloud as I tied a knot in the bobbing, fat balloon, handing it to her. "Can they get as big as they need to?"

"Prob-ly," she nodded. My answer, too. My hope, my prayer.

Lord, in stepfamilies, all things are continually being made new. Be with every family member in the reconstruction.

MAY 6

It was a dank basement room behind the belching furnace, but it took paint and de-humidifying fairly well. I set up a sandbox and picnic table and called it a playroom. It was not the best playroom, but the tired, financially strapped mind takes what is available.

The kids loved it.

On rainy days, we played there, taking off on jaunts of imagination, up, up, and away to lofty tree houses aboard rainbow railroads.

And on Sundays, we dined on my finest china—never mind that the oldest child was not yet through first grade, the youngest not yet through diapers. They were careful; I was attentive as our best selves were reflected in polished goblets. Candles stood tall in homemade juice-can candelabra; cloth napkins mopped up drippy chins.

We communed over baked beans and hot dogs, animal

crackers and chocolate milk. Love, when taken in and passed around our rickety picnic table, was a transforming moment, as all gatherings around the family table can be.

Lord, show us where the bright spots wait for us to find them in the chaotic days of mothering. Help us pull them from behind furnaces, frowns, sad days, scary days, lonely days. May we remember to enjoy the "best china" moments now, rather than saving them for later; regret for having missed opportunities for celebrating the bright spots of life would make a bitter dessert in years to come.

MAY 7

Training wheels thrice rolled their way into the memorabilia of our family, carrying two-wheeling children on wobbly new ventures as I watched with a lump in my throat as big as any speed bump.

I'm uneasy with wheels, I've decided, for they take children away. Today, a two-wheeled bike; tomorrow, a car; the day after, a family van.

I mourn each passing childhood stage; time turns page after page before I'm ready. For years I whined, "I wish I could stash the kids in the deep freeze; they are at such cute stages."

Who wouldn't trade a tempestuous two-year-old for a gurgling baby? Who wouldn't rather bounce an infant on a nursery-rhyming knee than chase a willful, disobedient, stubborn four-year-old?

Then I think of all the women who can't even fathom such silly questions because they can only dream of the day when they will have children of their own, and I am ashamed of my insensitive shortsightedness. How grateful I am for the gift of motherhood—for the discarded training wheels and the paths through my life they foreshadowed. My tears of separation, as

I watch children's taillights even today, spring from joy in their perpetual movement.

O Lord, be with those women who long to have children but cannot—for whatever reason. And forgive us for our moments of seeming ingratitude.

MAY 8

There was no money, time, or energy that spring, but we needed a vacation from the daily routine and its reminders of what we didn't have.

Even a tent cost too much. And even if we had had one, we wouldn't have had anything in which to wash the baby's diapers, cook meals, or get us to a campsite, for we had no supplies, equipment, or dependable car.

We did, however, have a screened porch.

Memories of a great-grandfather who'd done a stint as a hobo sparked the idea for over-the-shoulder bandana carry-alls tied to sticks collected by the older children. Leftovers cooked over a campfire in the yard tasted better the second time around. The children's soft singing in their folded-over blanket sleeping bags offered all the benediction needed.

A 'possum stared at us from a midnight foray, bats flew by, and the first lightning bugs lit the soft spring-stirring night as we shared the night with its usual tenants.

We greeted dawn with the commuters leaving for work, and we "hiked home" twice around the house.

"A great time," I wrote around the margins of imaginary postcards, "was had by all."

With your loaves and fishes, Lord, you were the original improviser, the one who knew what to do when there wasn't enough to go around. You are still the well from which lives, parched and dry from too many demands and too little time, money, and energy, may drink. We are grateful for the veritable backyard feast you prepare for us.

MAY 9

"Hello?" I whispered sleepily into the telephone. "Mom," a hesitant twenty-three-year-old voice responded, sending me into bolt-upright terror; "I've had a bicycle accident."

For nine months we wait, and it is an apt rehearsal for what lies ahead: more waiting—for first teeth, first words, first steps, and a good night's rest as we forever sleep with one eye open and one ear to the ground.

Waiting is a long tradition of mothers. Moses' mother waited at home while her daughter waited in the bullrushes to see which way the tides would flow for the infant boy. Mary waited in a stable, in a temple, and on a hillside.

Mothers of inventors, artists, and pioneers wait to see which will greet their offspring: applause or jeers? Mothers of soldiers wait for the 6:00 P.M. news. Mothers of outlaws wait in courts. Mothers of ill children wait by bedsides. Mothers of starving children wait for food.

Mothers of all children: We are a sisterhood of waiting. And when a midnight call comes, all the waitings are "kaleidoscoped" into moments when waiting reaped good news, and we dare hope: Christmases, birthdays, report cards, proms, colleges, jobs, mates.

The prayer came unbidden as I waited to hear the next words over my husband's questions and my own thundering heartbeat, *"Dear God, wait with me."*

"Mom," the voice continued, "I'll be okay. I'm at the hospital waiting for the doctor to sew up a few places on my face."

"Hold on," I replied, leaping into action, "we'll come wait with you."

Lord, be with us in our times of waiting, and strengthen and sustain us with your reassuring presence.

MAY 10

In our tattle-tale photograph album, I tally books; blocks; crayons; papers; vehicles; clothes; and mugs, dishes, and forks emblazoned with the latest toy dolls that teach zipping, buttoning, and snapping.

How did Mary manage the long trip to Egypt on a donkey when we can't even go across town unencumbered? Car seats for all ages, toys and snacks, wet washrags, diapers—the list is limited only by what Mom forgets to drag along.

I once challenged myself, "If we had to leave right now for a new town, what would we *need* to take?" That list is short—probably could be whittled a bit more; the list of *wants*, however, is endless.

Could it be that "monkey sees, monkey does, monkey wants"? For as I fixed lunch today, I counted my appliances, accessories, and duplicate pans. Our bulging toy box was but a mirror image of my cupboards, drawers, closets, car trunk, and garage.

Could I fit all I need on a donkey or even in a station wagon?

Probably. Would I be willing? Probably not.

Lord, most of us are up to our necks in "essential" stuff. Help us clean house not only of too many things, but also of the drive to acquire. Help us to know when we have enough for our journey; the rest is excess baggage.

MAY 11

"Are you busy?" my husband asked. Apparently I seemed busy with nothing important, for I was obviously holding gazillions of diapers to be folded.

"Mom, where is it?" someone wailed at me, the great human pocket who should keep all their lost things.

Welcome to Mom's Hotel, where rates are reasonable, the food is homemade, and bedtime snacks are provided.

Not only can we have it all; we can do it all. By ourselves.

Yet do we put off feeding, comforting, and tending anyone under our roof? Aha, how about ourselves? Taken-for-granted feelings are reality nudges, confirming we *are* buried beneath household demands. Yet we would not let anyone else in the family be neglected.

We deserve better treatment . . . from ourselves first. The others will follow our example of treating Mom better.

So I took my diapers and tears to a family meeting where even the youngest claimed a job: unloading the dryer! And I promised not to "correct" their efforts by reloading, redusting, or resorting. Many hands soon made short work out of diaper-folding; I kept mine from reshaping crooked corners, for they were folded with pride in being part of a family, a home—not visitors in Mom's Hotel.

Lord, help us learn to love ourselves so that we may better love others, and remind us to dig out from family demands that sound like bells ringing for "room service" in Mom's Hotel by asking for help.

MAY 12

It was useless to fertilize the lawn that spring, what with its already moth-eaten appearance. First and second base here; third base and T-ball home plate there; a race track encircling it all in a big bear hug.

We were the designated neighborhood playground, a role we'd inherited after a friend died the preceding fall—about the time his lawn succumbed to youthful football games.

His yard was a blessed gridiron; he'd gently chided those who sought to chase the kids off the expensive turf. It'll grow back, he'd assured.

Let them come here to play with my children, he had invited. The older kids in the backyard; the younger ones out front. And he hung a dangling swing from an oak tree to seal the invitation.

Drawn like moths to flame, neighborhood children spent his last months playing there, knowing themselves not to be nuisances but welcome guests at the party of childhood. Too soon, the scrimmage line was as bare as the grave site he occupied.

Kids grow up and away faster than a new lawn reseeds itself; life comes and goes faster than landscape trends and peer opinion. How often we send our children away from their own party, empty-handed and heads hanging as if their play is unacceptable in our neatly mowed lives.

Lord, remind us how quickly children move to larger playgrounds of school, adolescence, and distance. Help us to appreciate the beauty in the bare patches in lawns.

MAY 13

Like fans at a ballgame, the family perches on the edge of the couch. As one body doing "The Wave" in the stands, we move in a rippling motion to the left. Then we reverse and move to the right.

In front of us, oblivious to our efforts on her behalf, the baby tilts almost over on her left side, then on her right side. In silent, helpful, hopeful pantomime, we move with her, urging her on yet unable to do it for her.

It is no wonder we get weary, moving first to one side, then to the other, and finally remaining perfectly still, for the baby alone knows when to roll over.

The writer of Luke observes how God watches over us as a brood hen watches over her chicks, tucking them underneath her wings at night and clucking to them during the day as, underfoot, they scratch for food. Unable to do for us what we need to do to be fully, freely moving, God sits and watches, like the family on the couch, in hopeful support.

Sometimes, Lord, it seems that the most exhausting action is staying still, letting the chicks go where they must. Thank you for reminding us that you are at the edge of our lives, watching, straining, willing us to keep trying.

MAY 14

Spring arrived depressingly damp, and the children moaned at the rain-streaky windows.

The youngest, however, loved it. Raindrops for her face, puddles for her feet, and wriggle worms to adore.

She met the worms face to face, lying flat on her belly on the sidewalk, entranced that, without feet, they still arrived at their destinations, a little dried out but triumphant.

"Wigglings," she named them.

One of the neighborhood naughties, however, taught her to stomp them. Few creatures seem lowlier than worms, but they fit neatly into the echo-scheme of things, and I was horrified. Kitties, hamsters, even turtles rate backyard funerals. They also can scratch, hiss, bite, and show their displeasure at mistreatment. But worms? Nonetheless, they do warrant rescue.

"Let's help him instead," I suggested, interrupting her raised-foot aim at an unwary worm.

We nudged him onto a leaf that she carefully carried to the garden. "Here he can help our green bean seeds grow," I explained. Clapping as he inched away into the furrows, she nodded in understanding. Lots of worms were helped that afternoon, whether they needed it or not.

Lord, how quickly we learn pride in our destructive power. A raised foot to stomp worms can quickly become a raised voice, a raised fist, and later a raised hand ready to push a button launching nuclear destruction. Remind us, Lord, to teach our children by example to honor each part of your creation as lovingly as you do.

MAY 15

They'd been like brother and sister since their births the same week, enjoying a friendship as full as we, their mothers, shared. Equally at home playing house or trucks, they had crawled, creeped, and crayoned together at each other's homes.

The quietness sifting downstairs from my son's room one day should have alerted me, but I was busy starting supper. Besides, they had been four-year-old angels all day and had just gone upstairs for a minute. Ringed with toy-and-book-filled shelves, his room was little-kid perfect, and spring cleaning had left everything tidily in its place . . .

Until the blue bug wriggled its antennae at the two comrades building block towers.

Down came the books from their shelves; off came the cars, trucks, games, puzzles, papers, crayons, and stuffed animals from their perches.

Did they find the blue bug? Nope. Did I have help putting the things back? Nope, not much. Did they think they had done anything wrong? Nope. Did I punish them? Nope, not even a frown.

For they were so valiantly proud of trying to evict the dreaded blue bug—which has taken on gigantic, horrific proportions in the telling of it over the years—that I hadn't the heart to scold.

They did, however, promise to come get Mom next time they spotted an alien critter.

Lord, bless the messes children make; grant us wisdom to know the difference between what we call messes and their proud offerings of help. Help us to measure our responses to their intentions, rather than the results.

MAY 16

The baby redbird was dead; a rude spider scrawled nature's epitaph over its feathers where it lay still in the nest. The two other fledglings had apparently flown safely away.

Peering into the nest, I searched for the explanations I would need when the children made their morning inspection.

We had been delighted when the cardinals came to raise their family in our rambling honeysuckle. I was tempted to remove the corpse myself, sparing both the children and me a sad start to a busy day, but nature never lies, so why should I? And someday there would be grandparents, other pets, peers, perhaps. Better begin with redbirds.

We held a funeral in the backyard where the children prayed, "Here, God, take our dead bird to heaven where Baby Jesus can help it fly."

Life eternal in the theology of a child, and I added my "Amen" as we returned to the porch for lemonade and cookies.

There had been a moment when a comforting companion had joined us on a rustle of honeysuckle breezes, gently reminding even the oldest mourner that God is the first to mourn when we are sad. It was a good thought to sprinkle with the dust over the small grave.

Thank you, Lord, that you have given us turning seasons so that we are never stuck for long in bleak moments of loss. May we always feel your Spirit drawing us forward.

MAY 17

What, I suddenly asked myself as I brandished the glass of orange juice in the child's tearful face one long-ago morning, do I really have to gain by making her finish the last two gulps?

That I know better than she when her tummy is full? That I can force her to finish it, even if it gags its way up seconds later? That I can reinforce self-doubt, concocting it from disapproval of unfinished orange juice, pictures colored out of the lines, clothes happily worn inside out, and shoes proudly put on backward by a novice self-dresser?

What I have to gain is my image as Perfect Mother.

The world applauds children who dress, dine, and perform perfectly. The world also applauds mommies of these children.

Is the world really in our kitchens monitoring orange-juice-finishing, shoe-tying, shirt-buttoning? Yes, and often at our invitation, for *we* want to shine more than we want to learn from children who can teach us what they need.

First lesson of today: Enough orange juice is enough.

Lord, perhaps our grade books for rating parenting need to be replaced. Note unfinished orange juice, shirts buttoned crooked, and mis-tied shoes as homework evidence that we are teachable parents. We are grateful that you are in our kitchens, not disapproving but rather applauding our smallest efforts—even the backward ones. May we go and do likewise.

MAY 18

Helpless, I watched as my unwary son nibbled cotton candy; behind the neighbor's fence, a bully lay in ambush. Smack! Down went the spun sugar, taking my heart with it.

I longed to smack the rude child just as he had smacked my son's treat, flinging along with it childhood innocence, a brief visitor at best.

Before long, trusting hearts and outstretched arms have to grow callouses just as did their crawling knees, for the journey is rocky.

Training a child in the way he or she should go is not a solo parental task, for babysitters, neighbors, relatives, and even strangers write upon outstretched, unblemished baby palms seeking a response.

As the bullying candy-smacker laughed at my son's tears, I could see that my son was getting mad, too. Was he going to smack him back? Should I let him? Encourage him? Teach him how?

Those were easy questions compared to the one I knew was forming in his mind: "Why, Mommy? Why did he do that to me?"

Yes, "Why?" Lord. Why is there hatred in your world, from mean children to warring politicians and countries? Why do children have to learn it so early? How can we protect them? What can we do and say as we watch their innocence and their trust in goodness waver? We need help, Lord, although telling you about it helps. Send your wisdom, for the world is sometimes a mean playground.

MAY 19

While God may love a cheerful giver, my children weren't volunteering. I'd even concocted a cautionary tale of a selfish "Me-Mine Bird," for which there was no shortage of plot material.

Then they met the child with holes in his house.

Several church families had teamed up with welfare families that year to share economic problems and solutions, and my kids were curious about their companions' shabbiness, especially one little boy.

We drove past his patched house one day in our new car. They leaned from its shiny windows to stare, holding in their hands toy replicas of the new car, gifts from the dealer, which they treasured as much as I did the real thing.

The following day, however, my son was "Vroooming" an old car instead of his new one on the way home. "Where is it?" I asked, irritated he'd already lost it.

"I gave it away," he answered.

"Who to?" I challenged, ready to scold, when he looked at me in the rearview mirror with wiser eyes than mine. "I gave it to my new friend at church. He'll never have a new car unless I give him mine."

The "Me-Mine Bird" sat lonely in his tree that day, silent and still, with his wings folded in pouty consternation at such generosity.

Lord, help us not to pigeon-hole our children. The selfish can be unselfish; the greedy, giving. Remind us, when we hold on too tightly to a possession, of the joy of sharing.

MAY 20

"Remember playing doggy and kitty?" they asked each other.

I do.

I'd supplied them with towels for beds and food and water to "lap" from bowls on the floor. We still call corned beef hash "dog food."

It wasn't exactly listening at keyholes, but the effect was the same: I was eavesdropping on my grown-up kids' conversation instead of cleaning the kitchen, having shoed aside their offers to help. Together for my fiftieth birthday, they were "remembering when." Backyard circuses, doll hospitals, truck stops, inventions, books—their lists, as their play had been, were endless.

In none of these freeze-framed memories, though, is there a tally of dust bunnies, dirty dishes, or my other housekeeping failures. For I, too, enjoyed playing.

The life we live today is tomorrow's home movie. What images will I want flickering across memory's screen? The clean kitchen that—once again—was trying to take me from communion with this trio? Or heads bent close together in laughter, conversation, play?

"Hey, Mom, are we having 'dog food' for supper?" they hollered. Once again laying aside a dishrag, I yielded to temptation and joined them, giving my answer in person.

Lord, remind us that we can clean an empty house later. Keep us in the picture today; clean kitchens don't rate star billing.

MAY 21

The moving van was coming in the morning; the new neighborhood waited 150 miles away, but it was difficult to picture clearly through the swarm of butterflies we all had.

In response, the children squabbled, whined, and regressed; and I regretted the move almost as much as I did being a mother. "Get a grip, you guys," I wanted to say; "we'll have a better house, bigger yard, and finer job."

And then I remembered my move just across town as a child. I was plain old scared, for it meant a new library, new bus stop, new kindergarten, new bullies, new tries . . . and maybe there wouldn't even be a tree for my swing. I had been plain old scared, just like my children.

Fear was almost a familiar feeling from my most recent "first day": going to college as an adult. Talk about being scared!

Later, splitting a pizza with my children on a packing-crate table, I recounted how frightened and yet how excited I was on that first day with my new college sweatshirt, new books, and new writing tablets. They listened in rapt, calmed attention, nodding as we shared our fears and our dreams that begin with first days, first steps toward the unknown.

Children, better than we, can understand two things being true at the same time: New is good; new is scary.

Take our hands, Lord. We all need a companion for the journey between the old and the new.

MAY 22

I knew if I heard, "Come here, Mama," one more time, I would scream. The words were ready to spill out like laundry from the dryer. For on any given day there were potatoes to peel, dogs to dip, plants to tend, clothes to mend, phones to answer, errands to run, and spills to mop. In the midst of it all, my youngest daughter was hosting yet another tea party.

Guess who was the guest of honor? That's right: Mom.

Did I dare send any regrets? Could I explain that Mama's too busy right now with more important things?

Just as I was about to let the words "No, not now" fall from my lips, I considered which of us needed to learn patience.

This morning, years later, I found one of those tiny glass tea cups in the sewing basket. Cup in hand, I called this tea-loving, now out-of-town daughter, inviting her to meet me for lunch next week. Chinese food and endless pots of tea.

How many cups of make-believe tea does it take, Lord, to fill up a little one? How many pretend nibbles of clay cookies to satisfy small-fry cooks? Help us realize that imaginary adventures, like clay cookies, are best when shared with Mom. Remind us how briefly we will meet at their tiny tables. And remind us that interruptions are really disguised invitations into the lives of our

135

children to be sought after, treasured. They are not lightly offered.

MAY 23

"*I hat you*," proclaimed the note I found slipped beneath my bedroom door. Printed with angry pride, despite mis-spellings and erasures, its intent was plain.

My temptation was to "hat" the little nuisances right back, for it had been a bad day and "hat" was in the air.

The two older ones, playing ball in the house, broke an antique lamp, first offense before breakfast. Next, they refused to give the baby the cereal toy, although it was her turn. Finally, they dawdled into being late for a swimming lesson. Hence, they were plucked from the pool, dripping and sob-bing, before free swim.

They did, indeed, "hat" me.

Better notes than fists, we agreed later, figuring other ways to dilute understandable, forgivable, legitimate anger: punch-ing pillows, drawing pictures, talking it out. For it is easier to re-focus a child's expressed anger than it is to uncork stuffed, hidden, and suppressed anger.

We later shared mutual anger at child abuse, pet abuse, pol-lution, and hunger, which spawned polite letters of protest and petition for change. They'd had an early start in writing letters. Thank goodness—we laugh now—they learned to spell.

Lord, help us to remember that anger can be constructive and creative, depending upon its roots. Help us understand that to be angry on behalf of someone is not the same as being angry about sharing toys, traffic lanes, opinions, or borders.

MAY 24

I distracted them before the "diagnosis" was made, politely closing the door on the "doctor's office" my children and their friends were innocently playing. And then I took two aspirin and vowed to call someone wise in the morning.

Children will touch, ask, show, and tell. And we will squirm in embarrassment, stupidity, shame, and awe at the power of sexuality to render us drawn and repelled simultaneously.

The parenting task of teaching privacy and pleasure, curiosity and restraint, boundaries and celebration is enough to send everyone to that simple one-word pronouncement: "Don't."

Yet *don't* is not the only word in a theology of bodies, those glorious temples given as good gifts by a generous God.

Teaching children about their sexuality invites them to question and ponder; it gives them real names for real God-given parts, for a child who respects the parts is more likely to tend them wisely, at all ages. Books, videos, and even "pregnant" mommy dolls can help us explain facts; faith in all good gifts can help us believe what we say about them.

And if we don't want the job, others will explain for us: graffiti, older kids, movie screens, TV screens, stereos; they, however, neglect the crucial second part about all good gifts.

Lord, we know that you do not want us to be ignorant, ashamed, or prudish about your wondrous, sacred gift. Help us to look up to you when we speak of our sexuality to our children, for you cloaked us not in shame, but in beauty.

MAY 25

The toddler pinched my arm, catching me by surprise. She wanted her way. I wanted mine. Naptime battle lines were drawn.

Cars, lawnmowers, even microwave popcorn come with instruction labels; why not children?

They do; we just neglect to read them.

"I, me, mine," the labels instruct. Somewhere in childhood, we learn to negotiate selfishness, to share even naptime decisions. Never, however, do we completely remove our labels.

Why, then, do we try to break children's wills and sassy spirits in ways we wouldn't want to be broken? Would we have God do unto us as we do unto these little ones?

Stitched in fine print is a final instruction: "Handle with care." This is how to expand "I, me, mine" into "ours, us, we": by teaching, modeling, explaining—over and over again.

O Lord of unbroken spirits, remind us that to bend is not to break; to mold is not to reshape; to challenge is not to defeat; to offer options is not to argue; to negotiate is not to lose; to break is not to win. For of what use, Lord, are broken-over stalks in the wildflower garden of your creation? They cannot see the sun, cannot feed bees and birds, cannot yield harvest. Remind us that broken-over children cannot easily become who you intend either, for they can only look down in defeat; and that we can reach you best when we are standing on tiptoes.

MAY 26

For her fifth birthday, she requested a pet snake.

Yuk.

She loved snakes that spring; she poked into holes, beneath logs, around the porch, and under plants in search of a snake to study.

"They're not mean when they hiss," she explained. "They're just scared of us."

I also learned their skin feels cold, having been forced to touch the one at the petting zoo. "Just once," she'd benevolently agreed.

Snakes are primitive fantasy cousins to those other monster-
ish creatures—bats, dragons, dino-monsters—that live in children's closets and beneath their beds.

What we had was a child adopting her nightmare, not a
child planning to become a reptologist.

Did we become snake experts from books read aloud, a
video, nature coloring books, and a zoo visit? No, but we
learned that to name something is to know it, and to know it
is to love it, or at least like it.

She also wanted to learn where snakes go when it snows,
looking ahead to winter when she might still worry, "What's
under my bed?" Now she could know, "Can't be a snake, they
are sleeping."

There's a Nightmare in My Closet, by Mercer Meyer, should
be required adult reading for understanding children's ways of
cozying up to their nightmares. Ways we might adopt, perhaps, instead of denying our own nightmares.

*Lord, thank you for the gift of curiosity that leads us from night-
time terrors into daylight explanations. Let us be lights at the
edge of our children's darkness, as you are for us.*

MAY 27

Clumps of mud in her hair drizzled lines of mischief down
her smiling face; her brother was no better, a veritable mud
man.

How proud they were.

They had been planting a small garden when the combination of dirt and water became too tempting.

One poet calls spring puddles "mud-lucious," and, after a
brief hesitation, I agreed. Once again, the children were leading me to an enjoyment of creation rather than my own modi-
fication of it.

They made dams and rivers, floating leaves and stick rafts on the water; they made mud pottery, leaving their creations to dry on the sidewalk; they made mud pies and stews; they eventually made a soggy garden. They made a mess.

I hosed them off when their wallowing was done; it took two showers to finish the task, but what memorable moments are pressed between the pages of our photo album. Now separated by 2,500 miles, this brother and sister can be instantly reunited by the word *mud*.

Lord, did you keep your hands clean during creation or did you get down on your hands and knees while planting your first garden? Did you get wet as you waded into those first lapping tides and streams, skipping a stone or two across the surface of your smooth lakes and rivers? Bless the messy moments of childhood, Lord, and lead us too-tidy folks into them, the best spots for continuing your creating.

MAY 28

Kids play on teeter-totters; mothers live on them. Up and down in perpetual motion, I moved before dawn's first light, usually attending to some child or another—teeth, dreams, fevers, excitement for a new day.

Life was so different before children. Then I *"knew"* what working full time was. After children, working full time no longer meant forty-hour weeks; it meant perpetual vigilance, even at night.

Sometimes I liked being a mother; other times, I was not so sure, for I didn't seem to make a difference in the lives of children who rejected my meals, ignored my directives, and displayed appallingly lazy habits despite my best interventions, leaving my self-confidence in shreds.

I thought the parenting payoff would be different—a more even pace, a lighter toll on my self-esteem, and more sleep.

Ha! And I never imagined just how far down the swoop of the teeter-totter would take me—or how high.

Lows and highs. One cannot exist without the other, and it was at that pivotal point of balance where the children and I met for a brief moment powerful enough to get me going again.

Lord, level us off from the extremes of mothering with reassurance that to be ambivalent is neither unreasonable nor unforgivable. Help us keep the teeter-totter moving between false highs and inaccurate lows. Tiredness slows our movement. Restore us, Lord, to green pastures where we can lie down by still waters, at least for five minutes.

MAY 29

The children ran away from home on an unseasonably hot day much like today. I watched from the window as they loaded up the red wagon with toys, food, pajamas, and their little sister.

Away they went, pulling their load with a toy tractor.

"Meanest Mother in the World." That's me, because I wouldn't let them jump on the bed.

Logic—"a bed is not a trampoline"—didn't work; bargaining—"jump on the old inner tube"—didn't either. And threatened punishments resulted only in indignant departure.

And all because I didn't want them to suffer the consequences of jumping on the bed: possible injuries.

They, of course, felt punished; for children—we, too—can't distinguish clearly between consequences and punishments. Consequences, preferable by far, are by-products of actions.

Leave a toy in the rain: it rusts; don't feed a kitten: it cries; tear a library book: help pay for it; break a friend's toy: help fix it.

Obviously, the consequences of raising independent children are that they will act.

It struck hot noon, and I retrieved them for lunch. Afterward, I promised to return them to their red-wagon load of anger. They could decide then: proceed or return, each direction with its own consequence, including lugging the stuff home.

Help us follow your example, Lord, of parenting with consequences, for consequences offer us chances to learn on the long, hot walk home. Be with us when our consequences are too much to bear.

MAY 30

Her dog sits on my feet; her cat dozes on my front porch in the spring sun. "Keepers of children's things; that's all mothers are good for," I muttered to the tail-wagging mutt, as much mine now as my daughter's.

But my daughter lives in an apartment, and she is unable to take the dog who would be heartbroken to leave here, although she longs to be reunited with her "mom."

Does this grown-up young woman share the dog's feelings of ambivalence: Glad to be with me, her adoptive mother, but longing to be reunited with another?

I know I should be mature about adoption searches, and with my head I am. I, who have encouraged every question, every thought my daughter has ever had, completely support her if she opts for a birth-mother search. With my heart, however, I sometimes suffer selfishly at having to share her at all.

My anguish is likely pale beside that of the one who gave her up totally, relinquishing flesh of her flesh. Testimony to this love are photographs she took during those first hours of her baby's life, sending reprints via the caseworker to me.

When I looked at them again last week, I knew that I, too, would welcome her were we to meet, sharing a glance of companionship over the head of the daughter we both love.

Lord, give us courage, as you did the mother taken before Solomon, not to allow our children to be "chopped in half," especially by ourselves.

MAY 31

The children and I picked as many flowers as our arms could hold, arranging them in bouquets to decorate relatives' graves while en route to a Memorial Day service.

How quickly the month had passed, its now vibrant spring beauty providing a backdrop for this annual event, the family picnic. This picnic, like its forerunners, would not be complete without a family picture to chronicle the changes since last year. Marriages, births, deaths, babies now toddlers, toddlers now big children, grandbabies.

As I watched the children distribute their bouquets, I realized that through me, they are now connected to these ancestors as well as to who they will yet become. For mothers are the great connectors, linking childhood between history and promise—a momentous calling, an exhilarating, tiring task. And, like spring, we are best at being in the middle of creation.

Lord, as we enjoy spring, so much like childhood itself with its wondrous moods and humbling complexity, we are grateful that you are the pivot upon which the seasons of mothering turn. Remind us on this Memorial Day, as we honor who we have been, that you honor all families—big, small, single-parent, rich, poor, happy, and sad families—as we move on toward who we are yet to become. Be with us in the spring plantings of our children's lives; we want to tend them as lovingly as you do ours.

JUNE

Cherished Moments

SHERON C. PATTERSON

JUNE 1

obby is a four-year-old terrorizing, huggable, brown-skinned wonder to me. There are times when I want to give him a good old-fashioned thrashing. There are other times when I want to declare him the world's best boy and pin a gold medal on his chest.

He talks with his hands in such colorful ways that I did not teach. He shares his perceptions and experiences to my delight in pure childish animation. He sings to himself when he thinks that I am not listening. His imaginative lyrics and melodies make me chuckle secretly to myself.

I know that he is a boy now, but I still remember the joys of cuddling him in my arms when he was an infant. Occasionally I'll crave that maternal sensation, and I'll scoop all forty-five pounds of him into my arms and say, "Robby, be my baby again." Sometimes he complies and utters a few perfunctory coos. Other times he reminds me that he is a boy, not a baby.

My task is to love him whatever age he is. I must not try to lock him into the days of infancy but pray him into the days of young manhood. I must cherish what was and wait patiently for what is to come. It is a blessing to be in such a classroom of life.

Dear God, my arms still tingle when I remember rocking and cuddling the infant who is no longer a baby. Help me to grow along with my child, and let me be the appropriate kind of mother my child needs at the appropriate time.

JUNE 2

"I'm going on bacation," Robby cheerfully announced as we packed our luggage for a morning flight to Florida. We had anxiously awaited this family time. Vacation for him meant endless fun, no naps, and every meal at McDonald's. I wanted him to enjoy himself, but not to harm himself!

During that week we spent vast amounts of time walking at amusement parks, beaches, and other tourist traps. I am still alive, and I am grateful. I managed to survive long lines, humid weather, sand, and sunburn.

To be honest, I did not want to go to all of those places. A quiet cabana with a good novel is my ideal vacation, but I went on *Robby's* vacation to bring joy to my child. Such choices are a part of motherhood.

Much in the same way, our God brings joy to our lives, walks through life by our side, and never gets tired. And best of all, God does it by choice!

Dear God, I make choices every day for the good of my child. Thank you for enabling me to make right choices and for giving me the physical strength often required to follow through. And thank you for choosing to love me.

JUNE 3

It's after 10:00 P.M., and the day is just ending for me. A meeting at church lasted two hours longer than scheduled. Robby went with me and endured it the best he could. What he needs is to be bathed, dressed in his pajamas, and tucked into bed.

Yet all I do is sprawl on the sofa and wish. I wish I weren't so tired. I wish I didn't have to attend so many night meetings. I wish there were more hours in the day. I wish I could buy time, because I'd surely save mine and use it during times like these.

I thank God for the extra pair of hands attached to my husband, who picks up the weary child, prepares him for bed, and then comes back to help me. It is during the times of tremendous fatigue that I reflect on the non-stop energy of God—energy that allows me to get up as well as lie down. I think about the quiet waters described by the psalmists and yearn to be there.

Dear God, rest is what I need, and you are best prepared to give it to me. Help me put away the cares of today and place my slumbering hours in your hands.

JUNE 4

One afternoon meeting hit a boring and tedious stretch. My eyelids felt like weights, and my mind wandered from the printed agenda before me. The reality that I was pregnant added some legitimacy to my lethargy.

Drowsiness threatened to overtake me, when all of a sudden I felt a fury of tiny taps from within my slightly extended tummy. I'd been anxiously awaiting these first fetal movements. They brought joy and excitement to me and turned that boring meeting into an all-important occasion.

My head was no longer drooping. My eyes were wide open, and there was a smile on my face. Something got a hold of me; it was the feeling of a brand new life. I had felt the movements during my first pregnancy, but once again there was something new and exciting about me—and God was responsible for it. The first kicks energized me because they confirmed the reality that I was carrying a living, breathing person. From then on, how could anything be boring?

Dear God, I praise you for the opportunity to carry a life within my body. Make me a worthy vessel of this young life.

JUNE 5

As I pushed my shopping cart along the grocery store aisle in peace and quiet, it suddenly dawned on me that the calm I experienced was possible because my four-year-old was not with me today. There was no crying out, "Momma, there's the cereal I saw on TV!" There was no yelling about my decision to skip the toy section. "What a pleasure," I thought.

Strolling the aisle at my own pace, I watched other mothers encumbered with demanding, screaming youngsters. I chuckled to myself and savored every second of my freedom. The time away, the occasional opportunity to shop alone is something I long for as much as I long for the wet kisses and hugs and whispers of "Momma, I love you" from my son.

Walking the aisle in silence gave me the chance to hear myself. I heard my needs, my wants, my wishes—things I sometimes neglect. Just this one time I stuffed the cart with things for me, too: fancy bubble bath, nail polishes, and even a gourmet chocolate chip cookie.

Every now and then, we mothers need to mother ourselves. If we don't, who will?

Dear God, thank you for time just for me, wherever I may find it. Let me be receptive and ready to relish these rare times. Remind me over and over again that your eyes are on the sparrow and that you are watching me too.

JUNE 6

On the way to the daycare center this morning, Robby turned to me in the car with a snicker and said: "Mommy, you're not the only one with a baby in your stomach. I've got one, too." This caused me to pull off from the road to examine my child for some genetic mishap. But he quickly followed his declaration with a giggly, "I just kidding."

He wanted to make sure that I knew *he* knew what was going on. In his own way, he was staking a claim in my pregnancy; he was expressing love for the sibling he longed for.

Sure, he had no idea what the word *pregnancy* meant, nor how his mommy became pregnant; but he understood that something special would be coming his way, and he wanted a piece of the action now.

Robby's love for his unborn sibling reminds me of the words God spoke to the prophet Jeremiah: "Before I formed you in the womb I knew you" (1:5). It is good to know that God's love was waiting for us even before our birth.

Dear God, a child's love for a sibling is a blessing. I pray that you will be a force in my children's relationship with each other, helping their love to rise above jealousy, shared toys, and small insecurities.

JUNE 7

This Father's Day I gave tribute to my dad the best way that I know how. I treated him with the same concern and love that he's shown me all the days of my life. To me, Father's Day is a time to reward good men for being good fathers.

My dad lives a thousand miles away, so I mailed him his gifts in a brown box. Inside the box was what he said he wanted: a pair of brown, size 9½ leather loafers. It felt good to give him what he wanted. Finally he has learned how to be specific with his requests.

That was never a problem for me. When I was growing up, I could rattle off a list of things I wanted at any time. And whether it was a trip to the snow-cone stand, red sneakers, a mood ring, or a new puppy, Dad always came through.

The gifts were nice, but his was more than just a material love. We spent lots of time together doing father-daughter stuff. He listened to me. He encouraged me. He stood by me in the difficult times of my life.

It's good to have an earthly father who loves and cares for me, but it's even better to have a Heavenly Father who has an even greater ability to give us the desires of our hearts.

Dear God, thank you for my childhood and my father. Enable all fathers to be loving fathers, and help all children to appreciate the tangible and intangible signs of good fathering.

JUNE 8

A preaching engagement called me away from home for a week recently. My husband and son took me to the airport and waited patiently until the flight was ready to board. As we waited, we talked cheerfully among ourselves in the bustling airport. Robby was enthralled by all the coming and going around him.

My flight was ready to board, my seat was called, and I kissed my husband good-bye. Then I bent down to kiss Robby, who, to my surprise, grabbed my neck and burst into tears. "Momma, I don't want you to go!" he cried.

Robby is a loud and articulate crier. He might as well have used the airport public address system. Everybody heard him, it seemed. I felt that the eyes of all the boarding passengers and the airline check-in personnel were glued to me and my wailing child.

This dramatic moment made me feel like a character on a television program. I had a difficult situation on my hands, and the world was watching me solve it. I was leaving to go preach the gospel, but my son was asking me to stay home and be his mom.

I asked Robby if he would lend his mom to some other people for just a few days. I told him that I had a message from Jesus for them about love. "A message from Jesus," he said. This reason was good enough for Robby to release me. He calmed down and kissed me good-bye. Even Robby could understand that Jesus has enough love for our family and everybody else's. What an important lesson for our children—and us—to remember.

Dear God, your love is too deep to measure, too complex to compute. I'm just glad it exists and that there's enough of it for me, for my family, and for all your children.

JUNE 9

The toys scattered all over the floor of our den are a safety hazard. If the super-heroes' playhouse doesn't trip you first, the roller skates wait for you patiently under a jumbo coloring book, miniature race cars are strewn here and there, and three decks of flash cards are hopelessly jumbled together in a heap.

This place looks as if a tornado hit the toy chest. Robby finds joy in this cluttered den. He feels comfortable and safe surrounded by the piles of toys.

There are many things about childhood that I do not understand, and my son's ability to be happy in clutter is one of them. However, I can learn from my son that it is possible to find joy anywhere. When trials and tribulations surround me like the toys in the den, when my hope is crushed by what feels like a deck of life's hard-luck cards, and even when there seem to be enemies lurking at every corner to make me stumble, there is joy to be found.

The apostle Paul once wrote about life's turmoil and our abilities to overcome them in II Corinthians 6:4-10. It all boils down to how we see ourselves and how we utilize the power of God in our lives. With the right attitude, a jungle of distress can become a small patch of weeds.

Dear God, empower me to see the good when all about me seems bad. Open my eyes wider than my current distress. Allow me to see you in all things. Give me the eyes of a child.

JUNE 10

Growing up as an only child, I know the value of having extra people around who love you in a powerful way. When a child knows that she has more than one set of hands and hearts and hopes wrapped around her, insecurities vanish and self-confidence flourishes. The aunts, uncles, and cousins around me made my life full and rich in relationships.

On a recent trip back home to North Carolina, Robby was overwhelmed when he found himself surrounded by a houseful of smiling, hugging, and kissing relatives. Aunt Meece wanted to put him in her lap, uncle Mac wanted to shake his hand, and a slew of cousins his age wanted him to romp around the back yard with them.

Their smiles, outstretched hands, and genuine love convinced my shy boy. Soon he was lost in a sea of relatives. As the day wore on, it was not my name he called but names of other members of the family, and I was glad for him. He grabbed someone else's hand to help him cross the street. He asked someone else to tie the strings on his sneakers. And when it was time to eat, hands other than mine prepared his hot dog just the way he likes it.

Robby had found family love amongst his kin folks, and their love made him one of the richest little boys in the world.

Dear God, thank you for the rich blessings that are found in our families. Make us wealthy in mutual love, unity, and peace. Allow our surroundings to serve as fertile ground for the children, so that they may grow strong in the ties that bind.

JUNE 11

Robby has an attitude of gratitude. He has learned to say a blessing over every meal. His Sunday school teacher teaches the class a new blessing every week, and he shares them at home in a piecemeal fashion that makes it hard to tell one from another.

It does not matter to me that he jumbles his words together and combines the various blessings in a mismatched way. I'm just glad he knows he is supposed to be grateful to God. I'm glad he knows that God has given him everything that he has.

Unlike many adults, Robby is not ashamed to bow his head and pray in public. He can get loud as he prays, too. One night, as we ate at a restaurant, Robby led the family blessing so loud that the people at nearby tables turned around to see what was going on.

I can't tell you all the words that he says in the blessings; but I'm sure God knows, and that's what counts the most.

Dear God, I find that my faith is increased by my praying child. May you always keep words of gratitude and praise for you on my child's lips.

JUNE 12

At some point in every day now, a set of bright, small eyes meets mine and a question is asked: "What shall we name the baby?" Robby is on top of the world. His baby sister is on the way. He has the ability to offer names for her. This ability makes him proud, responsible, and most of all, involved in the pregnancy.

He always has a list of names. Connie, Brenda, and Kimberly are some of the common ones. Shalisa and Laquida are some of the uncommon ones that spring from his four-year-old imagination.

Today when he came to me with his list of names, his eyes were brighter than usual. His smile was more intense. "Momma, I have the baby name. It is Copper," he announced. This name appealed to me. The others had bounced off like rubber balls, but this name sank in deeply and felt good. Copper is a beautiful name. It has meaning. The way I see it, Copper means that she'll be strong, brown, and beautiful. This important gift from Robby reminds me that children do have valuable thoughts to share. We should take the time to listen.

Dear God, open my ears and my mind to the thoughts of my child. No matter how small the contribution may be, it has value. You may be speaking to me through my child.

JUNE 13

Writing sermons every week is a labor of love. Good sermon illustrations are the backbone of a sermon, and I constantly search for them. Sometimes I can't find them, and that's when desperation sets in.

Late on Saturday night I was stuck. My sermon was going no place fast. It needed a strong opening thought, and I'd exhausted my collection of colorful illustrations. I turned to book after book, but nothing surfaced. My sermon was based on Paul's conversion along the Damascus road found in Acts 9. I needed an illustration that centered on the topic of change.

It suddenly dawned on me that I had read Robby to sleep that night with a Dr. Seuss book about change. The main character was a big, bearish creature who changed constantly. The character fit my plans, and, after all, I could not be too choosy about illustrations after midnight!

Sunday morning came. I "preached" Dr. Seuss, and it was one of my strongest sermons. We can never tell where important lessons will come from. Oftentimes these lessons—especially lessons of faith—come to us mothers as we share experiences with our children or our children's worlds. The point is always to be ready and open.

Dear God, give me open eyes and a willing spirit so that I may receive your blessings whenever and however they may come. Thank you for the many new opportunities to experience your goodness that are mine because I am a mother.

JUNE 14

If there is one word that constantly springs from the mouths of young ones, it is the word *why.* Robby must use the word ten to eleven times per hour. This heavy usage has made him quite proficient and me quite weary.

Today he asked about day and night. "Day comes when the moon goes to sleep, and night comes when the sun goes to sleep," I said. I had explained the situation in simple language that a four-year-old could understand, I thought. He seemed to comprehend my explanation, and he even repeated what I had said in a tone of confidence.

I felt proud that I'd finally taken him to a new level of understanding, but I was able to revel in my accomplishment only a few seconds because another round of questions bombarded me. "Why do the sun and the moon have to go to bed? Where are their beds? Do they have pajamas like me? Who tucks them in at night? Do they have a mommy and a daddy?"

His questions covered me like a tidal wave, and I was on the verge of anger. Yet I also was impressed by the yearning in his questioning. There was a joy in his stream of queries, and that joy revived me.

The constant questioning of children pushes us to also look at the world and wonder. Some things need to be investigated and examined.

Dear God, help me see the best in my child's questions. Let those questions lead me to a greater curiosity of my surroundings. Let me not hesitate to ask how, where, when, and, most of all, why.

JUNE 15

Robby was eager to tell me that he'd learned a new song in Sunday school. "What is the song?" I asked. "Moo Va Yah," he said with pride. Obviously he had misplaced a consonant here and there and had turned the song "Kum Ba Ya" into a tune that sounded like something cows might sing. But he was oblivious to the error; he was in complete bliss with the song as he had pronounced it.

The joy that Robby experienced with his newly learned song is much like the joy that new Christians experience when they first come to know Christ. In their initial excitement they usually don't know all the words, and they may misplace a consonant here or there. Yet it is experiencing even some of the joy of knowing Christ that catapults them forward. That little bit of joy keeps them on the road of faith, so that one day they will get the words right.

I can't wait to hear what song Robby learns next week. It matters not that he pronounces some of the words incorrectly. What does matter is that he has started the journey of faith, and the joy in his heart will carry him down the road.

Dear God, keep songs of praise in my child's young heart.

JUNE 16

Recently I was asked to address a women's conference. After I concluded my remarks, one woman from the audience approached me to say how much she enjoyed my speech. "You certainly must have had a lot of encouragement while you were a young girl to have enabled you to do so much as an adult," she commented. I took her remark lightly and responded on a superficial level.

This was not enough. The woman probed further, this time coming closer and looking into my eyes. "You must have had a lot of encouragement while you were younger. Who helped you?"

This time she got through to me. She had pushed my mind back to the supportive parents I had and the church they took me to every Sunday. This persistent woman forced me to mentally run up and down the aisle of my home church, remembering the faces of those persons who loved me and nurtured me. They made me feel that I mattered and that I could do anything. How dare I forget them and refuse to acknowledge their contribution to my life!

Our children's lives are also touched and blessed by many people, and for this I am grateful.

Dear God, help me not to forget that you bless us in many ways. You bless us through people, places, and times in our lives. I give thanks for those persons who have blessed me and my child, and for those persons who have yet to touch our lives.

JUNE 17

Bedtime is always difficult. Robby will do anything to delay getting to sleep. He will kick, scream, and roll on the floor. If that does not work, he shifts gears and moves into the role of the eloquent negotiator.

One night when his array of tactics had failed, he made his last resort a real humdinger that was guaranteed to reach my heart. "Momma," he said softly and sincerely, "I just want to stay up a little longer so that I can love you a little longer."

Love me a little longer? *What does love have to do with resisting bedtime?* I wondered. Before I could blurt out the automatic line we mothers use so often, "Go to bed because I say go to bed," I was consumed by the weight of his words—particularly the word *love.* Suddenly I understood what love had to do with it. Loving a sleepy child who won't go to sleep is what moms specialize in.

I allowed Robby to climb into my lap. We talked for a few minutes and sang a couple of songs. Soon he was fast asleep.

Dear God, your love gives mothers the strength, patience, and power to love our children. No matter what situations we encounter with them, love is always the answer.

JUNE 18

I feel as if I've spent a greater portion of my years of motherhood here under the "golden arches." The weekly visits to the place are rituals for my son. If Robby doesn't get a Happy Meal at least once every seven days, he thinks he will cease to exist.

The one positive in this predicament is that my son has found a place where he feels comfortable and happy. He sings cheerful songs on the way to the restaurant. And once we pass through the doorway, he is grinning ear to ear.

If only I could "transfer" Robby's contentment from the fast-food locale to our church. That would be a real treat. But I realize that such a transition will have to begin with his parents. So I must ask myself, does Robby see excitement in us as we prepare for church? Does his dad feel comfortable and happy sitting beside him in the pews? Will our Sunday morning ritual ever provide the same pleasures of the restaurant? I think so. One thing I do know: It is up to us parents to pass along to our children the excitement we have for Christ in our hearts and in our deeds.

Dear God, help me remember that I am a role model for my child, who will learn much from me whether I intend it or not. Keep me on my toes, and empower me to let my light shine.

JUNE 19

Robby's best friend, Elliot, moved to Indianapolis recently. We were heartbroken to see him lose such a compatible next-door neighbor. The two boys were born four months apart and were inseparable since birth. Worst of all, there were no other children in the neighborhood as young as Robby. This left him with two choices: stay inside and play alone, or venture out and play with the big boys.

As his mom, I worried about him. On one hand, the big boys might view him as a baby and reject him. I hoped that they would not tease him and make him cry just to flex their eight-year-old muscles. On the other hand, playing alone in the house on sunny afternoons while his older neighbors frolicked on the front lawns might plant seeds of resentment in his soul. I waited for him to make the decision.

Today he informed me that he was "ready" to play with the big boys. I complied, opened the front door, and scanned the lawn where a spirited game of baseball was in progress. Robby leapt from the front porch and turned to wave good-bye. I waved back and watched with anxiety to see what would happen.

One of the big boys saw Robby slowly approaching the group, and he yelled out, "Hey, Robby, come on over! Do you want to play baseball with us?" My child was accepted, and I felt good.

It took a lot of courage for Robby to venture out to play with new and older friends. He was lucky; the situation might not have been as pleasant. But I would have been waiting just inside the door to comfort him.

We know from our own experience that it takes courage to face new situations, but we often forget that God is always near, ready to help us or comfort us when we need it.

Dear God, help me to be as brave as a courageous child when I face new situations. Give me the spiritual guts to know that together you and I can handle anything.

JUNE 20

Child rearing experts agree that young children are enriched by being allowed to help in the kitchen with small tasks. Today I invited Robby into the kitchen to help me make a pound cake for a bake sale at church. I allowed him to stand on a chair next to me at the counter as I prepared the cake batter.

His eyes sparkled just to be in the helping environment. He was delighted to crack open eggs. He squealed with happiness while pouring milk and measuring sugar and butter. To my amazement, he was quite a baker—though a bit clumsy. I was proud.

When the batter was being poured into the cake pan, he had reached his zenith and could no longer control his movements. He let out a big "yippie" and flung his arms into the air, throwing the full cake pan to the floor. Cake batter covered the kitchen. Robby began to cry, and I felt like joining him.

I had to think of a quick way to cheer us both up. I thought about the reality that failures do arise in our lives, yet they are overcome when we have the courage to try again. Together the two of us cleaned up the mess, made the batter again, and successfully baked a good-looking pound cake.

Dear God, help me to teach my child that when we fail, we must try again. Thank you for the courage to defeat disappointments and for the hope that overcomes fear.

JUNE 21

One of Robby's most cherished possessions is his bicycle. It is lime green and yellow and has cartoon characters all over it. When he pedals quickly, the streamers attached to the handlebars blow and crackle in the wind. He has a serene look of accomplishment when the wind hits his face. I like to watch him.

It wasn't always like that. First there was the fear of getting on the bicycle. Then there was the fear of pedaling. The largest hurdle was the fear of going too fast.

I'm glad that my dad was there to coach Robby on these techniques. My dad has patience, a gentle voice, and a wellspring of encouragement. Each time Robby would fall down, Dad would verbally encourage him to get up and try again. Just being there for Robby meant a lot. Often that's all Daddy had to do—just stand in the driveway and be there. As long as Robby knew his granddad was somewhere around, he felt comfortable and confident on the bicycle.

Those early bicycle days remind me of our faith. Regardless of what we are going through, just knowing that God is there with us helps us make it through.

Dear God, I want to keep feeling your presence in the driveway of life. I will stumble and fall along the way, but it helps just to know that you are there.

JUNE 22

The sweet disposition of a happy child can melt the most frosty of hearts. When I find myself burdened by the cares and concerns of my job, it is usually my son and his laughter that lift and cheer me.

When Robby laughs, his eyes light up, his nose crinkles, and the place on his cheek where he almost has a dimple, dimples in anyhow. I chuckle at the sight of him, and eventually I forget what had me so down.

I believe that God placed something within children to make them centers of joy and laughter. I believe that their carefree attitudes are examples to us of how we ought to be with God. Children can relax because they know their parents will take care of them. That's why their laughter is so infectious. As mothers, we can learn from them to rely on God more often and to laugh more often.

Dear God, help me to abandon more of my cares, to let go of the stress, and to turn my back on hard times so that I may laugh like children who know their parents will handle everything that comes along.

JUNE 23

Family walks in the evening after dinner are a personal favorite of mine. The setting sun, cooler temperatures, and full tummies are the perfect ingredients for a neighborhood stroll.

Usually all three of us can walk at a brisk pace and cover the ten blocks of our standard route in no time. However, while carrying the extra pounds during my pregnancy, I was slowed down a bit.

In fact, the slowness irritated my husband and son so much that they decided to run the last block home one evening. Off they ran to our front steps, and then they watched me waddle in from a distance.

As I walked the last block alone, my steps were slowed when a batch of premature contractions set it. It was an effort just to put one foot in front of the other. With my head hung down, I struggled. Much to my surprise, Robby got up and ran back to meet me.

"Momma, I've come back for you," he said. That simple gesture showed me so much. Robby had concern and compassion on me. That small act gave me a glimpse of the loving person that my son really is. I liked what I saw.

What tremendous blessings God gives us in our children's simple acts of love!

Dear God, thank you for giving my child the ability to love me and the ability to show it.

JUNE 24

All the lights were off in the kitchen. Robby's request for chocolate milk meant a visit to that dark kitchen. Before I had a chance to flip the light switch, he yelled "Momma, hold my hand! I scared!"

Robby is afraid of the dark, and that surprises me. Surely he knows that there are no ghosts or monsters lurking about. His life has been free of trauma and disasters. So what does he have to be afraid of?

I grabbed his hand and turned on the light simultaneously. A trusting hand to hold on to and a bright light to illuminate his path made his fears vanish and a smile erupt.

In the same way, God knows that we have no reason to be afraid of the dark situations we encounter, but we are. When we ask God to hold our hand, he does so.

Dear God, please understand that, like a small child, I also get scared of dark times. I don't always have a reason either; the fear just comes. Keep hearing me when I call.

JUNE 25

It is 6:00 A.M. I rise from my bed, leaving a happily snoring husband to sleep a few more minutes. The house is quiet and calm. There are a handful of moments when all is calm around here, and I've learned to seize them.

Instead of burying my head in the morning newspaper, I stand in the doorway of Robby's room. I look, listen, and marvel at the gift God has given me. As he lies there so still, I am free to go closer, kneel beside his bed, and examine the pint-sized miracle. I begin to dream about his future.

Will his soft facial skin someday be engulfed by a moustache and beard? Will those small hands in the years ahead become strong and sure enough to assist him in whatever occupation he chooses? Will that squeaky voice of his deepen, giving him a commanding speech that captures everyone's attention? Will his three-foot frame expand three more feet to tower over me?

All of this and more I want for him. I want him to grow up into an intelligent, articulate, compassionate, well-mannered man who loves the Lord. I want him to go to college and get married and have children and bring them to see me. I want a nice card and flowers from him on Mother's Day. I want the nice card and flowers hand delivered, of course, by the man who used to be a boy, who will say, "Thanks for being my mom," and then kiss me on the cheek.

I want all of this, but right now I just want my small, squeeky-voiced boy to be a boy I can watch and marvel at as he sleeps.

Dear God, each day there is newness about my child. I don't want to miss a thing. Keep me alert and keep me grateful.

JUNE 26

Looking through some of our wedding photos, I hardly recognize myself. Something has changed me; I don't know the old me anymore. We aren't alike at all. We talk differently, think differently, and even walk differently.

I am different now because I am a mother. The very existence of my child makes me somebody else. Because he is my son, I am a mother; because he needs food and drink, I am a provider; because he needs to learn, I am a teacher; because he thrives on security and love, I am a nurturer.

I am happy because he is happy, and I realize that my capacity to be all that I am comes from God. God enables me to be a mother with all the trimmings.

Dear God, I am somebody new. I am a mother. Motherhood is one of the greatest events in my life. You shape and mold me so that I can handle the job, as though I am clay on the potter's wheel. Keep your hands on me.

JUNE 27

Kim was a good friend of mine. We were about the same age, we had been married about the same amount of time, and we both had a slight addiction to the shopping malls. Even though we have so much in common, there was one area where we were painfully different. I had a child and another one on the way, and Kim was battling infertility and seemed to be losing.

Over the past eight years, she and her husband had tried everything that medical science had to offer—from the expensive to the embarrassing. We remained close friends throughout this process. I provided a shoulder to cry on and an ear to listen whenever she needed me. In fact, I became accustomed to the disappointments, and I kept a mental file of positive words and Scripture verses to share during her down times.

Tonight when the phone rang, there was a new low in her voice. She was calling from a hospital room, and the news she shared sounded like the end of her world. Some unforeseen complications had set in, and she was rushed into the hospital for an emergency hysterectomy. With this news all of my pre-meditated answers flew out the window, and we cried together. All we could do was cry, but God still heard our tears.

Dear God, my heart breaks today for all women who desire to produce children in their wombs but cannot. Dry their tears, bolster their faith, and direct them toward other avenues of motherhood.

JUNE 28

The daycare center director didn't look pleased when she summoned me this morning after I dropped off Robby. She led me to her office, and, along the way, my mind raced through a list of the things Robby could have done. Did he pull a girl's pony tail? Did he wet his pants? Did he refuse to eat his green beans? I decided to brace myself for the worst because my son has quite a tenacious streak.

"Your son is somewhat of a bully. He has been hitting other children," the director said. Her words hit me like a slap in the face. All at once I was embarrassed, shocked, and hurt. I wanted to shake my head in denial. Surely my sweet boy could not hurt any other child. Maybe she had him confused with someone else.

I accepted her words and held back my tears until I got home. Then I immediately phoned my mother for advice. She had always been a good mother to me. She would know what to do. What had I done wrong?

After calming me down, she told me to talk the situation over with Robby and to discipline him if necessary, and to pray, pray, pray.

There are some things that come along in this motherhood business that are easy and fun. There are other things that come along and knock you flat. When we feel flat, the best thing we can do is begin to pray, and pray mightily.

Dear God, your scriptures teach us that in this world there will be trials and tribulation, but you have overcome them all. I believe your words, and I will hold on to the promises so that I can survive the hurtful times.

JUNE 29

My church sponsors a daily senior citizen's program that includes a Wednesday morning sermon from me. This Wednesday morning I allowed Robby to spend the day with me. I wanted to show him what his mom, the minister, does all day.

He promised me that he'd be good during my sermon, and I wanted to believe him. Trusting those innocent brown eyes,

I held his hand as we walked to the pulpit before the service started.

I seated him beside me on a bench directly behind the huge, wooden lectern where I would preach. All he had to do was sit there quietly and watch Mom "work." No one could see him; no one knew that he was there.

All was well during the pastoral prayer and hymns. He sat on the hem of my skirt. But while I was preaching I looked down, and, to my dismay, Robby was standing behind me, clamoring for attention. I patted his head and scooted him back to the bench without missing a beat of the sermon.

However, my son reversed his steps while my back was turned. Ever determined to get my attention, he did the unthinkable. He marched around me in a circle singing "Ring Around the Roses."

The congregation was oblivious to the playground scene behind the pulpit. I kept on preaching, and Robby kept on marching. No one ever knew, and who would believe me if I told them?

This experience from a mother's "believe it or not" category reminded me how often we are like children, sincere in our promises yet short in tolerance. We grow tired of being faithful or of waiting for our own satisfaction, and we desperately seek recognition from others and from God. Sometimes our actions are as innocent as those of a little child, but sometimes our actions are selfish and demanding. Even so, God is always patient and forgiving.

Dear God, I so want to be a more patient and forgiving mother. Thank you for the gentle reminders my child unknowingly gives me. It's not always enough to be patient; how grateful I am for your patience with me.

JUNE 30

My college roommate was in town this week, and we had lunch together. I had not seen her since we graduated ten years ago. When we greeted each other, the first words out of her mouth caught me by surprise. "Motherhood sure agrees with you," she said. It was a pleasant compliment, but, in reality, I feel the opposite is true: I have agreed with motherhood.

It was a conscious decision to share my life with a new life, and it was a hard decision. I knew that my way of life would never be the same after the birth of my child, and I was reluctant to give up what I had become accustomed to. I said good-bye to self-centered shopping sprees and so long to quiet, romantic evenings at home with my husband.

This was something that I walked into with my eyes wide open. I agreed to allow my body to host a growing baby. I agreed to endure fourteen hours of labor. I agreed to wake up and feed the newborn every few hours. I agreed to have baby vomit all over my clothes. I agreed to change hundreds of diapers. I agreed to potty train, teach ABC's, and watch "Sesame Street" rather than my favorite shows. And I would take nothing for my trouble.

I have agreed with motherhood. May God enable me to always be an agreeable mother.

Dear God, you gave me the courage to begin this new life and you strengthen me from day to day. Help me to keep agreeing and to remain agreeable to the challenges ahead.

JULY

A "Real" Mother

ANNE L. WILCOX

JULY 1

e was so unexpected. His persistent knock could barely be heard above the din of our busy lives. As usual, I had been juggling house guests, piano students, home remodeling, and team ministry with my pastor husband. With heart and hands full, I threw open the door. It took only one look—I dropped everything and slammed the door. With a racing heart, I bolted the front door and ran to secure the back door as well. He would never be welcome here. We were young and full of high hopes for a family. Infertility would have to find other lodging.

In the months after our first encounter, we discovered he could pass through locked doors. As months changed to years, we realized he had not come to visit but to establish permanent residency. I despised this devourer of our nursery, but my anger could not evict him.

We had heard the proverb "Hope deferred makes the heart sick" (Proverbs 13:12). Therefore, how could we withstand not only the postponement of a hope but also its permanent destruction? Our only comfort came from one who had composed the following words in a time of hopelessness:

> Why are you cast down, O my soul,
>   and why are you disquieted within me?
> Hope in God; for I shall again praise him,
>   my help and my God. (Psalm 42:11)

JULY 2

The psalmist had called it *cast down* and *disquieted* in Psalm 42. As the years passed by and I discovered that our desire to parent might never be fulfilled, I called it *restless*. Finally I decided that if the psalmists were somehow helped by prayers of complaint, then maybe I needed to join them:

Lord, once again I come to You with a restless heart,
Year after year I place my request before You.
How long will You be silent in the face of my need?
How long will my circumstances remain unchanged?

My desire is not just for a baby to fill my empty arms,
I ask for a child whose heart is wholly Yours—
One who will delight in Your Word,
And stand steadfast for You in the midst of wicked times.
I long for the privilege to teach little ones Your ways
That righteousness may characterize the next generation.

Lord God, You appoint the seasons of our lives,
You alone are the Giver of life.
You are the God of Sarah,
A Giver of children at an impossible, but perfect time.
You are the God of Hannah,
A Giver of godly children in an era of ungodliness.
You are the God of Elizabeth,
A Giver of children in time to prepare a nation for Messiah!

Lord, You know I am a different race than these women,
And I live in another moment of history,
But You are the same God.
Therefore with confidence I bring my petition
To the One who has grafted me into His gracious promises.
Hear my desire to participate in the lineage of faith,
That Your name might be praised from generation to generation.

JULY 3

Infertility refused vacation leave; we were never without our uninvited guest. Holidays proved the most difficult times to endure his company. Therefore, I was startled one Fourth of July weekend to see his repulsive face begin a metamorphosis. The taunting sneer I had always seen in the midst of family picnics became less apparent. In its place, intermittent expressions of kindness and even compassion seemed to appear. I began to have strong doubts about my ability to perceive. Was he changing, or was I beginning to see with different eyes?

All these years I had raged at him—and rightly so. He had robbed us of the most important things in life. But this particular holiday, when not only freedom but also its great cost are celebrated, I began to see infertility differently. Maybe loss could sometimes—if not always—be a professor in disguise.

For the first time, I removed the cataracts of hostility and began to notice not only what infertility had stolen from us but also what he had given to us. Without his thievery, I might never have seen through the debate about when life begins. Without him at my elbow, I would never had learned to value each child with wonder. Without his pain, my weeping might have had little resonance with which to comfort others.

Although his courses are often still painful, I have ceased to view him as only an enemy. Now I recognize that loss can also be a master teacher.

JULY 4

If loss truly could teach, then maybe I needed to join the psalmist again—this time with a prayer of acceptance:

O Lord, You alone are the comfort of those who wait,
Their only hope through years of deferred hope.
Through the crucible of unchanging circumstances,
You skillfully purify hearts.

Lord, my heart was anxious and restless,
I could not accept Your answer to my prayers.
I was angry with Your timing,
For You were withholding something good from me!

But rash indictments cannot change You,
With loyal love You endured my grievances.
Patiently You began renewing my spirit,
Your Word enlarged my understanding.
Through disappointment and delay
You lovingly deepened me.
You carried me through sorrow
That I might learn to comfort others.
What a privilege to be taught by One whose power
Can refashion pain and endurance into proficient tools for maturity.

Master and Teacher, if You still answer my petitions with no,
Shall I bring more accusations?
If You ask me to wait more years,
Shall I nurture bitterness?
How can I mistrust and be bitter toward Him
Whose body was broken that I might live,
And who is now lovingly maturing me?

O Lord, only You are my comfort in waiting,
You alone are my expectant hope through years of silence.
May You always be my first love,
Above all petitions and desires.
No perfect thing do You withhold from me,
Your timing is ordered by omniscient love.

JULY 5

Adoption! Why hadn't we considered it before? Forming our family through adoption would be a delightful adventure!

It wasn't long, however, before our naive zeal sent us thundering over unexpected cliffs, leaving us bruised by the sharp rocks of reality below. Everyone had a story for us— stories of waiting forever for a child, stories of enormous costs, and stories of birth mothers changing their minds—all horror stories for those who wait.

After months of falling, we gently bandaged our wounds and slowly began to accumulate adoption agency forms with the detachment of those sobered by fact. Suspicious of hope and afraid of more jagged rocks, we no longer pranced enthusiastically. Tentatively we put out one foot, tested the ground beneath us, and then—only then—took another step.

Surely there was some way to walk more securely, despite the unexpected. Surely there was a way to intertwine the intense desire to parent with the setbacks often encountered in adoption—without getting hopelessly tangled.

David wrote in Psalm 40 that the Lord had set his feet upon a rock. No more unexpected cliffs sounded good to me. But David was not guaranteeing smooth terrain. The psalm is full of difficulties—more numerous than the hairs on the psalmist's head! Instead, the secure place to stand came from patient waiting on a God who hears (Psalm 40:1) and from a sincere desire to do the will of God (Psalm 40:8). Renewed hope had some maturing to do.

JULY 6

During all the adoption red tape, unbelievable news came. A private adoption looked promising. However, the lawyer advised us not to begin a nursery. There were too many *ifs*. We would be selected to parent this child *if* the state deemed us worthy to parent, *if* we could pay the medical and legal fees, *if* the birth father signed the papers, and *if* the birth mother did not change her mind. How could we sort through our feelings? In six months we might have our first child—or we might be thrown back to childlessness with one unresolved *if*.

This adoption news had come just as I was dashing out the door for, of all things, a baby shower. I drove in a daze. As I walked into the party I could hardly keep my mind on the joyous chatter. My eyes kept wandering to the expectant mother. Was I expecting, too? Even if I were, it would never be obvious. Even if I were, my preparations would be quiet and tentative. There I sat admiring booties and quilts and hiding our news in a heart that had become very cautious. In six months my arms would be filled with a child—or more stacks of adoption papers.

Anticipation with a *maybe* is the most awful kind of waiting. Where was that rock to stand on? It seemed to come from another of David's psalms. In Psalm 139, David understood that God knew all the days ordained for him before he was born. The child I now waited for was also being "knit together" in a mother's womb—and had not escaped the sovereign ordaining of her days by a gracious, all-knowing Creator.

JULY 7

"Do you mind if the child is short?"
Surely the lawyer was kidding. The physical size of the child

seemed unimportant, especially after years and years of waiting. But he was serious, and he interpreted my hesitation as reluctance.

"I know that your husband is over six feet tall, and no one on the child's maternal side is over five feet tall."

Instead of becoming angry that size would even be addressed, I informed the lawyer that it would be a delightful novelty to have someone with a smaller stature in a family whose men on one side always used Tall Shops and whose women on the other side wore extremely large shoes. A bit of "medium" or "petite" added into the lineage might be quite refreshing. At that the lawyer grinned—but then began pushing toward other areas.

"If something goes wrong, you can still change your minds. You know that, don't you?"

Those who wait so long for children can be terribly stubborn. I remember blurting something about being surprised that a warranty was expected when adopting a child. There are no guarantees. All parents take a risk, whether a child joins their family through biological reproduction or through adoption. Warranties do not accompany children.

If the item I'm shopping for is supposed to fulfill some need in me or to perform some task for me, then I want a warranty. But if what I am seeking is not an object but a person on whom I wish to direct my love—a child of God—then there is no need of a warranty. God requires no warranty, and neither do parents.

JULY 8

Twenty-four hours ago you were placed in my arms. We are mother and daughter, but this is the first day we've ever spent together. I had no part in your conception. There are no memories of your prenatal stirring. Someone else panted and pushed to bring you into this world. And yet, yesterday we became a family. I wonder what you think of this new heart-beat.

After your last feeding, I should have let you sleep, but it's so good to finally hold you. I wonder if you're comfortable in *my* arms. You've made so many changes, taking in oxygen through lungs and learning to depend on sucking for food. And the voice most familiar to you has become silent. Now other voices nurture you. I wonder what we sound like to you.

I suppose it's time to stop wondering and just get on with the process of bonding. What a fascinating mystery is this nonverbal dance of initiation and response between parent and child. If *I* take getting used to, dear daughter, I'm not the only one. Part of bonding is the anticipation of a child's appearance. Because the lawyer said your biological heritage was predominantly French, we used a French spelling for your name, and we pictured a baby with dark, thick hair. So here you are almost bald with strawberry blonde fuzz.

Finally, all of us can stop guessing and begin the joyful, face-to-face task of bonding. We've missed nine months of it, but it won't take long to catch up. Always know that this different heartbeat means a family where you will always be cherished.

JULY 9

Jaime, how will I tell you that you're adopted? I guess I'm not wording it right even now. Your adoption is past, so referring to it in the present is incorrect. *Adopted* does not define who you are; adoption is the process that brought you into this family. You are not adopted; you *were* adopted. You *are* a little girl who was conceived and born like every other child before you. Adoption was the legal procedure that brought you into a family where you will always belong. Birth is how you made your debut into the world. Adoption is how you made your debut into our family.

There is no reason to have any secrets about your beginnings. You have a very real set of biological parents, in addition to us. They have provided your genetic structure, which determines much of who you are. We will not pretend they don't exist. But they have relinquished you to us, and we are not temporary parents. No, through the act of adoption, we are a real family. All the rights, privileges, responsibilities, and especially love you have in this family are no different from those which would be enjoyed by a child coming to us through birth.

So when we talk about these things, I won't tell you that you *are* adopted. I will tell you that you *were* adopted. I will tell you of the pain of waiting, the hard decision made by your birthparents, and the celebration of your homecoming.

There will be no secrets. We are a family now, and how that has come to be is a story worth hearing over and over.

JULY 10

I hopped out of the car and opened the back door to release my priceless bundle from her car seat. I chuckled at the memory of shopping for this safety device. We had poured over the features of every car seat ever manufactured. Firstborns in any family must endure multiple acts of overprotection. When firstborns arrive after long years of adoption procedures, it's a wonder they survive all the fuss.

As I turned to dash into the store, an older woman approached us. "How old is your baby?"

When I answered, "Two weeks and one day," she seemed astonished.

"I've never seen anyone in such good shape with a baby that young. My, my, you must have had an easy delivery."

A mischievous impulse grabbed me. Should I flash her a radiant smile, utter a glowing thank you, and stride into the shopping mall? Honesty was stronger than mischief—this time—so I explained, "You're very kind, but I was never pregnant. Our little girl was adopted."

"Oh—that explains everything. I had three children, and I was miserable through every pregnancy. And then the deliveries—oh, they were terrible. Believe me, honey, you're doing it the easy way. Well, good luck."

She was gone as quickly as she had appeared, and I was left stunned by her words. This was the easy way? I slowly entered the mall and began to absently windowshop. Is it the easy way when your pain spans years, instead of the intense hours of labor? Is it the easy way when you cry out in the night, not with the birth process, but because another month has passed leaving you childless? Is it the easy way when one woman courageously gives birth but must go home empty-handed, entrusting the lifetime nurture of her flesh and blood to another woman? Dear mother of three, this should *never* be called the easy way.

JULY 11

"Hi, Anne. How are you managing with your new little girl?"

"We're doing just fine. We're so thrilled with her. All the years of waiting have been worth it."

"That's great. I've never been close to a family who has adopted before. Do you think you'll ever feel like a *real* mother?"

I almost dropped the phone. If she had come to my door, she would have witnessed the reality on my end of the line.

All week my two-month-old daughter had battled illness. The first night I was left to that anxious guessing game parents are forced to play with infants. My normally cheerful cooer would awaken in the night screaming and gasping for breath.

Eventually I calmed her enough for sleep to return, but within an hour the scene would replay itself with greater intensity.

The minute the pediatrician's office opened the next morning, I was standing at the door. His examination revealed infections in both ears, so antibiotics were administered to her at a tender age. After another marathon night, I hoped the medicine would take hold and give us some sleep on night three. It might have, if the flu hadn't struck.

Severe vomiting and the fear of dehydration sent me rushing back to the doctor. Special liquids would help her through the flu, but we had to continue fighting the infections. Since she couldn't keep the medicine down, shots were in order. The injections had to be given three times a day and they could be obtained only at the nearest emergency room. By the end of the week, I could drive to the hospital with my eyes shut—most of the time they were!

Finally we began gaining ground. The baby could keep a little nourishment down, and she awakened only three or four times a night. I began to hope that we would live through this after all. But flu bugs have no discretion. This one took full advantage of the tender closeness of mother and feverish daughter. It was my turn to lose my dinner.

When my friend called, a trembling hand had lifted the receiver. The flu and the night shifts had taken all I had—but before I collapsed I had a question to answer. Would I ever feel like a *real* mother?

I toyed with two approaches. Should I describe my week to my friend, or should I invite her to spend the night? I was tempted to prepare a guest bed next to the baby's crib. I *was* a real mother—and this week I had definitely felt it!

JULY 12

Last night was impossible. How I wish this baby could talk and tell me what hurts. Is it teeth? Stomach? Ears? Who can tell when she's this little? How do I know what to do when I have no specific information? All I know for certain is that this night was a blur of crying and fussing. The strangest part I remember from those foggy, sleepless hours was the way my daughter frantically pushed away from me—as if I were the source of her pain. It must be impossible for babies to discern from where their pain originates because she spent most of her energy fighting against me, her only source of help and comfort. How do I help her understand that I am not the enemy?

I wonder if I often act like my infant daughter when I experience discomfort or frustration. Despite my supposed maturity, I, too, often accuse the Source of All Comfort of being the author of my pain. I wonder if the same one who said, "Jerusalem, Jerusalem. . . . How often have I desired to gather your children together as a hen gathers her brood under her wings, and you were not willing" (Luke 13:34), is the same One who tries to comfort me as I frantically push away. I need to grow up. I need to understand more clearly the origin of my pain and frustration. I wonder if my Heavenly Father is also saying, "How do I help her understand that I am not the enemy?"

JULY 13

The courtroom was packed with strained people. Familial disputes carry their own unique kind of stress. The judge seemed austere in his long black robe, and his face bore the lines of one burdened by refereeing angry family members. Soon it was our turn to approach the bench. As our papers were handed to him, his countenance changed. He grinned, scooped up our documents, and invited us to join him privately in his chambers.

Over my shoulder rode a six-month-old charmer. She was ready to coo and bubble despite the solemnity of the occasion.

Six months ago we had become parents of a two-day-old little girl, and now we were in court to finalize the adoption.

After we were seated in his chambers, the judge resumed his expression of gravity and began asking us serious questions about parenting. Only after he was fully satisfied that we understood the immensity of our responsibility did he sign the official documents of adoption. Then he rose and threw off his robe. He reached out for our squirming bundle and began bouncing and tickling our child like an adoring grandparent. Our daughter was unimpressed, however. Her attention was drawn to one endeavor—munching the priceless papers he had just signed! The judge threw back his head and laughed. For a few moments, the things that tear families apart were forgotten. He had just taken part in putting a family together. It would all be final—if he could salvage the documents from slobbery little gums.

JULY 14

I'd spent three years in college studying the meaning of Ephesians 1:5: "He destined us for adoption as his children through Jesus Christ, according to the good pleasure of his will." Many volumes have been written about God's sovereign will and about our entrance into his family. The mysteries and complexities of both topics could hardly be resolved in one— or even two—term papers. But now, several years later, I had a new reason to explore the wonder of adoption through Christ.

Professors of law have looked long and hard at the implications of adoption in the Bible. One expert in Roman law observed that Paul used the metaphor of adoption five times in his epistles because Roman adoption laws were highly sophisticated and widely known. Roman law enabled the person who was originally separated from a particular family to become fully a part of that family with all the rights, privileges, and responsibilities of a biological child. Therefore, it gave

Paul a perfect analogy. This practice provided yet another way to describe first our separation from God and then our full restoration through Christ.

All of this doctrinal insight was helpful, but that was before I became a parent through the process of adoption. The experience of adoptive parenting unraveled the theoretical packaging of my former study. Adoption was not just a doctrinal definition of our standing before God; it was an analogy of intimate relationship with a loving Parent.

JULY 15

Before I experienced adoptive parenting, Christ's work of redeeming or saving us had always made me think in legal terms. Previously, I had consulted the book of Ruth to define redemption. In that poignant short story, the one being redeemed had to meet specific legal requirements. Therefore, New Testament redemption was Christ's unique fulfillment of the legal mandates required to achieve eternal redemption. I had not intertwined redemption and adoption as Paul does in Ephesians: "In love he predestined us to be adopted. . . . In him we have redemption through his blood" (1:5, 7 NIV).

Now, with an adopted child placed in my arms for lifetime care, I began to see a new side of redemption. It was still true that the legal transaction required to secure us in God's family needed more than drafting and a signature. It required blood. It was still true that our redemption into God's family had vast debts to pay with only one Person capable of making payment. And it was still true that through Christ the requirements of God's holy law were met—at tremendous cost. But something more was there.

God's forethought was not just to repair the breach of legal standing between fallen creatures and a holy Creator—as profound as that reparation was. His forethought also included this tender cradling—this hilarious joy! With love, he intended our adoption. Beyond the blood and legal requirements of redemption, he intended familial intimacy—closeness, support, nurture, strength. Just as we had drawn this child into our family for more than legal implications, so also God intended not just merciful justice but familial love.

JULY 16

We're wasting time right now—you know. All we're doing is enjoying each other's company. Why do you look so pleased when I sing softly to you? Why so content? Why am I—the overachievement addict—finding it so easy to simply sit?

There is a unique fulfillment in simply enjoying the company of another person. These moments contain no expectations, no requirements, no hurry-up-to-get-there pushing. I guess some would call it a waste of time. I'd call it our oasis of affirmation and love. Christ's words in Matthew 11:28 seem to invite us into his company in much the same way: "Come to me, all you that are weary and are carrying heavy burdens, and I will give you rest."

But I feel the busy, bustling years coming soon. Some say that these quiet moments evaporate the minute a child starts walking. At the rate and intensity with which you're crawling, I believe them. I also know that, as in any relationship, expectations and requirements must multiply between us in order for us both to mature—and survive.

Yet, as the years go by, I hope you can always find me ready and eager to join you for a few hallowed moments of acceptance and rest. Even during the spirited years and even during times of conflict, I hope we can waste a bit of time on quiet love and affirmation.

"Oh, you're ready to get up now? Okay. You want to try to stand? Good girl. Oh, my word, you're walking!"

JULY 17

There's such a wide, wonderful world for you to explore now that you're walking. However, with this new freedom have also come new restrictions. The electrical sockets, though fascinating, are a definite "No!" But don't forget, all your toys are a "Yes!" The staircase is great fun, but it comes with a "No, unless accompanied by an adult." It won't be long before you can negotiate those on your own. However, until then the restriction remains. Don't forget—all of your toys are "Yes!" I realize that the stereo, TV, and VCR controls are at your eye level now, but they are also a definite "No!" Why aren't you trying out all your toys?

I see—because the glass music box now has your full attention. Well, let's compromise. Let's learn that instead of most things being "No!" some things can be touched gently. No grabbing of glass knick-knacks, but you may explore carefully. I'll let you know what's okay by saying, "Touch gently."

Our toddler became fairly good at learning the difference between mauling an object and touching it gently. However, one morning I caught her trying to insert a paperclip into an electrical socket. As I frantically jerked her away and spanked her, she instructed me to "Touch gently!" She obviously wanted her mother to treat her as she had been taught to treat the glass music box. She was told that when she is about to electrocute herself, Mommy cannot be gentle. It's too dangerous. In most other situations, however, Mommy will make every effort to touch gently.

God has made us caretakers of this beautiful world, and he has asked us to "touch gently." But, like small children, sometimes we forget—or even ignore—God's warning, and our careless actions hurt God's creation—and ultimately ourselves and others. Though we might wish that God would reach out and grab us to prevent us from making such destructive mistakes, God has given us the freedom to make choices and to live with the consequences of those choices. Although we do not deserve it, may God "touch gently" with his forgiveness and help us to become wiser and more gentle stewards of the earth.

JULY 18

I had hoped to spark a love for language early in my daughter's life. After one tiny flame, a bonfire ignited. At naptime when she should have wanted her "blanky," she called out instead for her books. When I thought she was old enough to begin speaking in complete sentences, she was verbally exploding in paragraphs. Instead of learning "Jesus Loves Me" in Sunday school, she was composing words for forty other verses. We eventually had to invent a signal to extinguish the verbal exploration for a few moments so Mom and Dad could remember if they had anything to say.

Then the love of riddling took hold. At least there was quiet between the presentation of the riddle and the answer while a certain little person was thinking. We found riddles and guessing games everywhere, from ancient riddles in Greek literature to spellbinding riddle games in Tolkien's *Hobbit* to silly riddle books for kids. It was the silly riddle books for kids that made me realize we needed a bit of balance in our city-dwelling lives.

We had been laughing through a few riddles when we chanced upon this one: "What has a mane, wears iron shoes, and lives in a stable?" My daughter didn't even need to think about this one. Her eyes sparkled with immediate recognition while she blurted, "I know—baby Jesus!" That was the day I determined that we would balance our trips to Sunday school with a few trips to the farm!

At least I knew that not only had I succeeded in sparking a love for language that would stimulate my daughter's mind, but also I had sparked a love for knowing about Jesus that would—one day, I hoped—fill my daughter's heart.

JULY 19

When our daughter was two, she charged into the kitchen, grabbed hold of my leg, and beamed, "I'm adopa-did." I was glad adoption was becoming a familiar word for her, even if her pronunciation could use a bit of work. I didn't want to make the error of secrecy—an error often thought appropriate in the past. Often parents would wait five to ten years before revealing the child's adoptive heritage. Some attempted to keep it a secret forever. It seemed to me that nothing but mistrust and shock would result with that approach.

I also was wary of overusing words like *special* and *chosen*. I thought our daughter would begin to think she was different from everyone else and expected to perform up to higher standards than anyone else based on a unique beginning. Both extremes—the secrecy and the overemphasis—seemed inappropriate.

But there was a two-year-old beaming at my pant leg, trying to learn to use *adoption* as appropriately as *Daddy* and *kitty*. I bent down to her level. How could I tell her that, on the one hand, she was the same as other children, and, on the other, she was completely unique as all other human children are unique? She needed to know that some children join their families through birth and some through adoption, but they all are still children. But with a two-year-old attention span, I simply said, "You were adopted—that's how you joined our family. You are a little girl."

JULY 20

At a very young age, our daughter would try to mimic the moustache fiddling her father did when he was thinking. It was rather difficult to manage on a bald lip, but she never stopped trying. She also liked Grandma's doughnut dunking. Whenever coffee and doughnuts were served, she made sure she had steaming cocoa so she could match Grandma dunk for dunk. I also began noticing that the tone of voice she used with her dolls resembled a certain mother's. It was rather disconcerting, however, to hear the impatient tone used more frequently than the gentle, soothing tone. In the midst of all this eagerness to mimic came two questions about physical appearance.

"Will I be as tall as Daddy someday?"

"Will I ever have your brown eyes, Mom?"

With a six-foot-four-inch adoptive father and a five-foot birth heritage, the probable answer to the first question was no. And since she had clear blue eyes already, the answer to the second question was definitely no. At first she seemed quite sad to hear the answers, until we talked about what it meant to resemble one another in a family.

She was fascinated to learn there were other ways to resemble one another that were just as delightful—and sometimes more important—than matching eye color and height. Together we read Ephesians 5:1, which shows how members of God's family are to resemble him. The resemblance and imitation expressed there are concerned with character rather than physical likeness.

Therefore, even if she is never as tall as Daddy, she can still enjoy and mimic his sense of humor and his kind heart. Even if she has blue eyes and I have brown eyes, we can resemble each other in our love of people. We might even want to work together on making the tone of our voices more gentle, more often!

JULY 21

You've been overhearing us talk about adoption again. This time we have to fill out papers for an agency. They want us to specify our preference regarding the gender of the child. It feels so strange putting in an order for a person. I feel like adding, "We would also prefer a child who sleeps through the night, eats all of his or her vegetables, and is always good-natured." How absurd—but necessary for the maze of adoption paperwork.

You heard us decide to specify "male." And you must have heard why. I thought it would be nice to invade my side of the family with a male child. I grew up in a family of three girls, and all three of us have had daughters—so why not a prince among all those princesses? However, you must have thought girls weren't special anymore. Believe me—nothing could be further from the truth.

You looked so serious and so worried when you asked, "Mommy, did you want a boy better than me?" No, precious little person, a thousand times no! I only knew I wanted you. When we discovered you were a girl, then I knew that was exactly what I wanted!

Male and female humans are both required to reflect the image of God. Neither gender is inferior to the other; neither gender is more desirable than the other. In some cultures and eras of history, men were preferred to carry on family names. In some cultures today women are preferred for the same reason. However, in this family, in this culture, in this period of history, *you* are who we wanted. And as the years have since passed and our adoption attempts have fallen through, we realize even more what a privilege it is to have *you*.

JULY 22

When a friend visited two weeks before the birth of her fourth child, our daughter's questions erupted. With three-year-old wonder she asked, "Is there really a baby in there?" Fortunately, my friend was very relaxed, and she let Jaime feel the kicking evidence of a real, live human.

A few days later, Jaime began sorting this new information and relating it to her relatives. She asked if Derek grew in Aunt Cathy's womb. When I praised her understanding, she tried another deduction, "Then cousin Sean grew in Uncle Ken's womb—right?"

It took every ounce of self-control to greet this honest inquiry with a straight face. We tackled it by explaining that babies are made by both the mommy and the daddy, but the babies are all carried by the mothers in the family. She was thrilled with the new insights and went through all the cousins, telling me which aunt's womb they each grew in. After she scored 100 percent, I smugly congratulated myself on our first sex education lesson.

But the questions weren't over. "That means I grew in your womb—right, Mom?"

I stopped everything and picked her up. "You grew in my heart, but you didn't grow in my womb. Remember the talks we've had about adoption? You were adopted into our family, which means you grew in someone else's womb, but God intended you to be a part of our family."

She looked up at me with confusion and said, "Well, where's my other mommy? What's her name?"

I couldn't believe she was asking these questions so early. I took a deep breath and proceeded to tell her what we knew and what we didn't know about her birth mother. After listening quietly for a while, she hopped out of my arms with another extremely important question.

"Mom, may I have some gum now?"

JULY 23

Today was a day to forget! First I baked a pumpkin pie and burned it. Then I baked pumpkin bread from a recipe that had been copied incorrectly. It wasn't even salvageable. After furiously cleaning all the cooking dishes, I decided to make jelly.

My three-year-old had been toddling in and out of the kitchen, happily waving measuring spoons and spatulas. She looked up from her play only when my frustration over the latest cooking failure became loud enough to distract her. Then she would pause and study my face intently. I'm almost sure she was deciding that one day when she was in charge of a household she would forget the hassle and simply go to the bakery. Wise little woman!

However, the jelly making finally caught her attention. Rows and rows of blueberry-colored jars won over the measuring spoons completely. Before I could catch her, she tugged on the tablecloth to achieve a better view. Five jars smashed to the floor. That might have been bad enough, but the contents of the jars revealed that the gelatin had not worked. I had just made three batches of blueberry mush. It could possibly be saved for syrup, but that verdict would have to wait. It was time to fix supper.

Surely we needed biscuits to go with the ham, so I pulled out a five-pound bag of flour. Somehow the glue on the bottom of the sack was ineffective. Flour flew everywhere from the sink counter to the table to the floor. Two little stubby legs ran for cover while big eyes peeked out to see what Mom would do. If I hadn't been so tired, I probably would have exploded. Instead, I sat down in the midst of the flour and said to one in particular, "Well, we have a choice here. We can get extremely upset—which might take all the energy I have left—or we can laugh. Which should it be?"

Preschool giggles started under the table, and they are so contagious. Soon we were laughing together helplessly. What a priceless gift from God are children who rescue us from the intense, serious pace of adulthood and help us live more playfully.

In the end, we sent out for pizza, but first we learned to trace a few alphabet letters in the white flour on the dark linoleum.

JULY 24

Many times the most valuable learning experiences happen unexpectedly. One of those moments occurred when Jaime was four. One Sunday after church, a young woman asked to speak to me. In a few short days her first child would be born, and she had to decide whether to relinquish her baby to adoptive parents or try to parent the baby herself. All I could do was listen and share her tears.

Jaime was all ears, and she crawled into my lap to ask why we were both crying. How could a four-year-old understand such things? But she could see the tears and feel the emotion, so she deserved an honest explanation.

I began by explaining that Diane would soon have a baby. Jaime rolled her eyes impatiently and said, "I know that, Mom." She'd seen other pregnant women and was as eager to address the real issue as I was hesitant to explain. With Jaime's prompting we charged right into Diane's dilemma about who should parent her child. Then I said Diane's tears came because she loved her baby very much, and, if she chose adoption, it would be very hard to say good-bye to the baby.

Jaime had heard the term *birth mother* in our discussions of adoption. She knew she had one, but in those brief moments with Diane, the term *birth mother* became incarnate. I could have spent hours explaining birth parents and the difficult decisions they must make, but nothing would have communicated as effectively as this unrehearsed experience of life.

JULY 25

I used to pray sequentially. My meticulous notebook had ordered concerns and praises I would bring before the Lord daily. It also had specific topics to address for each day of the week: mission concerns on Monday, government officials on Tuesday, local church leadership on Wednesday, and so forth. Seven o'clock to eight every morning was my prayer and study time. There were no interruptions, and my sense of spiritual well-being seemed sustained by that regimen.

Now I'm a mother. Sequential anything—much less prayer—is impossible during the preschool years. The thought of being meticulous is completely laughable. The idea of specific things to consider—in prayer or otherwise—on specific days of the week is also ridiculous. After all those sleepless nights, who can even remember what day of the week it is? And to think of one hour with no interruptions is now another world away.

My only regimen now is to learn winsome flexibility—a much harder task than sequential consistency. But I wonder if this is where true prayer is born—in the midst of the mess. Some days I still feel prayerless, mostly because my prayers resemble many of my thoughts—interrupted mid-stream. But then I realize that prayer has become as necessary and as automatic as breathing. Somehow this entire parenting adventure seems more like real life than the predictable, ordered past.

Lord, take all my moments as prayerful offerings to You, especially in these years when the preschool attention span is rubbing off on me!

JULY 26

Today you became acquainted with an earthworm. At first you were afraid to touch it, but soon you loved the idea of letting it squirm and tickle your hands. Soon you had built a shoebox house for your new pet and had named him Slurpy, because you were certain that the moisture left on your hands was his way of giving you a slobbery kiss.

After bringing the critter into the house, you held it up so that it could watch the news. No worm could go on living without a bit of TV. You filled a clam shell with dirt for its food, and with a gentle voice you told it all about life in our family. Then, with less than gentle hands, you gave Slurpy a "ride" across the kitchen linoleum.

Two hours into all the handling and anthropomorphizing,

poor Slurpy stopped wiggling. This new world you thought would be perfect for him was looking quite toxic. It was difficult to begin to see that though worms are alive, they do not like—or need—the same things as humans. Finally, you realized that the only hope for Slurpy was to return him to his natural habitat.

Ceremoniously, we dug a nice hole in the dirt for Slurpy. With a few tears you said good-bye and watched as the wriggling slowly returned. He had survived, and you had respected his needs above your own. You had discovered that other living things are a delight, but their unique needs for habitat must be respected if they are to survive. You had taken a huge preschool step in becoming a wiser steward of God's world.

JULY 27

As I was fixing dinner, Jaime ran to me with "Starved!" and "Can't wait!" pleas. In order to divert her attention and let her help, I asked her to go out to the garden and pick an onion for the salad.

Her little eyes lit up, and her shoulders straightened with the importance of her task. She reveled in thinking she could contribute something useful to the family's needs. After marching out the door, she sheepishly peeked back around the corner to ask, "Where are the onions?" After I told her, I could tell she wasn't completely confident. But away she went, anxious to complete such a significant responsibility for a preschooler.

After a few minutes I realized she had not returned, so I peeked out the window. She was standing by the garden sobbing. I dashed out to see how she'd been hurt, and she wailed, "I've looked everywhere, and I can't find them!"

I realized at that moment how important it was for her to please me. I wanted to pick her up and say, "You please me, Jaime. You always will. What you can or cannot do doesn't

195

change that. I love you for who you are." However, I knew these words would not communicate it thoroughly to a four-year-old, so I tried another angle.

I said, "Here, I'll help you find them, and then you can pick one yourself." After showing her the proper plants, she instructed me to leave so she could fulfill her task alone. I ducked back into the house and soon heard her steps on the porch. With great importance, she knocked twice on the screen door and smashed her little nose against the glass. Bright-eyed and straight-shouldered again, she handed me the perfect salad onion.

Will I remember as the years go on to give her responsibilities even when it's easier to do them myself? Will I help her learn new tasks without doing too much for her? Most of all, will I remember to tell her how much she pleases me—and God—just because of who she is?

JULY 28

Crumpled in a desk drawer were carefully laid plans for a birthday party. Ten special friends had been invited—more than you'd ever been allowed to have before. The sheer excitement of the numbers had been thrilling for the last three weeks!

But things do not always go according to plans. Cancellation after cancellation came. Up to this point in your life, I had been fairly able to make your dreams come true. This time I could do nothing. I had struggled with powerlessness over making some of my own dreams come true, but it didn't hurt as much as watching your disappointment. I tried to come up with several alternatives, but nothing changed the fact that only two people could come.

We finally managed to rework the party into a swim time, which seemed to delight you and your guests. However, when the gifts were opened, both items were duplicates of things you already had. You courageously thanked both friends for their thoughtfulness—a phrase we've talked about using when the actual gift is a disappointment—and made it through the rest of the afternoon.

When everyone left, the tears came. It had not been as you had expected—it had been a huge disappointment. I don't even want to begin telling you that there will be more days like this. I hope I'll know what to say—and what not to say—as you work through them.

Somehow I hope the arms I put around you now to comfort you will help you begin to understand that God will comfort you in the days ahead. The arms and hands he comforts with are marked with nail scars—evidence that he not only wants to comfort you, but also that he has the power to transform the deepest sorrows into life and hope.

J

JULY 29

The old black-and-white photos were carefully preserved in a leather-bound album. This mother of four had a prestigious lineage—and was very proud of it. We had been discovering through the pictures that many of the great-grandparents and great-great-grandparents were reappearing in the new generation. The shape of one face austerely preserved in a black-and-white portrait completely matched the face of the child dashing past the table where we sat. The stature of another grandfather was exactly duplicated in the young adult shooting hoops in the driveway. The heritage, the line, the family tree would all continue for many more generations.

I left this woman's home thinking, what of my family's lineage? When forming a family through adoption, genetic codes stop; ancestors do not make a second debut for all to say, "She looks just like Aunt Ethel." But heritages do not stop. Our legacy to our adopted child will go on. To her, all the generations will continue to give love, hope, truth, belonging, and support. From this particular family with grandparents that pray for her, she will receive a lineage of faith. She may not have the shape of their face, or their stature, but she will have the choice to imitate their wisdom, their passion for Christ, and their prayerful priorities. There is no more venerable lineage than that.

JULY 30

Hindsight from a former preschooler:

Sometimes when you're little, it's hard to tell a mom you're afraid.

One night I was in my room in the basement with a 100-degree temperature and the humidifier was on. I kept yelling for Mom, but she thought I was just stalling about going to bed. Shadows of the trees started to dance on the walls, keeping time with the noise of the humidifier. My fingers started to get numb, and I had the sensation of sand between my fingers. When the wind whistled, it sounded like someone talking very, very slowly—also keeping rhythm with the humidifier. All these things made me so afraid.

By now I was mad at my mom because she kept thinking I just didn't want to go to bed. Finally I fell asleep. Not until eight years later could I tell her my fears of the basement. When I get a fever now, some of these same things happen, but now I can tell someone.

Jaime Lynne Wilcox

My memory of those days with basement bedrooms includes the certainty that my daughter could write a book called *101 Ways to Stall the Bedtime Hour*. I often thought for sure she was just refusing to go to bed, and I was through being patient! This particular night she has described was the night I had decided to put my foot down on the bedtime routine. I thought we had done all we could to soothe the sickness needs, and now it was time to be firm.

Years later as Jaime described what was really going on, I

realized I had made the wrong choice that night. Preschoolers can and do manipulate the bedtime hour—but, as Jaime taught me, they also have needs that they are still too young to articulate or even understand themselves.

As we seek to be sensitive and responsive to the needs of our children—especially those needs they cannot fully understand or express—let us remember and be glad that God knows our every need, even those we cannot fully understand or express.

JULY 31

Tonight we lit candles and made tea for a special mother/daughter ceremony. We both had heard recently of several mothers and daughters having difficulty with communication. We decided we wanted to be best friends when we grew up.

My daughter had a good giggle at the thought of her mother still needing to grow up. But maybe that will be one of the keys to our friendship—a realization that we are both "in process" on this life journey. We even had a toast—with peanuts—to our relationship. Eight-year-old Jaime said, "To Mothers!" and I replied "To Daughters!" Then we each popped a peanut into the other's mouth.

It was a special moment, but my thoughts took me far away. We're still so new at this mother/daughter work. In many ways we're just getting started. There have been some misunderstandings between us already, but we've been able to work through them. But we haven't even started into the adolescent years—those years when daughters try to gain more independence and mothers think overprotection is still quite appropriate! How will we do then? How can we build a strong friendship that forges through whatever the future holds?

At that moment Jaime broke into my thoughts with a question: "Mom, what's the kid like that you've always dreamed of?"

How could I answer that one? Any time two people are together for any reason—not only mothers and daughters—two sets of expectations are operating, consciously or unconsciously. I prayed silently, "Lord, help me first to understand the needs behind my dreams and expectations of my daughter. Then give me a gracious willingness to adjust all of them to the individual you've made her."

I told Jaime she had asked a very important question—one that I wanted to answer always like this: "You are the daughter I've always dreamed of, and now that we're together in a family, I want to learn to dream *with* you. I want to share *your* dreams and be the support you need to fulfill them."

AUGUST

God's Blessing

KATHLEEN F. TURNER

AUGUST 1   Read Psalm 139:13-16.

ugust 1, 1986, was the day I became a mother. As with all births, our daughter came into the world through pain and some trauma. Her advent was marked by a few medical complications that caused several grown-ups to scurry. Because I was already two weeks overdue, labor was induced. Everything went well until it was discovered that the baby was not receiving enough oxygen. I was immediately given a caesarean section.

But when all was said and done, there she was—ours! Beautiful, perfect, and—as every parent knows—the most wonderful baby in the world. As we looked her over from head to tiny toes, we laughed. She was a little female version of her father. The resemblance was just that unmistakable.

We also were totally awed by her birth, her uniqueness, her very being. We had been partners with God in creating a soul that would live somewhere forever. How incredible!

Even though she was born in the evening, and her aunts thought she should have been called Twilight, we named her Dawn. She was the beginning of our family. She was also the dawn of a new awareness of God's radiance shed upon our lives.

When God wanted to bless women of the Bible, he gave them children. There *are* days when I wonder about this. Yet since August 1, 1986, there has been an undeniable richness to my life, and I know that it comes from God's blessing—being a mother.

AUGUST 2 Read I Samuel 1–2:21.

How can I write a month of devotions for mothers of young children? I don't cook enough vegetables for my children. I yell at them. I don't pray enough for them. It seems that all the wonderful "mother things" I want to do stay in my mental Donna Reed video. I *can't* do this!

I wonder if Hannah said, "I can't do this," on the morning she took Samuel to the Lord and to Eli. Samuel had just been weaned. What great emotion Hannah must have felt: Pain to be separated from that little boy who had been her hope and life for years—oh, where had the years gone? Joy that this moment was possible; she had been barren so long. Could she make it through the coming days without his voice and chubby face?

These things may have been in Hannah's heart that day, but she did go. She kept her promise. And God blessed her integrity with joy.

She had five more children after she gave up Samuel. When she returned home, she didn't know there would be others. It must have been hard to go home alone, but her prayer gives a clue to her faith: "It is not by strength that one prevails" (I Samuel 2:9*b* NIV).

I see Hannah cooking, cleaning, working at her tasks, making little coats for Samuel and finding that God helped her to be useful, faithful. She cheers me to believe that whatever God has for me, I *can* do it!

AUGUST 3 Read III John, v. 4.

I stared at the paring knife at my feet. That alone meant leaning over my expanding middle. Picking things up was not convenient. I looked at my husband. He took pity and retrieved the knife for me.

Pregnancy and motherhood are two things that no woman who has experienced them would ever call convenient! Morning sickness, physical exams, and waddling around like a walrus are not convenient. Nor are wiping noses, answering countless questions (often the same ones), picking up toys, and washing piles and piles of laundry on the list of most-sought-after jobs.

Convenience is the byword of our society. Unfortunately, much of what truly matters in life is not convenient. Imagine associating "convenient" with God. John 3:16 would take on new meaning: "For God *found it convenient* so he gave his one and only Son, that whoever believes in him shall not perish." Suddenly salvation is reduced to something "doable."

Motherhood and salvation have little to do with convenience and everything to do with commitment. Commitment means doing all the things that are not easy but necessary. Commitment gives immense value and dignity to all that is done, because commitment *is* costly. Commitment cost Jesus his life. Commitment costs a mother time and energy.

But, oh, the rewards! Would any Christian wish that Jesus had chosen convenience? Does any mother who knows that her children are "walking in truth" think of her sacrifice?

Today I choose commitment over convenience, and I pray for help to live that way.

AUGUST 4 Read I Samuel 1:27.

It was my fourth-month visit. I sat in a chair in front of my doctor, who sat at her rather imposing desk.

"Since you are over thirty-five, we'll need to consider amniocentesis," she said.

"What is its purpose?" I asked.

She explained that it would detect any abnormality, and she stressed the importance and urgency, because the legal cutoff point for a termination was fast approaching.

"No," I said.

"I don't think you understand," she responded.

As I signed a form stating I was aware of the possibilities and released my doctor from responsibility, I thought, "No, you don't understand."

I had prayed for this child. For months, I had asked God for a second child. How could I say to God, "I don't trust you, so I'll have an amniocentesis"? No. I trust you, Lord. Like Hannah, "I prayed for this child, and the LORD has granted what I asked of him" (I Samuel 1:27 NIV).

Our second daughter was born with four very distinct "strawberry" birthmarks, and she later developed a protruding belly button. Most of these markings are now indetectible. We loved her before the birthmarks faded. We loved her before she was born. This child has brought delight to our home. In fact, her middle name is Joy. When I think of her, "My heart rejoices in the LORD" (I Samuel 2:1 NIV).

Children have a way of working themselves into our hearts—something no medical tests can predict.

AUGUST 5 Read Psalm 32:8.

The stove desperately needs cleaning; the frig needs defrosting. The ironing pile looks like Mount McKinley. The desk is a wreck, and the bathroom drain is sluggish. I'm into "reclamation"—reclaiming living space and any resemblance to cleanliness!

Being a mom has not only complicated the stuff and location of life; it has made relationships more complex. Before our second child was born, my first child easily gained my attention. Soon after daughter number two came, things were very different.

One afternoon our oldest called insistently from the bathroom for help; she was being potty trained and needed assistance. Meanwhile, I was frantically trying to change a diaper and prepare a bottle for our infant, who was crying as if she hadn't eaten for a year—though she was only a couple of months old! It was a tense moment, because I honestly didn't know who to help first.

No matter how hard we try to shake it, we seem always to be haunted by the tension between what we need to do, can do, and want to do. Often those categories blur.

Looking at a situation squarely can be helpful. Looking to God is even better. "I will instruct thee and teach thee in the way which thou shalt go: I will guide thee with mine eye" (Psalm 32:8 KJV). As we learn to look where God is directing, we will be guided. Sometimes this may mean that the pile of ironing gets higher while a story is read, or that there are leftovers for supper because someone is rocked to sleep. Let's keep on making eye contact with the Instructor, taking time to ask him to help us know what to do. He will enable us to focus our minds and choose what is most important.

AUGUST 6   Read Psalm 18:28.

"Mommy, I'm scared of the dark!" It's not a statement of fact; it's more than that. It's terror!

The little body is tense under the blankets. Fingers desperately clutch the edge of the sheet and hold it tight at chin level, lest someone or, worse yet, some*thing* yank it away.

What are my children thinking in those black moments? That there are alligators under the bed, as I believed as a child? Or that there is a moose in the corner, watching every move?

"I'm sorry, sweetheart," I apologize, turning on the night light. "I forgot to turn it on."

We wipe away the tears, and gradually the tense little body relaxes. That small bulb and its soft glow provide immeasurable comfort. Who knows how many alligators and moose have been sent packing?

Like my children, I need a night light. How many times I've said, "God, I'm scared of the dark!" The path ahead of me seems impossible to travel. There isn't enough light. It isn't alligators or moose that frighten me now. It's other things—grown-up things—that scare me. I think they might be out there in the dark—somewhere.

It is then that God turns on the night light—the promises. They provide comfort and courage, not in myself but in God. "I will not neglect your word" (Psalm 119:16*b* NIV). I will ask God to help me keep this promise so that God's light will illuminate my darkness.

AUGUST 7 — Read Jeremiah 31:3.

I was preparing supper in the kitchen. She was in the living room, watching television. All was well.

Suddenly there was a horrible noise. Dashing into the living room, I saw the TV set crashing to the floor. My terrified daughter stood close by. I snatched her and raced from the room, making an incidental mental note that popcorn was strewn all over the carpet.

When my heartbeat slowed to only double time, I retraced my steps and unplugged the set. It had to be ruined. My daughter, too upset to even tell me for several days that she had been "swinging" from the TV set, cowered on her bed. I was too upset to deal with her; I waited for her daddy to come home.

The TV set was indeed destroyed. The popcorn was cleaned up. And although we were very upset by the destruction and our daughter's behavior that had caused it, she was still our daughter. Even a "Black Thursday" doesn't change the fact that my daughters are, and always will be, my beloved children.

I've had my "Black Thursdays" with God—days when I've spiritually pulled down TVs and tossed popcorn around. I know God wasn't pleased, but he was patient. I was still his child. Nothing could change that, for God assures me, and all of his children, that his is an everlasting love. This assurance is a great comfort for all God's children on any day, but especially for mothers on "Black Thursdays"!

AUGUST 8 Read Romans 8:26.

"Doughnanas," "forkshops," "Old Maple," "constructions," "tomarvin"—all those are words that you might hear at our house if you were to visit. They are among others that are part of our "family talk."

As children copy us and learn language, sometimes they don't quite get all the letters correct. Then those wonderful "family words" are created, those words no one outside the household may be able to understand.

I often feel that I pray with as much finesse as young children speak. Sometimes I think I know what to pray, but I can't get the words out in a very clear way. At other times, the words flow, but I am not certain just how to pray about something.

At times like this, it is comforting to know that God understands "family talk." When we do not know how or what to pray, God sees beyond our inadequacy. We can count on the Spirit to intercede for us "with groans that words cannot express" (Romans 8:26c NIV).

Just as I know that "doughnanas" are bananas, "forkshops" are porkchops, "Old Maple" is Old Maid, "constructions" are instructions, and "tomarvin" is tomorrow, so, too, God knows our hurts, needs, weaknesses, and limited knowledge.

My daughters trust me to understand them. And we can trust God completely when we pray. He's fluent in "family talk."

<hr>

AUGUST 9   Read Romans 8:15-16.

It doesn't seem to take too long after a child learns to talk that he or she discovers that Mommy has a name other than "Mommy." It's usually a savored piece of knowledge, often mixed with a bit of mischief. Sometimes when we walk down the sidewalk together, my oldest has addressed me as "Kathy," with a can-I-get-away-with-it twinkle in her eyes.

"Call me 'Mommy,'" I tell her. "Anyone can call me 'Kathy,' but only you and your sister can call me 'Mommy.' I like you to call me that because it's your special name for me."

God has many names—Lord, Almighty, Holy One. They are wonderful names that help us understand God and God's qualities better. But when we become a part of God's family, as Paul says in Romans 8:15, "We cry, 'Abba, Father.'" Only God's children have the right and the privilege to address God by that special family name—Father—a name of relationship, of family, of intimacy. God is our Father.

<hr>

AUGUST 10   Read I Corinthians 1:3, 4.

She stands there silently, holding my hand while her sister is lavishly admired and cooed over. Is she hurt that she is momentarily a secondary thought to the neighbor? I wonder.

A woman and her son live on our block. There's speculation about her ethnic background. I hear she has been shunned by most of the neighbors because she and those she associates with don't fit in here. Horrible. Does she notice? I wonder.

Being ignored and shunned is painful. I know; I've been there, too. I can't take away the pain of my daughter and neighbor. Only God can do that. But I can extend God's comfort to them. I can teach and show my daughter how special she is to her family and to God—with kisses, hugs, words of praise, time spent with her alone. I can demonstrate how to accept her weakness by living that way myself.

How can I deaden my neighbor's pain? Maybe by taking over a plate of cookies and offering some time for friendship. And maybe I'll take my daughter with me. What better way to teach her about easing her pain than to help ease the pain of others?

AUGUST 11   Read Philippians 1:6.

Cheese, mustard, ketchup, pickle, onion, burger, bun. Every time we walk past the gigantic hamburger on the bus-stop poster, we identify each part of the sandwich—or rather, I do. My daughter points, and I identify. She never tires of stopping and pointing to the same things and hearing the names of the items.

Children enjoy repetition and familiarity. Whenever my children are exposed to a day or two of unusual activities, they have a delayed reaction to the changes.

Change comes hard; it's stressful. It also is an inevitable part of life—as a human being, and even as a child of God.

God is always bringing about change. He is committed to making us like Jesus Christ, to completing the work he began in us. This takes a great deal of change! Sometimes the changes that God brings about are subtle—gentle ways that he speaks to us. At other times, the changes we need can be brought about only by what seems like a gigantic upheaval in our lives.

If it were left up to me, I'd rather be like my daughter with the burger ad. I get comfortable in my rut. But some day, the add will be changed. And I, too, need to grow.

So I begin this day with confidence in the God who doesn't change (Malachi 3:6). Knowing I am in God's care, I can face the changes of the day.

AUGUST 12 Read Galatians 6:9.

"Do you work?" It's something I'm often asked. Since I have two young children, the question amuses me.

"Yes," I answer, laughing, "very hard!" Truth is, harder than I ever have in my life!

The truth also is that I don't like some of my jobs. I'm not fond of household tasks, although I like a clean home. I'm the same way about "mother" jobs. I'm not crazy about repeatedly wiping noses. Giving instructions and demonstrations day after day gets tiresome. Will they ever learn how to take care of themselves? And questions, questions, questions! A mother's job is hard!

But I do love my work. I love to see my oldest daughter's bed, though lumpy, made up. What a delight to peek in on my daughters and find one helping the other with an uncooperative toy! Or to see them willingly share with neighborhood kids without prompting. They *are* learning.

What thrills me even more is to hear, "Mommy, I love God with all my heart." "I was thinking about God today." "God gave me this idea." Or the spontaneity of our youngest, singing "Jesus Loves Me."

Today I really should have cleaned the bathroom and spent a lot of time with the kids, but the bathroom got a lick and a promise, and the kids got a bedtime story. I will pray for help to not grow weary and to keep sight of my work—the preparation of these children for this world and the next.

AUGUST 13   Read James 1:4.

If awards were being given out today for motherhood, it wouldn't surprise me at all to receive a plaque inscribed, "Most Impatient Mother of the Year."

The old adage "If you pray for patience, you'll get tribulation" always made me shake in my shoes. Why pray for patience? I have enough to handle!

Every mother knows all too well that patience is a wonderful, elusive quality that mothers need desperately. You know— "I want patience, and I want it *now*!"

Yesterday I tried an experiment. Instead of praying that God would help me be a good mother or help me understand my daughters, I flinched and prayed for patience. I had doubt, but I also had a flicker of faith that maybe, just maybe, I really could tap into God's storehouse and hang on through the ups and downs of our household's late afternoon craziness.

And it happened. It actually happened! A spirit of peace and self-control, even in the midst of quarreling, boisterousness, and a fast-ticking clock carried me through those normally tense hours.

So this is what it's like to pray for patience? I think I'll do it again tomorrow!

AUGUST 14   Read Psalm 121:8.

The car drove past us, running the red light, while we stood in the middle of the street. The driver, oblivious to our location, stopped, reversed, and then stopped where he should have. We still stood in the middle of the street, waiting for the danger to end.

With a youngster on each side of me, I finished crossing the street. Amazed, angry, shaken, I thanked God for his care. For the rest of the day, however, I couldn't get the what-ifs out of my mind. Finally my oldest said, "Mom, forget about it; it's over!"

She was right, and she made me smile. Sometimes, though, the physical dangers my children can face overwhelm me with fear. There are so many things that could harm them.

Sometimes it's hard to think of the mothers in the Bible as ordinary, everyday mothers. Then I think I hear Leah say, "Get away from that camel, Reuben! You know they are mean animals, especially that one!" Eve might have said, "Abel, get away from the snakes. Now! They're more poisonous than you know!"

A child's safety is always on a mother's mind. And everything can seem hazardous to a child's life. Often we worry about what can happen to them when we are not with them, and even when we are. Worry can paralyze us. But we must remember that God is *always* on duty, watching over us and our children—our comings and goings, all day long.

AUGUST 15   Read Psalm 119:165.

I go in their bedroom sometimes once, sometimes twice, sometimes three times each night. One constantly rolls out from under her blankets. The other always seems to have her nightgown hiked up. Checking on the kids usually is the last thing I do before crawling into bed.

There are times when I don't go in to check them. I go in just to look at them. One breathes heavily, the other like a baby—whisper-sweet. Dark and golden hair tousles over pillows in spite of nightbraids, as we call them, which are supposed to prevent such annoyance.

How I love them!

Love surges into motherly protection. Unbidden, exhaustion and love mingle to parade fears before me. Will they grow up to love God? Will they be snared into drugs, premarital sex, AIDS, divorce, alcoholism? What does the future hold for my children? Will they make the right choices?

I begin to plot and plan ways to help them do the right things. Then my ideas crumble. How ridiculous to think I could perfectly guide my children through every choice in the minefield of life.

While I watch them sleep, bits of Scripture come to me. Peace comes, too. God's Word, always faithful and true, has guided and comforted me through the choices I have made. I know it has preserved me. So I will teach my children to love God's Word. Then they, too, will be able to know peace and walk confidently, without stumbling.

AUGUST 16 Read Proverbs 31:28.

She used to want to be a firefighter. Now she says, "Mommy, when I grow up, I want to be a mother." I say, "Thank you," but underneath, I am unable to accept the compliment without feeling a little uncomfortable.

Why does she say that? I think I need to stand up straight and check to see if my "mother slip" is showing. What does she think a mother does? Sometimes even *I* am confused!

Mothers serve by influence, example. What do my children see and hear? Yes, they know how to pick up and put away toys. They know to fold their hands when we pray. They also have heard me say things I wish they didn't remember. When our oldest has had to clean the bathroom sink, I've heard her annoyed voice call out, "I'm not a slave!" Ouch! Now where did she hear that?

There are days when my influence is negative. On those days, it seems I'm saying "I'm sorry" from morning till bedtime. Amazingly, because children have such big hearts, I keep hearing, "I forgive you, Mommy."

She wants to be a mommy. I am blessed and challenged by her compliment and aware that her footprints seem to be in mine. Maybe she does understand. Mothers are people who succeed and fail and ask for forgiveness. Perhaps, once in a while, she is actually seeing Christ in me!

AUGUST 17   Read Romans 8:38-39.

A few years ago, when we had only one child, I calculated that I had changed about 3,780 diapers! That must have at least tripled by now! The number amazes me, but I have never minded changing diapers. It's one of the things a mother doesn't focus on because her thoughts are on the little person who wears them. That is love.

Since becoming a mother I understand more about God. Being available around the clock is crucial but exhausting. God, our Father, is available twenty-four hours a day, but *he* never gets tired or bleary-eyed (Psalm 121:4). Just as a child cries in the night to be comforted, or during the day to be loved or helped, so also we can go to God.

When a mother becomes versed in the ways of her child, exhaustion, hunger, and frustration are easy to read. But some things baffle even a mother. What is the best thing to do? How do I know? God isn't baffled. He knows *all* about us. He knows the best way to test, discipline, and meet every need of his children. Mothers may have to guess once in a while, but God never does (Psalm 139:2-3).

When I held our daughters for the first time, they didn't need to do anything in order for me to love them. They were loved. Neither you nor I have to do anything to keep God's love. Mothers sometimes express love in imperfect ways, but God's love for us is perfect and constant.

AUGUST 18   Read John 10:27.

Before I became a mother, I watched moms talk to their babies and young children.

"I can't do that," I thought. "I'll feel stupid. Besides, the baby hasn't any idea what is being said. Furthermore, how can I possibly keep up a running monologue? Dialogue is one thing, monologue another."

It's a funny thing, though—babies change grown-ups. It wasn't long after our first child arrived that I was talking a blue streak to her! The "impossible" monologues were taking place, and I didn't feel stupid in the least. After a while, I think both our babies knew what was being communicated.

Looking at our infants and speaking with warmth expresses a great deal—love, help, protection. Those kicking feet and flailing arms, and all those baby noises, are perfect proof.

Our Shepherd's voice is audible to his flock. At first we hear on a baby level. But as we grow, our understanding and our hearing develop. Then we notice that the Shepherd not only speaks to us, but he also knows who, what, and where we are in our lives. As our communication deepens, we follow him in confidence.

Today, listen to Jesus the Shepherd as your children listen to you—drawn by his voice, confident in his understanding, and trusting his guidance.

AUGUST 19   Read Deuteronomy 6:6-9.

I am always somewhat amused (and also dismayed) when people say that parents should stand back and let their children make their own decisions about God and religion, without an ounce of parental teaching. I always want to ask them, "Shouldn't we merely hand kids a spoon and tell them to feed themselves? Simply lay a washcloth by the soap and hope the idea gets across? Why bother to toilet train?" Should we waste the time, when sooner or later they'll get the point?

There may be some people who might rear children this way, but most parents wouldn't think of it. A great deal of effort is spent on all these skills, and more. God says that this is the way we are supposed to be teaching our children about him—actively, enthusiastically, constantly.

After God finished giving the Law, he told the Israelites: "These commandments that I give you today are to be upon your hearts. Impress them on your children. Talk about them when you sit at home and when you walk along the road, when you lie down and when you get up" (Deuteronomy 6:6-7 NIV).

Just as we teach children how to take care of themselves physically, so also it is vital to teach them spiritual truth. Without it, they will be unable to stand in an increasingly godless world.

With God's help, I will further lay the foundation of truth upon the hearts of my children.

AUGUST 20   Read I John 2:3-6.

My daughter came into the kitchen where my friend and I were talking. I watched her intently as she imitated a mannerism of mine. "Now where did she get that?" I asked rhetorically.

"I'll bet I know just what you do when you're on the phone, too," my friend said. Then she described perfectly my phone stance and the way I walk back and forth with the long cord. "That's how she," she said as she pointed to my offspring, "talks on a play phone."

Children don't miss a thing, as my mother would say. Although that gives me pause, it also gives me purpose. My Christian walk can have great teaching value.

My daily journey is like a honey container. No matter how hard I try to avoid it, every time I use a container to store honey, it ends up being sticky, and so do the things that surround the container and the shelf it sits on. Likewise, living a Christ-like life is "sticky business." It involves more than going to church on Sunday morning; it's a life-style.

Just as my daughter "learned" how to talk on the telephone, so also I want my oldest and youngest to learn about God's ways by watching their mother "walking sticky."

AUGUST 21   Read Galatians 5:13-15.

They're at it again. Sometimes it seems constant. The little jabs, verbal and physical, because one or the other or both are irritable. Then it starts to wear on me.

Please stop. Please get along. Please share that toy. Why doesn't one of you go do something else?

Reasoning with young children can be like reasoning with the weather—useless. By the time we have reached the picking stage, drastic measures may be required. Sometimes my girls hear my "pick-pick routine," which sounds unmistakably like the cluck-cluck of a hen. Then they dissolve into laughter.

Their picking is not too different from grown-up picking. Grown-ups pick at one another. Picking and bickering does not become God's children. Only God can help us love those who rub us the wrong way. As we commit ourselves to the good of our brothers and sisters in Christ, we will please God. Such love will draw people to Christ because they will want to know what—Who—enables us to do the impossible.

Even though my daughters can become the Pick Sisters, as we call them, there are those beautiful moments when we hear things like, "You're my best friend." This is what God has in mind for his church: choosing to love, befriend, bind ourselves together. By doing this, we can begin to see how God looks at us.

AUGUST 22   Read Galatians 5:24-26.

I love to watch my husband and daughter walk down the street together. Both my husband, at six-feet-four inches, and our daughter, at three-feet-ten, are a study in long legs. As they walk away from me hand in hand, they seem to flow down the sidewalk in perfect rhythmic motion. I find myself thinking, "How well she keeps up with her father." Then I ruefully remind myself that *she* isn't keeping up with him; *he* is gauging his pace to her ability.

Of course, she knows that if she dallies behind, she runs the risk of her father continuing on. This means she will be called to catch up. Running to catch up may involve a skinned knee. Dashing ahead is dangerous, too. Keeping in step *is* important.

Living the Christian life is much like our daughter's walk with her father. God the Spirit knows what kind of pace to set for us, and it will be one we can keep. In Galatians 5:24, Paul reminds us that we have died to our sinful natures—we should not lag behind in them. In verse 26, he cautions against conceit and envy, the I'm-a-better-Christian-than-you-are trip. It's the race to get ahead. Between these two verses, in verse 25, Paul says, "Let us keep in step with the Spirit" (NIV). It may be a rough walk, but it will never be a faster pace than we are able to travel.

AUGUST 23   Read Psalm 5:3.

It was the end of August. She had turned four a few weeks earlier. Although I knew she was ready and needed a little bigger world than her home, my daughter still looked vulnerable and very much like a little, little girl. I knew she was excited and apprehensive about nursery school. So was I.

We could and would walk to school together. Sooner or later, however, I would need to leave her to trust other grown-ups and learn how to face situations by herself. It was time to renew the tradition.

I cannot remember when it began, but I am still aware of the impact it had on my life. Each morning in my childhood home, my mother helped us memorize a Bible verse and then prayed with us before we walked out the door. She chose verses about God's protection and his constant and unchangeable love. I still remember those verses. Her prayers were for us and for the day we faced. They have meant much to me.

As our daughter went off to nursery school, I sent her with Scriptures and a prayer. Mothers can't go everywhere with their children, but God and his Word can.

Knowing this was a comfort for both of us on her first days of school. And they were happy days, as I saw her taking a new step, confident that God had spread his protection over her (Psalm 5:11).

<hr/>

AUGUST 24   Read I Corinthians 1:27.

I sat in the pew. Our six-week-old infant lay peacefully sleeping in my arms, with not a care, need, or fear, just being herself—small, frail, helpless.

Then the woman came up the aisle alongside us. She stopped, leaned over, and gazed at our baby. Tears came into her eyes. Her mother had died recently. Somehow the wonder and joy of birth and the sorrow and pain of death had commingled in her heart.

"What a blessing to see your new baby," she said. "Someone has gone and someone has come." She smiled through her tears. I was near tears myself, to think that God was blessing others with my daughter.

There have been times since then when my children have blessed me or others more than they knew. The sudden hugs and kisses on days when I thought my tears didn't show, but they did; surprise drawings with wild, cheerful colors that were meant to make Mommy feel better.

Others, too, have received colorful drawings. And spontaneous prayers have been offered on behalf of many. Though children can scarcely guess the things that trouble grown-ups, they do know when things are amiss. They bless others with their requests of God.

We tend to think that what appears helpless is powerless. God's viewpoint is so different from ours. He continues to amaze the world with little things, including little children. They are truly some of the most powerful people on earth!

AUGUST 25   Read Matthew 18:3.

Bubbles. They are there in the sink every day, usually more than once because I need them. They are very ordinary, really, yet not ordinary at all. The other day, while doing a mindless, mundane task, I stopped and enjoyed them. Was it because I live with small children?

I immersed my hands in the water below and lifted up mounds of them. My daughter came into the kitchen then. We oohed and ahhed over the bubbles together. "Mommy," she said, "they have rainbows on them." And so they did.

Regularly, my children make me see how jaded I am by my surroundings and the world. In amazement, they will see a rainbow in an ugly oil stain on a driveway, stare with wonder at a sunset, or try to figure out an insect.

How often I fail to see and hear all that God has given to bless me—beautiful things, useful things that lift and serve, in spite of the fact that we live in a broken world.

I need God's help to see creation as children do. I am too busy, too harried to stop and enjoy or investigate. I've lost the wonder and newness that children bring to this world. I am so thankful that my children have awakened me again by their freshness. Jesus said that we need to become like children to inherit eternal life. Today I will pray for help to become like a child so that I may receive all the ordinary/extraordinary things in store for me today.

AUGUST 26 Read Ecclesiastes 3:4*b*.

It was 2:00 A.M. My husband leaned bleary-eyed against the kitchen counter. The night light, the only illumination in the room, spread a dim glow behind him. I stood at the changing table with our infant.

The novelty of night feedings had worn off three years ago, with our firstborn. So we said very little in our sleep-deprived stupor. Our baby, though, was very much awake, with all systems functional.

I took the wet diaper off and situated a new one underneath her. Then, before I fastened it, she chose—or nature chose for her—to relieve herself. With amazing trajectory, the substance shot across the end of the changing table, over the space above the diaper pail, hit the wallpaper, and ran down.

Now we were all awake. Usually I immediately consider the toil of a mess, but this was too funny. We laughed and laughed. It was 2:00 A.M., and we laughed! She felt good, and so did we.

I need to remember that I am made in God's image and that, without doubt, laughter is an important part of life. I need to remember to see the humor in life with my little ones, and then laugh and laugh, for I think God does, too.

AUGUST 27 Read Psalm 91:5.

I know she meant well. She reached over and gently felt my daughter's upper arm. "Yeah, she's cold."

She crinkled her nose and smiled. I suppose to take some of the edge off the implication. Still, I felt the sting. Without saying a word, I went back into the house for a little shirt to pull over the sunsuit. Afterward, my daughter seemed just as content with it as without it. My neighbor then admitted that she was overprotective. Still . . .

That's not the first time someone has made a remark—sent an arrow—that made me flinch or deeply wounded me. There is something about becoming a mother that almost immediately makes a woman defensive and insecure. Maybe it's the possibility that we might do something wrong and prove what we fear—that we are not good mothers.

It would be nice if there were a perfect class to prepare women for motherhood. But even then, being a mommy would have surprises. It's rather like learning to swim. You must get into the water.

Motherhood—it's one of God's on-the-job-training projects. Easy? No. Vulnerable? Yes. But because motherhood is God's gift, we can redirect our focus when the arrows do come: "In God I have put my trust; I will not fear what flesh can do [or say] unto me" (Psalm 56:4 KJV).

AUGUST 28   Read Psalm 119:103-104.

Our baby was hungry. Her fists moved in the air, and even her little toes were tensely curled under.

Then as she began to hungrily suck her bottle, a gradual, amazing thing happened. Her tiny fingers were no longer clenched into fists; they relaxed. Her feet no longer appeared toeless. The tension went out of her body. She was content.

There are times when we are uptight—when we don't know what has happened or will happen. Fear, anger, tension creep into our spirits and bodies. Sometimes we clench our fists at others or even at God.

My mother has often said to me in gloomy times, "Eat something. You'll feel better." When we hit these uptight times, we do need to eat. We need to eat of the Word of God. The psalmist reminds us that God's words are sweet— "sweeter than honey to my mouth" (Psalm 119:103 NIV). It's not always easy to enjoy eating—food or words—when your stomach is in knots, but the psalmist knew what we too can know and experience: God's Word for our lives, God's Commandments, give us understanding that enables us to choose the right path.

Feeding on God's Word can refresh, build, strengthen us for the pits of life and prevent us from taking the wrong path of fear, depression, anger, or any other useless avenue. Then, even in rough times, we may be content.

AUGUST 29 Read Mark 10:27.

Dear Heavenly Father,

They came to me again today with happy, loving faces, and said, "You're the best mom in the whole world!"

I laughed and sagely said, "I'm the only mother you have."

At one time I might have said I'd like to be the best mother in the world, but I have two children now, and I think I know better than that.

What I would really like to be is a *good* mother—the kind of mother my girls need. Help me to be *that* mother.

A listening mother. Even when I think I don't have time or strength for one more discussion, help me tune in. It might be terribly important.

An encouraging mother. Lives can pivot on a word of criticism or encouragement. How well I know that myself, Father. Help me to not forget it. Help me to be a cheerleader for my children.

A mother of example. It's really true that "more is caught than taught." So help me to guard my tone of voice, the words I choose to speak, and the way I treat others. They do watch me.

To me all this is a big request, because I am only human. If I stopped there, I would fail. Help me, Father, to be a good mother—not because I can, but because "all things are possible with God" (Mark 10:27 NIV).

AUGUST 30   Read Luke 22:19.

One of us starts it; the other finishes it. Then we laugh. Those around us haven't the faintest idea why we said what we did, and they can't possibly imagine what could be so funny.

It's the stories, the stories we have read to our children over the past years. Mom and Dad haven't read them once or twice to eager ears, but countless—maddeningly countless—times. And now all it takes is a word or, even less, an idea to trigger a quotation begun by one and finished by the other. (Now, with the advent of the VCR, it happens with videos, too! Some videos have come dangerously close to being banned in order to maintain parental sanity in the face of endless replays!)

Even though we think we will never forget the lines from these stories, they will, in time, fade. There is one story, though, I *never* want to forget—the story of Jesus.

When Jesus met the disciples in the upper room, he broke bread, gave it to them and said, "Do this in remembrance of me." Remembrance—as if they, or we, could forget him! Could we? What a chilling thought! Have we heard the story for so many years that we unconsciously have taken the first step—familiarity—toward forgetfulness?

May we never forget all God has done for us, and may we always live in remembrance of our Savior!

AUGUST 31   Read Matthew 19:14.

"Breakfast is ready!" I called to my daughter one school morning. I didn't give much thought to why she was in the bedroom. Sometimes she likes to draw when she has a free moment.

She came into the dining room, stood by her chair, and looked up at me. "Do you wonder what I was doing in the bedroom?" she asked, a smile on her lips.

"Tell me," I said, thinking it could be almost anything.

"I asked God to forgive me for all the bad things I had done and to come live in my heart." Her face was still lit with a sweet smile.

I was thrilled and surprised, but I shouldn't have been. I reflected upon how many seeds of the gospel I had been able to plant in her life. I remembered that "Jesus Loves Me" was her favorite song—and the one I sang over and over to her when she had been hospitalized. We had memorized and illustrated the Twenty-third Psalm. We talked about God and Jesus when we went for walks. We prayed together. She enjoys sacred music.

My daughter had seen Christ and chosen him. Now she is not only my daughter; she is my sister in Christ. She has just begun her walk of faith, and I continue in mine. We both have much to learn; I have much to share. I look forward to our travel together.

SEPTEMBER

Heavenly Treasures

LEANNE H. CIAMPA

SEPTEMBER 1   Read Matthew 6:19-21.

I walked into the family room and discovered my two-year-old had torn out many of the pages from one of our picture albums and had the pictures all over the floor. They were bent, torn, and slobbered on. There was a picture from Britton's first birthday and one of his brother decorating Easter eggs. I was so angry that I cried as I picked up the pictures, trying to unbend them and dry them off where he had been chewing on them.

The more pictures I picked up, the angrier I got. Then I remembered the scripture about storing up treasures on earth. These pictures were earthly treasures, but the moments that they captured were treasures to store in heaven. I might not have the pictures of these important events, but I did have the memories in my heart forever. I felt a bit better, and then I ran to get the camera. I took a picture of the whole mess! Someday I will laugh when I tell Britton about the mess he made out of my earthly treasures. And as we laugh about it, we will be storing away another heavenly treasure.

O God, help me find more time just to enjoy my children. Help me find time to relax and play and laugh, for it is those times that I treasure most and will remember always.

SEPTEMBER 2   Read Matthew 5:14-16.

My children, like many children, will not go to bed unless their night light is on. The thing that tickles me about the night light, however, is that it really doesn't put out much light. For all intents and purposes, after I turn it on, the room is still dark. But in my children's eyes, that night light makes a very dark, frightening room a cozy, safe place to sleep.

That little night light has changed the way I see my role as a Christian in this world. I used to hear Christ's words about "letting my light shine" and feel really overwhelmed, thinking I would have to be a really outstanding Christian to even be seen in this dark world of ours. Drugs, violence, racial hatred, poverty—darkness is everywhere we look. And somehow Christ wants me to shine, to overcome the darkness. It seemed impossible until I thought about that little night light.

I may not be the best Christian in the world, but I try my hardest to shine. And just like that tiny night light in my children's room, my light may be all someone needs to feel safe and cozy in this scary, dark world. So like the night light, I'll keep on shining.

O God, let your light shine through me, and may I, like the light that brings so much comfort to my children, bring comfort and hope to others.

SEPTEMBER 3   Read Psalm 98.

A few weeks ago I arrived to pick up my boys after Sunday school, and my four-year-old came running to me saying,

228

"Listen to what I learned to do!" Then he let out the most blood-curdling scream I have ever heard as he clapped his hands. I thought, "Oh, my! Has he been yelling the entire time he has been here? They are going to tell me never to bring him back again!"

By now, both my children were screaming and clapping their hands. Then my four-year-old said, "Come on, Mom, make a joyful noise to the Lord like we are!" Not waning to do it, I said, "I don't know how." My son replied, "Well, I just think about God, and all this happiness pops out!"

Suddenly I didn't care if he had been screaming the entire time; he had learned a Bible verse I hope he always remembers: "Make a joyful noise to the Lord" (Psalm 98:4a). To me, and perhaps to God, those embarrassing screams suddenly became songs of praise!

O God, your presence makes such a difference in my children's lives. Help me to find that same joy in my life. I want to think of your name and let the joy "pop out," for because of you I have many things to sing and shout and clap about.

SEPTEMBER 4   Read Luke 12:6-7.

My son recently had to have his tonsils taken out. He and I had been sitting in a hospital room for some time. It was just he and I, since I am a single parent and my mother and father were keeping my other son. We sat there for a long time, just the two of us, talking about the things that would happen next. I tried to do the best job I could of preparing him for his surgery.

Finally the time came, and he was put on a cart and whisked off to surgery. I thought I was prepared for the moment, but my heart sank when they wheeled his cart away from me. My baby was going off to a new experience, and I could not go with him. It didn't seem right. I was

229

there when he learned to take his first steps, when he learned to say his first words, and when he learned to pedal his tricycle. I should be with him now! I knew he was afraid, and he looked so tiny and helpless as they rolled him into the operating room.

I wanted to yell, "Stop! Forget it! Just give him to me, and I will take him home." I wanted to jump on that cart and go with him into the operating room. I wanted to cry. I wanted to be strong. And then the words of Jesus suddenly came to me: "Even the hairs on your head are counted." I thought, "God, you know every hair on my little boy's head. I can't go with him into that operating room, but you can." I let my son go, and I felt better knowing that God went with him.

O God, if I could, I'd go with my children through every difficult experience they will ever have. I won't always be there when they need help and guidance, but you will. You know and love my children even better than I do. So when I can't be there, when I can't help them, thank you for being with them.

SEPTEMBER 5   Read I Samuel 17:48-50.

I love September afternoons when my kids are playing outside and I can peek through the kitchen window to watch them play all kinds of games and pretend to be all sorts of things. Today as I watched them, my four-year-old pretended to be David and my two-year-old pretended to be Goliath.

Goliath was very dramatic as he walked across the yard toward David. Both of his little legs were very stiff, his arms were stuck straight out in front of him, and his eyes were wide and a little glazed. There he came, walking and groaning across the yard as David yelled, "Come on! I am not afraid!"

and took out his pretend sling-shot and shot a pretend rock at Goliath. Goliath dramatically fell to the ground, and we all cheered.

My boys have no idea that there really are giants in the world—giants named hatred, violence, drugs, poverty, cancer, and AIDS. Someday they will come face to face with real giants, and I hope that they, like David, will face the giants bravely knowing that God has the power to help them.

O God, it seems that giants are everywhere I look. When the day comes that my children have to face a giant, let their hearts be filled with courage and hope as they rest in the knowledge that you are beside them, helping them every step of the way.

SEPTEMBER 6   Read Deuteronomy 6:4-9.

Whenever I see a yellow school bus, I wonder what it will be like to put my children on one and send them to school to learn how to read and write and add and subtract. I am glad my children will have trained teachers, for I am not sure I could teach them these things.

My children will learn many things at school, but there is much they will not learn there. They will not learn about God or Jesus or the greatest commandment or how to pray. No, I will be their primary teacher in these things. At times I feel unsure about my qualifications for the job, but I know that God will guide me and remind me of the importance of this task.

O God, help me to teach my children your ways. Help me to tell them stories of you and your Son and the Holy Spirit that they will understand and love. And, above all, I pray that my actions and words will teach them about faith and joy and the peace that comes from knowing you.

SEPTEMBER 7 Read Matthew 13:24-30.

I just picked a few squash and tomatoes from my garden. It won't be long until the first frost, and then the harvest will be done. I have to laugh at my garden now. I let the weeds grow until it is hard to tell a weed from a plant. But, somehow, the vegetables still grow.

My garden reminds me of Jesus' story of the weeds and the wheat. I have always interpreted the story to mean that some of us are weeds (people who do bad things) and some of us are wheat (people who do good things), and someday God will sort the weeds from the wheat (on the day of judgment). This is one interpretation; but, now that I have children, the story has another meaning for me.

It is clear to me that children—all of us, really—are weeds and wheat at the same time. My youngest son kisses one minute and bites the next. Children are wonderful and awful, fun and no fun at all. I see the wheat, and I see the weeds; but when I look at the entire garden, I see "wonderful"!

Now when I hear this story I think that perhaps harvest day for my children will be adulthood. I hope my children will grow into adults who have gotten rid of most of their weeds and have wheat abounding.

O God, help me to accept my children as they are: children who are learning and growing in many ways. As I guide them, help me not to become so concerned with their weeds—the things they do that bother me—that I forget to show them how proud I am of their growth. I pray that as they grow into adults, they will be like my garden—bursting forth with many vegetables, despite the weeds.

SEPTEMBER 8 Read Isaiah 44:2-3.

Nothing scares me more than a blood-curdling scream from one of my children. And when whatever it is that hurt my son is over, nothing makes me feel more useful than to know that he chose to come to me, his mother, for comfort and security. At scary times, it must be a universal reaction to "run to Mommy." Isaiah told Israel not to be afraid: "Thus says the LORD who made you, who formed you in the womb and will help you: Do not fear, O Jacob my servant, Jeshurun whom I have chosen" (Isaiah 44:2-3).

Sometimes when I am afraid, I wish I could run to my mother, be small again, and let her make it all better. But my mother is not always close by, and, the truth is, I am an adult and must handle things on my own. But I still get scared. And when I can't run to Mom, it is nice to know that God is waiting right there to hold me and to calm me.

O God, I am such a source of strength and security to my children. They have no idea that I am often unsure and afraid. I am glad that you are there for me and that you love me even more than I love my own children. That is an incredible amount of love. Thank you!

SEPTEMBER 9   Read Ecclesiastes 4:9-10.

My four-year-old has just crossed a new milestone. He has discovered friends. It used to be that when he was around other children, he would simply take their toys, push them down, or, if I was lucky, just ignore them altogether. But lately I have noticed that he is actually playing with the other children. They are pretending together, cooperating, and hugging a lot!

As I watch them, I think about my friends throughout the years—those I still keep in touch with and those I don't. I wish I could hug each one again. Friendships are important. I am glad my son is discovering that.

O God, I am so glad that my children are discovering how wonderful friendships can be. I pray that they are always surrounded by friends—people who will help them up when they fall. And thank you, God, for my friends—friends I have now and friends who have helped me throughout my lifetime. The words of the writer of Ecclesiastes are correct: Two are better than one!

SEPTEMBER 10   Read Isaiah 11:6.

When I was pregnant with my first child, my mother was diagnosed with a disease very similar to muscular dystrophy. One of Mom's biggest worries was that as her condition worsened and she required more equipment, my son would avoid her and perhaps even be afraid. But so far nothing has stopped him from sitting and cuddling with Granny. In fact, the more equipment she needs, the better he likes it.

He loves to ride on her electric wheel chair and go up and down in her hospital bed. He likes to put her foot braces on and walk like a tin soldier. He uses her walker as a jungle gym, doing push-ups and crawling through it. When he sees her, his first words are, "Granny, do you feel like cuddling today?" He never seems to get impatient with her slow speech, and when she spills her water or drops her plastic plate, he howls with laughter—and so does she. When she cries, he grabs a tissue and dries her tears. All this from a four-year-old. Who would ever imagine that a tiny child would be such good medicine for his Granny?

O God, remind me to stop feeling that I must always teach my children, and help me to let them teach me. For there are so many times when a child shall leads us.

SEPTEMBER 11   Read Genesis 1:29-31.

With children, you never quite know what kind of a day they are going to have. They are affected by the weather, the amount of sleep they had the night before, the new teeth that may be coming in, the emotional state of their mom on that day, and on and on. So, as mothers, we never know quite what type of day we'll have.

I must admit that on an average day, at least twenty things happen that I don't expect: a spilled cup of something, a peanut butter sandwich smashed where it doesn't belong, a temper tantrum, unexplained crying, a lost shoe, a soiled crib sheet, a tipped over lamp—you know, the usual daily messes! By the end of the day, I am usually worn out and feeling rather frazzled.

But then bedtime comes, the children are tucked in, and they are quiet and so peaceful. And there I stand, tired and frazzled but thinking, "This is good; this is very good!" I know how God felt after creating the world—the same way I feel after tucking my children in bed. It is good, very good.

O God, thank you for creating this family of mine. It is good; it is very good! Sometimes it is out of control, disorganized, and exhausting, but it is always good.

SEPTEMBER 12   Read Matthew 23:37-39.

The other day my two-year-old and I got into a major battle. I was cooking supper, and he wanted to take the corn bread out of the oven when the timer went off. We fought and wrestled, and he cried. Finally I had had enough, and I cried myself. I thought, "Why won't you just realize that I am keep-

235

ing you away from this hot oven because I don't want you to get burned?" He thought I was just spoiling his fun.

Then I thought about God and how often I ignore what God would have me do because I think my way will work just fine, even better. How often does Christ cry out the words to me, "I am doing this for your own good"?

In many ways we all are still children, wanting something so badly that we don't realize God's warnings are for our own protection—not for spoiling our fun. I guess part of growing up, physically and spiritually, is getting burned sometimes because we don't listen.

O God, we are still children in so many ways. We do not listen, and we do not understand your desires for us. But God, don't give up on us. Be our mother hen and keep pulling us under your wing, for we are growing and learning—often the hard way— that you want only the best for us.

SEPTEMBER 13 Read Luke 19:1-5.

The other day I bought my children a book and tape set of the story of Jesus healing the blind man, Bartimaeus. I played the tape, and my sons were spellbound—so still and quiet. But when the story came to the part when the man was healed by Jesus, my kids instantly jumped to their feet and began hugging and jumping and turning in circles as they yelled "Yeah!" They could not have been more excited if Jesus had actually walked into our home! They have never met Jesus, and yet they believe in him and get more excited about him than I do.

Zacchaeus, the short man who had heard stories about Jesus, got so excited when Jesus came to town that he climbed up a tree just to get a glimpse of Jesus. That is real excitement. I am so glad that through Bible stories my children can experience the kind of excitement that Zacchaeus had. They will never get to welcome Jesus into their home to eat supper as Zacchaeus did, but perhaps they will welcome him into their hearts.

O God, thank you for the precious stories of faith you gave to us. I pray that the enthusiasm my children now have for Jesus, the unshakable belief they have in Jesus, will remain with them always.

SEPTEMBER 14   Read Luke 15:8-10.

No matter how many pacifiers I buy, it seems there is only one at any given time in our house. And this one pacifier is easily "lost." My youngest son, like many children, will not go to bed without his pacifier. When I am so tired that I think I am going to fall over as I try to get my kids to bed, it is not unusual for me to be searching for the lost pacifier. I crawl around looking under beds, in drawers, and even in the diaper bag. I look everywhere. Then, just as I give up all hope of ever finding it, there it is! The lost pacifier is found. For me, there is never a more joyous moment at the end of a long day.

In the parable of the lost coin, a woman loses a coin, searches carefully until she finds it, and then rejoices. Who would ever guess that finding a lost coin—or a lost pacifier—could bring so much joy?

Sometimes we are like lost pacifiers or lost coins. We lose our way, we sin. But God does not stop searching for us until we are found. Some might say that pacifiers and coins are silly things to search for so diligently, but, to those who have lost them, they are treasures. Some might say that there are people who are not worth caring enough about to search for, but each of us is priceless to God. This is God's promise. I am reminded of this promise every time I find a lost pacifier!

O God, the simplest things often bring us joy. The simplest stories often tell us so much about your love. Thank you for thinking that

I am so important that when I am lost, you will search for me, and when I am found, you will rejoice.

SEPTEMBER 15   Read Isaiah 66:12-13.

One night, very late, I heard an awful noise coming from my son's room. I ran in and found him sitting up, crying, and making a terrible barking noise. I later learned that he had croup, and that September is one of the months when croup is most common. But, common or not, I had never heard a sound like this. I was afraid and unsure what to do—and so was my son. So I sat down and held him as tight as I could for a few moments until we had both calmed down.

These words from Isaiah remind us that God will comfort us like a mother when we need it. Sometimes when we are afraid and unsure, we should just sit down and get really close to God until we calm down. It worked for me and my son, and it works for me and God.

O God, when I am afraid and unsure, hold me close and calm me down. For you, and only you, can give the comfort and security I need.

SEPTEMBER 16   Read Genesis 25:22-23.

My two sons are fighting again. They fight over everything! I get so tired of it. I am never sure how to stop them. But most of all, I want them to be friends.

At times like these, I remember the story of Jacob and Esau, who started fighting in their mother's womb and continued fighting for years. Then I remember that when they met as Jacob was returning home, they embraced! Yes, even Jacob and Esau ended up being friends. Maybe there is hope for my children as well.

O God, help me to know what to do when my children fight and argue. Give me guidance, wisdom, and, above all, patience.

SEPTEMBER 17   Read Deuteronomy 5:16.

It wasn't until I had my own baby that I knew just how much my mother loved me. I looked into his eyes and realized how much love a mother is capable of feeling.

It wasn't until he talked back to me and said "I hate you" for the first time that I knew how much a child's words can hurt a mother. I thought I would burst into tears at that very moment.

A mother's love is a precious thing—so strong, so constant. But a mother's heart is a fragile thing, breaking at even the smallest hurt.

O God, I wish I had listened more closely to your commandment and honored my mother more constantly. So many things I did and said I wish I could take back. Now that I am a mother, may I treat my children with love and respect so that honoring me is an easier task.

SEPTEMBER 18   Read Matthew 26:10-13.

I had a terrible day. I was tired and sweaty and just plain worn out. So I tired to sneak away from my children and take a nice hot bubble bath alone. But I had no sooner gotten into the tub than the door flew open and there they were. I could have cried. I said, "I am so tired!" And then my oldest son said, "Will it make you feel better if we wash your back?" They soaped and scrubbed and rubbed, and you know what? I did feel better, much better. They did what they could to help their poor mom feel rested and relaxed; they washed my back.

I felt loved and cared for. Perhaps that is why Jesus got so upset when the woman who poured ointment onto his head was crossed by Judas. She had done what she could to make Jesus feel loved and cared for. Sometimes the simplest acts done in love are the best kind.

O God, let the acts I do to others be acts of love and kindness so that I, like the woman so long ago, might bring joy and peace to others.

SEPTEMBER 19   Read John 14:1-3.

Sometimes I look at my children and think, "What would you do without me?" I feed them, bath them, and give them shelter and security. They often seem so strong, so able to do for themselves, but still they are babies needing their mother's love. And they never question that love. They know that if they need food, I will get it for them; or if they need a blanket on a cold night, I will get it for them. There is no need that, if I am able, I will not provide for them.

That is what Jesus was talking about when he promised to always care for us. He promised to go prepare a place for us and return to take us there. And we, like children depending on our mothers, can depend on his words. For Christ will provide all that we need, not only for this life but also for our life eternal.

O God, thank you for providing all the warmth, love, and security we will ever need. I look forward with confidence to my life and the lives of my children that will be spent in eternity with you.

SEPTEMBER 20   Read Psalm 136:1-3.

Today was a beautiful, cool fall day. On the spur of the moment, I decided to take my kids to the zoo. They were thrilled, especially my two-year-old, who did not remember ever being at a zoo. Every time he would see a new animal, he would shout, "Oh, Mommy, look at the elephant!" (Or some other animal name.) The funny thing was that he did not know which animals were which. He would point to a hippopotamus and say, "Oh, Mommy, look at the monkey!" Or he would point to a giraffe and say, "Oh, Mommy, look at the tiger!" He shouted with such enthusiasm and confidence! But even though he didn't know the names of the animals, he made one thing perfectly clear: The animals were the greatest things he had ever seen before.

Julian, my four-year-old, was listening to his brother's excitement, and he said, "Britton, do you know who made all of this? God did! And God is the only one who is smart enough to think all these animals up." When Julian said this, the words of the psalmist rang in my ears: "O give thanks to the LORD, for he is good" (Psalm 136:1). And I thought, "You are good, God. This creation of yours, these animals, the sky, this world—it is so good that even children realize your power and wisdom. Thank you for moments like these when I am reminded of your good works."

O God, we certainly have much to shout about! I give thanks to you, for you are good!

SEPTEMBER 21   Read I Samuel 1:19-28.

Some close friends of mine recently adopted a new baby girl. What an exciting time! The baby is so tiny and sweet, and she has been welcomed into a home where all hopes for ever having a child were nearly gone.

After trying for some time to get pregnant, my friends had to wait a long time to be accepted by an adoption agency. Then they had to wait until the agency found a baby for them. But now their home is filled with joy and happiness, and I doubt that that child could have found a more loving set of parents!

It must have been difficult for the birth mother to give up her child. I think of Hannah, who had promised God that if she could give birth to a child she would let him grow up in the Temple and serve God all of his life. She did have a baby, Samuel, and she let him grow up under the care of a priest, Eli. As difficult as it was, Hannah gave her baby into the care of Eli and then sang a song to God. She knew that sometimes God has a plan for children to grow up with parents other than their natural parents, and she trusted God.

I hope the birth mother of my friends' baby knows that God took care of her baby and found loving parents for her, just as God took care of Hannah's Samuel.

O God, I pray for birth mothers everywhere who feel it is best to give their babies up for adoption. May their hearts be full of songs of joy and peace, and may they rest knowing that you have found loving parents for their babies.

SEPTEMBER 22   Read Ecclesiastes 3:1-8.

Besides becoming a mother, nothing has ever been more thrilling to me than becoming an aunt for the first time. I will never forget how precious my new niece looked when I saw her through the glass of the hospital nursery. I stood at that glass with tears pouring down my cheeks. I was so happy, so proud—and this brand new gift from God was my niece! I recently watched that "baby" walk into her new high school for the first time, and I wondered how she could be so grown when it seemed like only weeks ago when she was born.

Now I look at my two toddlers playing with their toy cars. Tomorrow you'll be driving cars of your own. Today you have to be helped up and down the front steps of our house, but tomorrow you'll own your own homes. You don't know how to read yet, but tomorrow you'll be writing me letters from college. Time passes so quickly. I am thankful for the time we have now to play, for tomorrow you will be grown.

O God, time goes so quickly. My babies will not be babies very long. I have so much to teach them, and they have so much to teach me! Please help me to realize what a precious time we have together right now. Help me to slow down, to listen, to enjoy them, and to savor this time while they are little.

SEPTEMBER 23   Read Matthew 22:34-39.

When I was growing up, I often heard the story of the lawyers who came to Jesus and tried to trick him by asking him to tell them what the greatest commandment was. Jesus responded with the Great Commandment: "You shall love the Lord your God with all your heart, and with all your soul, and with all your mind. . . . [and] your neighbor as yourself" (Matthew 22:37, 39). I always assumed that the entire passage was a "new" commandment that Jesus gave on the spot. But then one day I was surprised to find the first part in the book of Deuteronomy: "You shall love the LORD your God with all your heart, and with all your soul, and with all your might" (6:5). I later learned that this is the passage that Jewish children often learn first. They recite it much as my children say the prayer "Now I Lay Me Down to Sleep." Mary probably taught this scripture to Jesus long before any other. It was central to his faith-filled upbringing.

So when asked to name the greatest commandment, Jesus

responded with scripture he had learned as a child. But he did not end there. He added onto the passage and said, "You shall love your neighbor as yourself" (v. 39). Jesus had taken what his mother had taught him, pondered that, and then added a new commandment.

As mothers, we can teach our children the Scriptures and lessons of faith, and we hope that, in time, they will reflect on them and grow with them. Our children may not grow up to believe exactly what we have taught them, but we hope they will always *remember* what we have taught them. Jesus was the Son of God, and he would have answered his questioners correctly regardless of what his mother may have taught him; but, as a mother, I hope that all I do to help my children grow spiritually will not be in vain. Perhaps, like Jesus, my children will listen to their mother.

O God, let me teach and guide my children so that when they grow up, they will have a solid foundation of faith to stand on, just as Jesus did so long ago.

SEPTEMBER 24 Read Daniel 6:1-9.

When I hear the story of Daniel in the lion's den, I usually focus on the part when Daniel faces the lions. But the last time I read the story, I was struck by something else. Daniel had done no crime for which to be put into the lion's den. Instead, he was "set up" by the king's advisors who purposefully tricked the king into signing a law that Daniel would not obey. These men knew that Daniel would not worship the king in place of God, and this is why they passed the law. Daniel was a blameless, guiltless person who was hurt by others intentionally. But God prevailed and looked after him.

Although my children are not and will not always be blameless or guiltless, there are times when, despite their goodness, they will be hurt by others intentionally. Other children may say mean things to them and bully them on the playground. As they get older, peers may pressure them to drink, or drug dealers may persuade them to take drugs. I cannot be with them every moment to guard them from danger, but I know that God is always with them, and for this I am thankful.

O God, thank you for watching over my children. Whatever pressures or dangers they may face, I pray that they will lean on you and your wisdom for guidance.

SEPTEMBER 25   Read Exodus 19:4-5.

It was a wonderful fall day. It was cool, but the sun was shining; and there was just the touch of a light breeze. I was pushing my sons in their swings. Back and forth, back and forth. And each time I pushed, they yelled, "Higher, Mommy!" They laughed and giggled. They were as free as birds, flying higher and higher through the air.

The Bible says, "I bore you on eagles' wings. . . . Now therefore, if you obey my voice and keep my covenant, you shall be my treasured possession out of all the peoples" (Exodus 19:4-5). Wouldn't it be wonderful if my children stayed so close to God all their lives that they felt as free and empowered as they do soaring on the swings? I wonder why I feel so down and out a lot of the time. I wonder why I often don't feel that I am really soaring on the eagles' wings I have been promised. Perhaps I stray too far from God. Perhaps I need to listen more closely to God's voice. Perhaps I need to swing more often—to remember what soaring on eagles' wings feels like.

O God, help me to stop feeling burdened with life and instead fly with you as my guide. And perhaps if you and I show my children what flying on eagles' wings is like, they, too, will spend their entire lives soaring with you.

SEPTEMBER 26 — Read Matthew 9:9.

Lately, the first thing my children talk about when they get out of bed is what they are going to be when they grow up. Today they are going to be doctors, but yesterday they were going to be firemen, and the day before that they were going to be Batman. I have no idea what my children will choose to "be" when they grow up, although I am pretty sure that they will not be Batman! I just hope and pray that whatever they become, they will be people who love Christ and follow him.

Matthew was a tax collector, but when he met Christ, he followed him. James and John were fishermen. Mary Magdalene was a prostitute. I guess that is why the writers of the Bible were so careful to include the occupations of the people Christ called—to remind us that whatever it is we "are" when we grow up, we also are called to follow Christ.

O God, no matter what my children eventually choose to "be," please work inside their hearts. For no matter what they become, I pray that they will also grow in faith and love for you.

SEPTEMBER 27 — Read Matthew 6:5-7.

I had never given much thought to the scripture about praying in private, because I am accustomed to praying in my room alone. But one day my son entered while I was praying, and I said, "Wait just a minute, honey, I am finishing my prayers."

He started giggling, and then he said, "Mommy, I thought you only prayed at church." I said, "No, I pray in many places." He just giggled and giggled; he was so thrilled that I actually pray at home.

As mothers, we sometimes need to open our doors and let our children see us pray, for how else will they learn that we can pray anytime and anywhere?

O God, help me to feel more at ease about praying in front of my children. And help me to find places and times that I can pray with my children, for I want to show them how important talking with you is to me and how important it can be to them.

SEPTEMBER 28   Read Ephesians 6:1-5.

Most of the time I am happy and content in my role as a mother, but I admit there are days when I am so low I could just sit and cry. The things that get me low are things like having to pick up toys for the hundredth time, having to change a dirty diaper—again—and having a child hang on my leg while I am trying to walk across the room.

Now, to anyone except a mother, these things sound insignificant and maybe even funny. I admit it often is hard to find sympathy. That is why I am glad that I have friends with young children. They know just what I am talking about when I have had enough! They "bear my burdens," and I bear theirs. There is nothing like a good friend, especially when a glass of milk has been tipped over—again!

O God, thank you for the friends I have who understand my situation. They lift me up, and I pray that I may lift them up when they need it, as well.

SEPTEMBER 29   Read Hosea 4:16.

My two-year-old refuses to ride in a stroller anymore. But when he's not in a stroller, he strays from me. So I got a harness for him to wear. At first he loved it, but after a while he wanted to get away from me. He started pulling and tugging, but I held tight. Then he would not move as I tried to walk through the store; he lay down. I reasoned with him, I threatened him, I tried to pick him up; but he would not budge.

Suddenly I felt as if I was trying to move a stubborn heifer. The words of Hosea came to me, and I wondered how often I, like the people of Israel, have been like my son—a stubborn heifer who refuses to go in the direction that God wants me to go.

Of course, I did not leave my son. I stayed with him for what seemed like hours, coaxing and prodding and begging. And finally, he got up and went with me.

Sometimes I wonder if God has ever been so fed up with me that God was tempted to leave me alone. Yet I know that God always stays with me, even when I am a stubborn heifer.

O God, I know I can be awfully stubborn. Thank you for staying with me and never giving up.

SEPTEMBER 30   Read I Corinthians 13:4-13.

These words of Paul, "love is patient; love is kind" (I Corinthians 13:4), always seem to haunt me as a mother. There are many, many times when I am not patient or kind, especially with my children. I have a "trigger" inside me that says, "You are not being patient or kind or loving—in fact, you are being rather mean." I wonder why I don't have a trigger inside me that says at other times, "Wow! You were really patient and kind. In fact, you did great!"

It is so much easier to be critical of ourselves than to praise ourselves. But with the ups and downs of motherhood, we need to praise ourselves because, as you and I both know, sometimes we are the only ones who will.

O God, help me to know when I am being impatient or unkind, but also help me to pause and celebrate when I am being loving and kind. This is a hard job, and I need all the encouragement I can get.

OCTOBER

Autumn Reflections

MARY ZIMMER

OCTOBER 1   **Read Deuteronomy 6:4-7.**

I stood, ankle-deep in mud, cutting the rich, dark green stalks of broccoli. My husband and two sons stood on the roadside shaking their heads at my determination to have enough broccoli in the freezer to last the winter.

We were on our annual October ritual to a U-pick farm where we gathered broccoli, several kinds of apples, and cider to take home. We always stopped at a family restaurant to have a fried chicken dinner and stuff ourselves with fried biscuits. And Jacob and Michael got to pick out the largest pumpkin they could each carry from the field.

This family ritual has carried over to their teenage years, and they still look forward to it. Even though they have grown up in the city, there is something about even an organized U-pick farm that appeals to them.

When children are small, such family rituals can begin, and then the telling of stories about trips and activities will become rituals in themselves. As they grew older, one of my son's favorite things was to look at albums and hear stories about themselves over and over.

The writer of Deuteronomy knew how important this kind of family ritual was. The Hebrew people did most of their religious teaching in the home.

What are the rituals of faith that you will pass on to your children? What will you recite to your children and talk about when you are at home and when you are away?

OCTOBER 2   Read Philippians 4:6-7.

I was very excited to be a new mother because I had so looked forward to and carefully prepared for the event. But even with a husband and visiting mother, the anxiety mounted during each day.

For that first month, I felt that I had been plugged into an electric outlet. I worried if my firstborn son didn't sleep enough, and I worried if he slept longer than usual. I was breastfeeding; how would I know if he got enough to eat unless he was weighed often?

That "baby" is now six feet, three inches tall, has biceps he is proud of, and is making plans for college.

Sometime during the interim, I read the above verses from Philippians, and a new emphasis seemed to be written there. Instead of "stop being anxious when you already are," the emphasis was "be *not anxious*." Rather than getting in the vicious cycle of worrying, feeling guilty for worrying, and then worrying about feeling guilty, I learned to aim for the state of being not anxious.

Relaxation and breathing exercises helped. Yoga positions for stretching tense muscles helped. Prayer helped. Sometimes just gazing at the outdoor scene or at a book of beautiful photographs helped break the cycle.

Good mothering doesn't mean always being alert for what might go wrong. What prayer of supplication for your needs will you make known to God today?

OCTOBER 3   Read Matthew 11:29-30.

Having read all the major baby books, I fully expected to recognize my newborn son's cries and be able to discern whether food, comfort, clean diapers, or sleep was needed. Several weeks into my new career as mother, I was very disheartened to learn that each cry sounded much like another.

In the fantasies that arise from new-mother fatigue, I thought it would certainly have been a good idea to have lights on his forehead, each a different color to denote just the response required. In my not-too-humble opinion, God was guilty of a serious design flaw here.

But gradually, as Jacob and I got to know each other, I got better at a trial and error approach. Contemporary researchers have recognized distinct personality differences even in newborns and emphasize that the early months primarily involve getting acquainted with a new love who doesn't speak the language. It is this focused and attentive sensitivity that creates the empathy attributed to the role of mother.

Jacob and I just had to get to know each other in the dynamic of mother and baby. We had to "learn each other."

Just so, we often expect our relationship with Christ to be automatic and immediate. But we don't have to be experts. We are only required to be willing to learn. We only need to be ready to learn about walking in the way that leads to life.

What do you need to learn from Christ today? What do you want to share of yourself so that Christ may know you?

OCTOBER 4   Read Genesis 2:2-3.

Since mothering is a seven-day-a-week, twenty-four-hour-a-day job, sabbath may seem an impossible goal. Mothers cannot set aside one whole day from their responsibilities. So "sabbath time" has to become a matter of claiming those moments and, hopefully, hours here and there when we can rest and enter the place of the Spirit.

One day I tried beginning the day just as I would choose. I ate a good breakfast, read the paper, and went for a walk in the crisp autumn air before my prayer time. Two-and-a-half hours passed. Ironically, if the waking hours of sabbath are divided into sevenths, it comes out to just about two-and-a-half hours.

When my sons were very young and I was too tired to sleep, I found that just resting was very helpful. To just withdraw from the routine with no other agenda than resting is a concept that has almost disappeared from our lives.

Is that because this passage in Genesis really bothers us on some deep level? What do we do with our doctrines of omnipotence (God's unlimited power) and omnipresence (God's presence in all places at all times) if God is taking a nap one seventh of the time?

In our busy, overachieving culture, this passage in Genesis is a very important one. A resting God gives us permission to rest when we need it, whether we feel like we have earned rest by our accomplishments or not.

Instead of always aiming at the list of things that must be done, can you imagine having a period of rest as a goal for each day, a sabbath for yourself?

OCTOBER 5 Read Psalm 91:14-16.

A pastor friend of mine has a passion for polar bears. After a trip to Canada to see them in the wild, he showed a videotape of the bears. In one scene, a mother polar bear watched over her two cubs while they played and ate. She wasn't obvious in her vigilance, but her head and shoulders moved slowly from side to side so she could watch out for any predators.

Early on I knew I could be like the biblical she-bear where my children were concerned. I realized I was fully capable of violence should their safety be threatened.

My vigilance took strange forms. When Jacob was about four, we bought a tricycle from a friend. Jacob was just beginning to venture from his own yard to the sidewalk and the real world of the neighborhood. The tricycle had a serious squeak, which brought a complaint from a neighbor. But I wasn't about to fix that squeak. It let me know just how far Jacob had ventured up the sidewalk, and when I couldn't hear it, I knew to go looking.

One time I realized that God might interpret as prayer some of my thoughts and feelings that I didn't necessarily intend as prayer. What if God hears all our worries as prayer? What if those concerns that plague us are like squeaky tricycle wheels keeping us in range of God's loving attention?

According to Scripture, God is always vigilant on our behalf. What does it feel like to know that God is constantly on the lookout for danger, always ready to protect us?

OCTOBER 6   Read Luke 10:38-42.

A recent newspaper article described a planned community and the problems that one resident had when he painted his mailbox an unapproved color of green. More than one neighbor was upset, and apparently there was a community council meeting about the travesty. I always figure that people who have time to worry about such things need a good mission project!

I could never live in a community that was planned to that degree. Besides a major independent streak, I strongly believe that a house and yard where children live should be geared toward the children. The messes they make are time-limited, no matter how long one day with two preschoolers can seem.

I realized one day, when I just could not get the house

straightened up, that the boys and their mess weren't going to be here forever. In fact, out of my expected lifespan, kids' messes would only be around for about one-fourth of the time. So I relaxed.

I believe that a cluttered house and yard where children live is a sign of happy, contented children whose parents realize that room to make a mess is essential to the development of children's creativity.

With nonstop TV commercials for cleaning products always set in picture-perfect houses, we may find Jesus' words to Martha preposterous. Can we really believe that we should leave the mess and go to sit in prayer at the feet of Jesus and thereby learn from him?

OCTOBER 7   Read Luke 4:42.

A very wise young mother once passed on "The Rule" to me. "The Rule" for young mothers is, "Never do anything while the children are asleep that you can do while they are awake."

Does that make sense? What it refers to are those household chores that can be done, even if it means being interrupted, while children play at your feet or in their own room.

This rule is necessary because the hardest thing for young mothers to do is reserve precious nap and sleep time for themselves. That is the time to do what nourishes your own soul and heart, not the chores that could be done at another time.

The spiritual concept here is stewardship. But it is stewardship of the self. Jesus modeled this stewardship by retreating to a quiet place for prayer and meditation. Even the usual expectations of motherhood encourage women to give of themselves to such a degree that we risk turning around someday after the last child has started school and finding that we have given our entire selves away.

Nourishing one's self—that part of you that is made in the

image of God—may require the use of Mothers' Day Out programs or neighborhood play groups. Whatever the method, the purpose is time that is reserved for yourself as a person, without the immediate demands of the role of mother.

What are your preferred forms of self-nurture? How will you practice stewardship of the self for God?

OCTOBER 8   Read Psalm 5:1-3.

Watching a young child learning to walk is often both amusing and heart-rending. They have earned the name *toddler* because that is what they do. Learning to walk means "toddling" for a number of months before all the skeletal and muscle parts learn to work together smoothly.

Before children reach that stage, they go through a long apprentice period. This time consists of pulling up, letting go, trying with one foot and then the other, stumbling, falling, whimpering, or just sitting looking perplexed and then rolling over to start the whole process once again.

The spiritual gift of prayer is a similar reality for most adults. We decide to make prayer a significant part of our daily lives. Perhaps we buy a guide or book of meditations. But on a busy day, our quiet time for prayer, study, and meditation may often be the first sacrifice.

A life of prayer is a matter of adopting the toddler's approach to walking. There will be many attempts, some spills and dissatisfaction, and renewed efforts before we come to the stage of determined hunger to be a person of prayer.

There are some essentials—silence, solitude, and Scripture. But most people develop an individual style. Some, like the psalmist, prefer to spend quiet time with God in the morning; others choose the afternoon or evening. The elements of a personal style of prayer are related to personality and needs.

What are your expectations of prayer? What do you hope

will come from your time with God? What resources and guides do you need?

OCTOBER 9   Read Psalm 69:13.

After a few weeks home from the hospital, my new baby son took a seven-hour nap during the day. I knew that I was in for a rough time if he got his days and nights completely mixed up. After fretting about "on demand" schedules, I called the pediatrician only to be reassured that Jacob would be fine if I woke him up.

The question that came to mind was *Who was going to be in charge of the rhythm of my days?* Since I felt very uneasy not knowing what I could expect one day to the next, I decided to attempt to put Jacob on a schedule. Within a few days, he settled into a pattern of waking at 7:00 A.M. and going on a general three- or four-hour schedule.

Those who have studied and practiced a deep spiritual life report that there is also a rhythm to our sense of awareness and relationship to God. There is a regular ebb and flow, but we are not necessarily in charge of the rhythm.

One day while listening to the theme music from the movie *Chariots of Fire,* I heard a deep bass sound that surged and faded under the melody. I realized that, like the pattern of our breath, this is like God's presence in our lives. God does not leave and certainly does not abandon us, but sometimes God does draw away. It is this ebbing of the presence of God that pulls us even more to search for God. We seek the Presence because we are hungry or lonesome or in need of deep peace.

How do you experience the ebb and flow of God's presence in your life? How do you seek the Spirit of God?

OCTOBER 10   Read Matthew 5:6.

One evening during a women's spirituality group, a young mother spoke up. She lived in a two-bedroom apartment with her husband and three children under the age of five.

This mother had come to a point in her life where she needed some space in her home to call her own. She wasn't concerned about size or decorating, but simply a place in her home that belonged to her alone. The hunger and thirst of her inner spirit symbolized her unique individual search for the Spirit of God.

After we talked for a while, she realized there might be space in her bedroom on one wall between the crib and the bed. She could set a small table there and put up a shelf for books and a journal. My friend was in the process of creating sacred space for herself.

Just the summer before, after I returned from a significant retreat, I pulled an old table from the attic, covered it with a grandmother's dresser scarf, and set a candle, my Bible, and some stones gathered on retreat on top of the scarf. This was now to be my sacred space in my house.

In any house where young children eat, sleep, play, and ramble, a mother's personal space may become very limited and precious. Reorganizing rooms and furniture to "set an altar to the Lord" may take creativity and negotiation.

Where can you set aside sacred space for communion with God? What items do you need to enhance this space?

OCTOBER 11   Read Exodus 19:1-6.

Once my sons grew big enough to straddle my hip, I liked to carry them on my left side. I could manuever them more easily and still have my right hand free. Certainly, my hips were ample enough to carry the load! I could get a rhythm going, and they enjoyed the ride.

The day came, of course, for each of them, when all they wanted was "Down!" They were ready to explore the world on their own terms. But when fatigue or hunger or a bump happened, they were glad to be picked up to ride on my hip for a while.

A mother eagle teaches her young to fly by an instinctive gauge of their readiness. Then she launches them out into the wide space off a cliff and goes to fly just beneath them herself. When they tire, she is there out in the air to catch them and return them to the nest.

This image of God is one of my favorites because of the implications of God's strength and faithful providence. The word *wilderness* occurs three times in the Exodus passage for today. The chosen people of God have just left the homes and security they knew to follow this one man, Moses. Certainly they were tired and wondered how food and sustenance were going to be found.

God's word to the Israelites, who were sometimes fearful of their new freedom, is also the word of God to us: "I bore you on eagles' wings and brought you to myself" (19:4).

In what arena of life do you need to launch out and trust God's eagles' wings? What needs to happen so you can take that chance?

OCTOBER 12 Read Isaiah 49:15-16.

On an evening walk, I met one of the revered grandmothers in my church. She was worried about her middle-aged son and his family because their vacation travels were taking them through an area where a hurricane had landed on shore.

I was reminded that mothers never stop being mothers. The intensity and immediacy of demands and needs vary, but we don't get to a point where we no longer want to be available if needed. Many of us have a hard time letting go, even at the stages where a child's growth and development require independence. Our own development as mothers needs to be a gradual but intentional process of relinquishing power and control while conveying a ready willingness to be available.

God's steadfast devotion is the subject of Isaiah's psalm of praise in chapter 49. This fidelity of the Creator is compared to a mother's devotion to an infant. God is like a mother whose compassion remains available no matter what happens.

Have you had a dream or fear that you will get the car all packed with the children's things and blithely drive off forgetting the most important passengers? These verses promise us that even if we have forgetful moments as parents, God's compassion is assured for all of us for all time.

What is your prayer for God's motherly, steadfast compassion? How can you claim the fidelity of God for your life?

OCTOBER 13   Read Exodus 2:1-10.

Pharaoh's daughter doesn't get much space in the commentaries on this passage. Curious, isn't it, that only women are involved in saving the life of the boy who will become the deliverer of the Chosen People? But Pharaoh's daughter "took pity" on the crying child in the basket. It is her compassionate bonding that will provide the means of his escape from her father's command.

I found that I could identify with this woman from another time and culture when I went to stay with my sister and her family when each of her sons was born. Caring for a new nephew in the first days of his life, when a baby's vulnerability is so clear, was an experience of bonding for me. If, through some tragedy, I had been required to take him home and raise him, I knew I could do just that. There was no question in my mind.

One of the favorite rituals at my church is the dedication of infants. Before our pastor takes the baby in his arms to walk up and down an aisle to introduce us, we take a pledge to support the parents and their new child. We all accept the symbolic responsibility of Pharaoh's daughter to offer needed compassion to our "spiritually adopted" nieces and nephews.

Throughout our country there are still children as vulnerable as a baby in a basket in a river. Do you feel like Pharaoh's daughter toward any group of them? What child or children need the discipleship of your compassion as a Christian mother?

OCTOBER 14   Read Luke 12:22-28.

Porch swings are a necessity in my life. They are especially nice in October, when the world is ablaze with color. When my sons were small, the combination of being outside and gently swinging to and fro was very soothing to a cranky baby. One evening when Michael was about six months, I sat on the swing just after nursing him. I felt totally at peace with the world and then realized what the source was. Someone who could figure out how to mass produce and market nursing hormones could make a fortune!

Breastfeeding made me stop everything else I was doing; there wasn't any other task I could accomplish. I was quite literally "doing what came naturally"—just what my body was prepared to do.

I was not a fervent disciple of the breastfeeding movement. The decision was pragmatic—so much easier just to unsnap a bra than to keep up with bottles and nipples. But often enough, the actual experience turned into natural grace.

The passage in Luke often brings the protest: "But we all have to work." But during the times I was breastfeeding, I could begin to understand what Jesus meant in these images. When we get in touch with who we are in a specific life situation and appreciate the resources of the "sky" or "field" that God has given us, then we can stop worrying.

What support in your life can you lean into right now? What worry calls you to petition God for peace?

OCTOBER 15   Read Luke 15:8-10.

Societal changes that encourage one nuclear family to live on its own, far from extended family, have created an isolated life for some young mothers. This social isolation too often leads to loneliness and depression if friends are not available.

One day after a long winter at home with my first son, I realized that the only activity easily available for us to get out of the house was shopping. The only easy contact that American society offered me was the opportunity to buy something.

One generation ago, mothers in neighborhoods got together in the morning for coffee while children played together. But today over 50 percent of mothers with young children work outside the home. Maternity leaves for new mothers don't often coincide, and any one mother may be the only one home on her block for weeks or months.

Some communities provide drop-in centers for mothers and children that create conversation and support. This is a resource that local churches could easily provide.

But there will still be days when the loneliness of isolation rears its head for the at-home mother. This passage from Luke is a comforting one for those days. These verses remind us that no matter what crack of loneliness or depression we roll into, God will be "care-fully" searching for us and will celebrate with us when we are found again.

What do you need from God today? How can you call on God to find you?

OCTOBER 16
Read Psalm 62:1-2, 5-7.

My spiritual home away from home is the Sisters of Loretto Motherhouse in central Kentucky. I go there periodically for one or two days of solitude, silence, and replenishment.

Balance is a word that becomes more and more significant to me. There is a fine line between isolation and solitude sometimes, and the balance between human contact and solitude is important—especially for mothers.

I go on retreat to be just the person I am, without the needs and demands of the roles that I carry in daily life. There is a soul inside each one of us that is affected by all our roles but that is a unique and special creation of God. It is the part of ourselves created for communion with God alone.

Being on retreat gives me time and space to make room for those thoughts and feelings that are ignored or laid aside during ordinary, busy days. There is room for my soul to be nourished by the friendship of God's Spirit. Mothers whose lives are circumscribed by others' needs do well to stay in touch with this part of themselves.

How can you find the retreat mode for your daily life? What help do you need to nurture your spiritual self?

OCTOBER 17
Read Galatians 3:25-29.

Some community of family, friends, or church is a necessity for young families. Stories and jokes can be shared, help can be found, and wisdom can be passed down.

My family has been very blessed to find this in a couples' Sunday school class, which is extended family for us. As part of the larger community of God we know as our church, my sons have a sense of belonging and security that many of their peers do not have.

At the farewell party for one youth minister who had been very significant in Jacob's life, I tried to express my gratitude for his ministry by saying, "Thanks for helping me raise my kids." Camp and lock-ins and summer dialogues at various homes meant my sons had contact with lots of aunts and uncles who watched them grow up.

Contemporary life is too complex for children to get all they need from two parents. And my bias is that it is the place of the church to function as a base community for young families. Churches don't have a lock on spiritual expression, but they do offer a very humn connection.

Jesus' ministry was not separated from a human community. He called disciples who traveled with him and depended on women for financial help and their witness. His teaching about families indicates that our family of origin might not be our family of faith, but the family of faith is very necessary.

What resources do you need from Christian community? How can you find spiritual sustenance in community?

OCTOBER 18   Read Hebrews 12:11.

I started walking as a form of regular exercise because it requires only shoes, no ball or raquet, club or court. For discipline's sake, I mapped out a route that goes around two settling basins of the water company near my home. This is a popular place because the path is set up about two stories above the street; there is lots of sky and usually a breeze.

My favorite time is the beginning of the day. Early on, this was required because the discipline of forming a healthy habit came easier in the morning. When the boys were younger, I would get up early and walk while my husband, Steve, got ready for work. The first discipline was getting out of bed before I had to; the second was giving myself permission to do the first thing of the day for myself.

For the last two years I have had all kinds of music, thanks to the Christmas gift of a portable cassette player. The music, combined with days when the weather and natural world are just plain beautiful—like October days when the leaves are falling—makes for prayers of wordless praise.

Walking has taught me the truth of spiritual disciplines. In difficult times, spiritual disciplines carry us beyond what we can do by "taking thought." Walking has gone way past disciplined exercise to being a major source of God's grace in my life.

I now believe, like the medieval monks, that physical discipline is an essential part of the spiritual life. What discipline of the body do you follow or need to start?

OCTOBER 19 Read Psalm 91:11-16.

Have you ever gone in after your new baby is sound asleep and checked to see if that precious child is still breathing? Of course you have! Some mothers use mirrors; I always just used my hand. Bonding with and loving such innocence makes us fierce protectors of our children's safety.

The first night home with our oldest son, I initially attempted to sleep with my arm over the top edge of the bassinet, my finger securely grasped in Jacob's tight fist. Talk about a substitute umbilical cord! I was afraid to let go of my connection through that first long night home. The dark outside seemed much darker since I had a newborn baby to protect.

But we do have to give them up each night to God's care and any available guardian angels. We cannot be the absolute, omnipresent parent since we have to work, play, and sleep ourselves. When exhausted from a day with a sick child, I knew that at bedtime I would have to pray a prayer giving my son back into God's safekeeping, so that I could get rest for the next day.

And as they grow, we slowly but surely must gradually give them up to what life offers them that we cannot. To absolutely protect our children would rob them of the pleasure and accomplishment that life provides. Later on, as the boys faced different challenges, I had to pray a prayer of relinquishment so they could grow.

What worry or concern do you need to give up to God's protection? What is your prayer of relinquishment?

OCTOBER 20   Read Proverbs 22:6.

One young mother in a support group that I coordinated stated her intention to avoid telling her son no. Her logic was that if her son never heard the word, then he wouldn't say it— he wouldn't go through the defiant toddlerhood stage.

I smiled and tried to let her down gently. No from a small child is not intentional defiance. It is a test for parents. The only question is "Do you mean what you say?" Saying no and physical resistance are a preschooler's ways of experimenting in order to learn what the real limits are.

Children come with a built-in radar that makes them focus on nonverbal and voice-tone communication. We have all heard a parent direct or reprimand a child in a voice that clearly showed the parent had no intention of enforcing the rule. Any child knows whether a parent means what she or he says or not.

Setting limits for children is easier if we start thinking about our values and goals before that first, clear no is required. What limit do we face in our lives? What is our response?

Dealing with limits is recognition of our creaturely finiteness and fallibility. We cannot be everything and do everything as parents. We have to choose, sometimes between two positive options. And we will make mistakes because we are fallible human beings.

How do you discern what place finiteness and fallibility have in your role as parent? What do you see as God's teaching about limits?

OCTOBER 21 Read Song of Solomon 2:11-12.

I have always been a believer in the French proverb which states that if you only have two francs left, spend one for bread and the other for flowers. My thoroughly biased opinion is that flowers are proof of the existence of God because there is no need for such an abundance of color, shape, and fragrance in order for a plant to reproduce itself. For me, the beauty of flowers is evidence of God's infinite extravagance.

I started buying flowers for myself about fifteen years ago when I realized that I would get them sooner if I bought them myself, rather than hinting around for days. A flowering plant or vase of cut flowers is my defiant pledge for beauty and meaning when my days have been spent in John Bunyan's "Slough of Despond."

My family now knows that if they come in and there is a bunch of cash-and-carry carnations or Dutch irises on the dining room table, they are to be especially sweet to me. The flowers are a signal that I have been having a rough time and need beauty.

For young mothers, such a fragile gift to self may seem terribly selfish and impractical. But on a chilly autumn day when the rain outside is unceasing and the only smells you notice require laundry bleach, consider what claim you need to make of God's blessings in your life.

What is a primary symbol of God's extravagance to you? How can that symbol be provided in your life so that you can receive with open hands and heart?

OCTOBER 22   Read Psalm 27:7-8.

After becoming a mother for the first time in 1973, I read many child-development and parenting books. And I listened to all the advice that experienced mothers would share.

But then the day came when I had to learn on my own. One of the first things I learned is that we can never be the mother we plan to be before a baby is born. We cannot be a generic mother, but only a mother to a certain child with an individual personality and temperament.

When my son Jacob was older and astonished at my response to some issue between children and parents, he would ask, "How did you learn to be a mother?" The constant response was, "You and Michael taught me."

For mothering is on-the-job training. We learn by doing in the dynamics of interrelationship. In that way, mothering is like the development of Christian faith and discipleship. We can read all the recommended books and study the Scripture throughout years of preparation.

But until we step out in a leap of faith to relate in prayer to the Unseen One and in relationship to other human beings, we cannot "know" how to be a disciple. We only learn "the Way" of Christianity by walking it.

There is a seeker of Presence and meaning inside each of us that searches for the face of God in mystery, nature, and the faces of people we see every day. Thereby we learn who we are and how we are to be in the world.

What gift of the Presence do you need in your life today? Where and how will you seek it?

OCTOBER 23   Read Psalm 57:1.

During our children's young years, my friends and I would quote "Mother's Bad Day Verse": This too shall pass.

The most likely time for us to mutter it under our breath was 5:00 P.M. on a weekday, the time I began to call the "bewitching hour." For that is the time when everyone is tired, hungry, and cranky, and someone has got to feed everybody else.

Sometimes a day or a period in our lives is so overwhelming or painful that survival is the major goal. We find ourselves reducing the dreams of future blessing to a desperate hope that the next hour or day just won't get worse.

What we need is a repertoire of survival skills. Sometimes that requires lowering our expectations both of ourselves and of others. Sometimes it is music or a hymn that gets us beyond anxiety. Sometimes it is simply a matter of stopping in the middle of frustration to sit down and take a few deep breaths.

When life batters us down and we wonder whether we will get through the present hour, the psalmist promises us that we can seek refuge under God's wings of mercy. There, in that place of holy protection, we can wait until any storm passes.

What is the most significant storm in your life right now? How will you seek God's steadfast mercy?

OCTOBER 24   Read Genesis 3:1-7.

One morning Steve and I were awakened by Michael, then two years old, as he was vehemently practicing his independence. From the next room we heard, "I don't *want* to. I *don't* want to. *I* don't want to." Steve and I wrapped pillows over our faces as our bed rocked with laughter.

Children are not born into this world knowing they have a separate and originally blessed self. Their awareness of a self separate from the world develops gradually in the first year. As we point to them in the mirror and use their names over and over, the inherent human consciousness begins to grow.

Michael's "practice session" in ego development was absolutely necessary. To a significant degree, he would find out who he was by defining himself against parental expectations.

Do we dare say the same for each of us as adults finding our way in God's world? The story in Genesis reflects the fact that human free will is a part of our makeup as created beings. God did not attempt to determine our goodness and right behavior but made—and continues to form—a world that requires the use of a thoughtful free will.

Just as Michael would incur the natural consequences of his growing independence, so also each of us is responsible for our decisions and behavior. We are not puppets at the mercy of a controlling God, but we are free citizens with choices to make about our place in the Kingdom.

What choice about your search for God's purposes in the world do you face? How will you discern God's freedom of choice?

OCTOBER 25   Read Ephesians 4:14-16.

Sometimes we hear parents and grandparents say, "But she's growing up so fast. I wish she could stay little for just a while longer." But that is a wish against all the physical, mental, and emotional impulses of any child.

Children's growth and development occurs by change. Sometimes it seems gradual, and suddenly we notice a new skill. But preschoolers do not spend much time on developmental plateaus.

Often as mothers we just get comfortable with one "stage" of development when our child is on to the next challenge of growing up. And it is the child's changing that brings about our growth and development as mothers. We live in response to their changing needs and demands, letting go of our control over who they are going to be just a little bit more each time.

The same model applies to our own growth in faith. The faith we had as adolescents expands with spiritual experience as we grow and change. For some, this kind of change is the hardest to bear.

But our changing perceptions of God do not mean God actually changes. We don't have that kind of power.

The model of Christian growth described in the New Testament is one of growing up into Christ, facing new challenges to our faith and beliefs. Faith that does not grow becomes stagnant and turns in on itself.

How are you growing up into Christ? What changes do you need to make?

OCTOBER 26 Read John 4:5-26.

The Samaritan woman is one of my favorite biblical characters, partly because she is an irascible woman. I like irascible people because they are honest. The Samaritan woman doesn't play games with Jesus. She asks questions until Jesus convinces her of his offering.

It is to this hard-bitten and careworn woman that Jesus brings some of the best news of the gospel. The first is the image of a spring of water welling up for eternal life as the gift of faith in him. The second is the statement of what this faith is—worshiping in spirit and in truth.

One of the best images for stewardship of the self is that of a cistern or reservoir. Just as fresh water must constantly flow into the reservoir to balance the demands for water that drain it, so also we must keep an interior balance.

A wise "commandment" for mothers is related: Take care of thy self. If we are constantly giving emotionally and spiritually for others without renewing our selves, we will start to dry up and be unable to nurture others. A dry spirit is one that is unable to accept and hold joy.

We start by being honest with God in prayer about our own needs. We must tell the truth. This is what confession is, and we cannot know true worship without confession.

What feeds you emotionally? What nourishes your spirit? How do you open the sluice to the spring of water always welling up?

OCTOBER 27 Read John 3:6-8.

One day when Jacob was five years old, Steve found a nest of praying mantises near the side of the house. They caught one about half-grown and brought it inside. Even though Jacob had a cocker spaniel named Snoopy, this was a "found" pet—and so tiny and unsual that he was entranced.

The requisite mayonnaise jar with holes punched in the top was found. Grass was pulled for the bottom of the jar, and small rocks were gathered to give the slowly stalking insect something to climb. Jacob set about capturing other insects for food.

Of course the inevitable happened. One day Jacob went in and the praying mantis was dead. Whether from too little food or from confinement there was no way to know. But Jacob at a very young age learned that we do not possess living creatures. Sometimes we have no other choice but to let go—to say good-bye.

It was a lesson to us, also, as parents. Our children belong to themselves, not to us as parents. We are entrusted with their care and upbringing, but they are not possessions.

273

I am writing this as we prepare to take Jacob to college, five hundred miles away. The time to let go has come, no matter how vulnerable he seems to us.

Letting go is a traditional theme in spirituality. Today, what do you need to surrender to God's grace and mercy? What is your prayer about letting go?

OCTOBER 28   Read Psalm 63:3-8.

Like all children at the crawling stage, Michael loved to crawl up steps. Born in March, he was ready for this by the end of October. We had about six steps leading to our front porch, so after supper, Michael and I would go outside for climbing practice.

I sat on the edge of the porch next to the steps. Michael would crawl up the steps and hold his arms out to me, and I would lift him down to the sidewalk so he could start over again. He would continue this ritual every evening as long as my patience lasted.

My job wasn't to teach him how to climb steps. By trial and error he would learn that skill. My job wasn't to absolutely prevent any scrapes or bumps. That is an impossible goal for any child's physical development. My job was simply to be present and available to provide a lift when needed. I was to be steadfast—simply there to catch Michael if a serious fall threatened.

I believe this image describes the intention of God's providence in our lives. The constant free gift of God's love and grace is not a guarantee of perfect safety and security in a finite world filled with fallible human beings. While we grow from one place to another in our life here on earth, God is always close by, ready to provide a lift when we need just that. And God's constant, strong mercy is available to reach out and hold us whenever a serious fall threatens.

What is your need of providence just now? What reassurance do you need?

OCTOBER 29   Read Luke 1:39-45.

I am convinced that sharing the early months and years of our children's lives bonds women as friends for the rest of our lives. There is something about those consultations, often over the phone, about runny noses, temper tantrums, and sleep patterns that builds a kind of special trust. Perhaps sometimes it is simply not-knowing together.

One of my definitions of a good friend is one whose kitchen I know almost as well as my own. This comes from sharing endless peanut butter sandwiches just above the kids' clamor or many cups of tea for mutual comfort.

Mothers of young children need good friends. They need the connection, the sense of being part of a web that is the world of other women who understand what it is like to live in the stretch of maintaining a personal identity when most hours are devoted to others.

A primary characteristic of these friendships is mutuality. Much of the time, what we need is not solutions but a listening ear and empathy. Sometimes I call my dear friend to say, "I need to whine." So we take turns ventilating and sharing, talking and listening.

Many times I feel like Mary in this story, scared and excited all at once at unusual news. Then I seek out a friend who will affirm and support me. I am also glad to be Elizabeth to friends who need to lean and hear words of encouragement.

When you feel like Mary, who is your Elizabeth? If you need to find an Elizabeth, where do you look?

OCTOBER 30   Read II Corinthians 5:16-18.

In a book entitled *Motherhood and God,* Margaret Hebble-thwaite points out that we most need the sacrament of reconciliation at those times when we are most reluctant to participate. As mothers of preschoolers who must sometimes develop their egos and selfhood in defiance of our rules, we may need to learn, practice, and teach the sacrament of reconciliation.

On a day trip with a mother who apologized to her children for almost every slight disappointment beyond her control, I realized that she was setting herself up to be blamed by her children whenever anything went wrong in their daily lives. That is a tremendous burden—to believe that we are totally responsible for every reality of our children.

But the reverse is also possible. Some parents believe that an apology to small children demeans their authority, and so they refuse to utter the words *I am sorry* even when it is appropriate. Such parents will harvest the resentment children feel in the home of aloof pride.

The parent who apologizes all the time grants children much more power than they can handle. The parent who refuses to apologize when appropriate presents the illusion that he or she is not an ordinary human being.

Reconciliation always requires that someone take the first step. This is an important modeling for children, and something they learn only by our modeling.

Is there someone with whom you need to share the sacrament of reconciliation? How do you begin?

OCTOBER 31   Read Luke 18:15-17.

My church has a Writers Group that meets for feedback and discipline. Periodically, they present an evening of readings of their work. At one reading a particular sentence stood out to me: "I am doing the best at being me that I can."

That would be all children's sentence every day if they could pronounce the words and understand the meaning. It is an important phrase to remember as mothers of preschoolers. They have never done any of this before. They have very limited experience and must often learn new skills in order to make secure habits that at least show up when company is around.

The gift of a new baby is God's determination that life should go on. And not just that life should go on, but go on in the particular and unique personality that each child brings to interact in the world.

Preschoolers' delight in the newness of the world is one of the most refreshing human realities. They are seldom bored because they have a completely new angle on what seems tediously boring to us. Preschoolers can teach us to delight again in the joy of our five senses as they stroke our skin, chase a butterfly, and stomp in a mud puddle.

But we can only share the experience if we are able to let them be the selves they are at that moment. Preschoolers are very good teachers if we are willing to learn.

What refreshing joy do you need in your life? How can you "become like a little child" and be open to joy?

NOVEMBER

Lessons from Little Ones

HELEN HEMPFLING ENARI

NOVEMBER 1

It had been "one of those days." For some reason, everything Allison and Sam did seemed to rub me the wrong way. I had spent most of the day responding to tantrums, whines, demands, and fights. I had mopped up spilled orange juice, un-jammed the VCR, and scrubbed red crayon marks off the wall. At 7:00 P.M., I was counting the minutes until bedtime. After I gave the children their baths, Allison wanted to play in the tub, but Sam was ready to get out. I dried Sam off, put his diaper on him, and began to put his pajamas on him when the phone rang.

My telephone conversation could not have lasted more than three minutes, but by the time I hung up the receiver, Sam had pushed a chair over to the kitchen counter, climbed onto the counter, and managed to get to the bread on top of the refrigerator. I discovered what he had done when I heard him in the bathroom talking to his sister. When I looked in the tub, I saw a little boy sitting in the water, diaper and all, sharing a soggy piece of bread with his sister. Pieces of wet bread were floating all over the tub.

Allison could see the fire in my eyes as I glared down at the tub. "Someone sure needs a time-out," she said, trying to focus my attention toward her brother.

"Someone needs a time-out." Those words seemed to jump out at me. Yes, someone *did* need a time-out. *I* needed the time-out. *I* needed a time-out to be alone with God, to concentrate on building a stronger spiritual life. I needed a time-out to experience the serenity and peace that comes with solitude. I needed a time-out to re-energize my mind, my body, and my spirit so that I could cope more easily with the daily stresses of raising children.

"Someone needs a time-out." Allison was right. Mothers need a time-out, too.

Lord, help me take the time each day to be alone with you.

NOVEMBER 2

The other day Sam was playing happily with one of his toys when Allison decided that she wanted to play with the same toy. She simply went up to Sam and jerked the toy right out of his hands. Of course, Sam let out a loud scream of protest and was about to come running to me for intervention when Allison tried to explain to him the reason for her aggressive behavior.

"Sam," she said in a most serious manner, "you're supposed to let me play with it. Remember, God wants us to share."

God wants us to share, but on whose terms? More often than we like to admit, our sharing habits are similar to Allison's. We may be conscientious recyclers, but we tend to "grab away" more than our fair share of the earth's resources. We may give regularly to our church and other charities, but we tend to "grab away" our gifts when portions of the money are spent in ways we do not agree with. We may share our used clothing with the needy, but we tend to support economic policies that "grab away" monies that could be used to assist the poor in truly helpful ways.

Yes, God indeed wants us to share, but on whose terms?

Oh God, help me to understand what it means to be generous. Help me to share in ways that are pleasing to you.

NOVEMBER 3

I said something that hurt Sam's feelings. It wasn't intentional, but he was right to be upset. He came to me trying to hold back his tears. "You hurt my feelings," he said as tears spilled out of his big brown eyes. Then he hugged me, crawled onto my lap, cuddled, and continued to cry as I told him over and over again how sorry I was. Within ten minutes he was feeling better. He looked up at me with a smile and said, "That's okay, Mommy. I still love you." Then he ran off to play.

What a lesson in forgiveness! If we adults could do what Sam was able to do, we would be much healthier and happier people. As adults, we tend to deal with our hurt and anger in unhealthy ways. We hide our feelings. We avoid the one who has hurt us. We want to hurt the one who first hurt us. We are unable to forgive freely and fully. We are unable to go on with our lives.

Instead of running away in anger, Sam took the initiative to confront me with what I had said. Instead of holding me at arm's length until I apologized, he crawled right up into my lap. Instead of ignoring or avoiding me, he hugged me. Instead of holding in his feelings, he cried. And when he felt that his anger had been heard, he was able to forgive and go on with his life.

Gracious God, help me to forgive.

NOVEMBER 4

"Allison, put your shoes on. We're running late."

"But Mommy, I can't find them. I've looked everywhere." Glancing down at my watch, I realized that we really were going to be late if Allison couldn't find her shoes within the next thirty seconds. When I went into her room to help her find them, I saw her playing on her bed. Her shoes were right in the middle of the floor, practically in front of her nose. Obviously, Allison hadn't looked very long or hard for her shoes.

How long and how hard do we look for God in our lives? In our quest to find God in our lives, it is easy to become distracted and overlook God's presence, especially if we look only in the most obvious places. When we pray, our minds wander. When we attempt to read an inspirational book, our children demand our attention. When we read the Bible, unanswered questions keep popping into our minds.

We need to remember, however, that there are other ways that we can discover God's powerful presence in our lives. When we look into the eyes of our children and respond with love, or when we volunteer an afternoon a month at the food bank, or when we share mutual joys and concerns with another mother who may not have the skills and resources to provide for her family as she would like, we can find God.

God's presence surrounds us constantly. All we need to do is look in the right places.

Surprising God, startle me with your presence today.

NOVEMBER 5

I have never hidden the fact that housekeeping is not one of my strengths. Last year, when my husband was out of town, when I was eight and a half months pregnant, and when I had a viral infection that sapped my energy for two weeks, my house became so disorganized that I practically had to dig a path to get from the living room to the kitchen. I became so overwhelmed by the thought of housecleaning that I was practically immobile to do anything about it. Then I received a phone call from a dear church member. "Helen, I don't want to offend you," she began, "but would you mind if I round up a few women to come over and help you clean your house?"

Under normal circumstances, I might well have taken offense and refused her offer. But at that particular time, I received her offer as a true blessing. She is an excellent housekeeper, and she was offering to share her gift with me.

Isn't that what Christian community is about? Sharing our strengths. Being vulnerable with our weaknesses. Rejoicing in one another's gifts. Helping others in times of need.

As the women began cleaning, I can't deny that I had to swallow a little pride. But it was worth swallowing, because I had been blessed by their wilingness to share their gifts with me—and by the reminder that I can use my own gifts to hlep others, especially other mothers, in their times of need.

God, giver of all good and perfect gifts, help me accept your many blessings and return them to others.

NOVEMBER 6

My children thrive on routine and ritual. Their bedtime ritual seems to be the most important one to them. Every night I have to recite "eenie-meenie-minie-mo" in order to determine which child's favorite book I read first. And every night the one whose book isn't chosen first feigns disappointment, knowing that tomorrow night his or her book will be the first read. As I tuck them into their beds, their blankets have to be arranged in a certain way, the door must be left halfway open, and the kitchen light must be left on. They must have a hug first, then a kiss, then a lullaby followed by another kiss on the cheek. By following this ritual, my children sleep securely throughout the night.

Routine and ritual are important to children and to us as people of faith. Leviticus, Numbers, and Deuteronomy are filled with rituals that enabled God's people to remain faithful during difficult times. While most Christians think that many of the Old Testament rituals have little value for us today, we must acknowledge the need for ritual and routine in our own spiritual lives.

My daily ritual includes getting up before the family is awake, making a cup of tea, and sitting quietly at the kitchen table with a devotional book or a Bible. My weekly ritual includes attending church each Sunday morning. Whether our rituals are simple or elaborate, they help provide order in the midst of chaos, security in the midst of fear, and direction in the midst of confusion.

God, thank you for providing order and security in my life, and help me demonstrate for my children the value of an ordered spiritual life.

NOVEMBER 7

Sam and Allison came inside after spending all morning playing in their sandbox. When I looked at Sam's face, I saw wet sand in both corners of his mouth. "Somebody's been eating sand," I said, trying to sound stern. Sam looked sheepishly at me, knowing that he had been caught, and tried to minimize his actions by saying, "I only ate two bites."

How many times have we used similar excuses to minimize our own behavior? We tell the police officer that we were only driving five miles per hour over the speed limit. We tell our overweight selves that we are only going to eat one small piece of that high-calorie chocolate mousse. We tell our children that we have only one more task to complete before we can give them our full attention.

What excuses do we give God for the many times we have fallen short of our Christian responsibilities? Do we try to justify the times we have failed to respond to human need? Do we minimize the times our behavior has reflected values we abhor? Or do we confess our shortcomings, ask God for forgiveness, and try to live according to the principles dictated by our faith?

O God, forgive me for the times I have fallen short of what you have required of me, and help me follow you more faithfully day by day.

NOVEMBER 8

One day last fall our neighbors took Allison and Sam on their first fishing trip. When they returned from their expedition a few hours later, Allison's face beamed with excitement as she showed me her catch—a fifteen-inch catfish. Sam was excited, too, as he told me about the little fish that he caught but had to throw back in the water so it could grow some more. My children's faces were filled with sheer joy as they told me over and over of their afternoon of fishing. I delighted in their enthusiasm and excitement.

Jesus told those who followed him that they were to become fishers of people, casting their nets with enthusiasm and drawing in people to hear about the exciting Good News that he had to offer. Today we need to recapture the excitement of catching that first fish as we witness our faith to others. We need to recapture the enthusiasm of children as we tell people over and over again the stories that changed our lives and can change their lives, too. As fishers of people, we need to regain the sense of anticipation as we experience the sheer joy of sharing the Good News.

O God, help me witness my faith to others with childlike enthusiasm.

NOVEMBER 9

There is something special about a mother's kiss that makes "owies" go away. My children come to me screaming in pain, showing me where they bumped their heads or where they scraped their knees or where they stubbed their toes. I take them in my arms, tell them how sorry I am that they are hurt, and gently kiss the exact spot that is causing them so much pain. And with that kiss, their tears immediately dry up, a smile replaces the frown, and they run off to play, completely cured.

As mothers, we often see ourselves as the primary caregivers and nurturers in the family. Because of this, it is often difficult for us to allow another to take care of us when we are hurt. Although many of our own "owies" can't be healed as easily or as quickly as our children's, our hurts can be healed if we allow ourselves to be vulnerable to God's nurturing power.

Throughout the Bible, God promises to be with us, to nurture us, to sustain us, and to protect us. The Psalms are filled with words of comfort and assurance. The Beatitudes can be a source of great comfort. Many of Paul's writings affirm God's constant and nurturing presence in our lives. It is important that we know where to look when we are in need of comfort.

God, you are our great Nurturer. Help me bring my hurts to you so that I can experience the healing comfort of your embracing arms.

NOVEMBER 10

I have a collection of the most beautiful rocks in the world. Never mind that most of them are pieces of gravel found in alleys and driveways. Never mind that a good many more are small red lava stones used to landscape neighbors' gardens. They are still the most beautiful rocks in the world. They are Sam's favorite rocks chosen carefully and given with love. To Sam, each rock he gives me is unique and special. He keeps track of them and becomes greatly offended when he catches me weeding my rock collection.

What a gift it is to be able to see value and beauty in the most ordinary things! Yet, if we think about it, there is nothing that is ordinary about God's creation. Each part of God's creation has its own unique beauty. When we look at our surroundings through the eyes of a happy and curious child, the world becomes an amazing place—a place where acorns are transformed into diamonds and ladybugs take on their own personalities, where swing sets become ships and pine trees become castles, where full moons become vanilla cookies and crescent moons become bananas. The world is, indeed, a marvelous place.

God, help me marvel at the beauty that surrounds me every day.

NOVEMBER 11

"Tell us that story again, Mommy," Allison and Sam begged. I had just finished telling them the same story for the third time, and yet they wanted to hear it again. My children never seem to tire of listening to stories. Although they enjoy books, they are especially fond of the stories I make up. Most of the stories I tell are about situations that are familiar to them—lost kittens, birthday parties, chipmunk families, and little boys and girls going on outings to the park. Allison and Sam relate my stories to themselves and become personally involved in the outcomes.

Jesus was well aware of the powerful nature of storytelling. The stories he told, although they were about ordinary people and events, captured his listeners' attention and fed their hunger for a new way of living in the world. Those who listened and heard went home transformed. Those who listened but did not hear went home angry.

Jesus' stories are well worth retelling to ourselves and to our children. The more we tell them, the more we become personally involved with the characters and the outcomes, and the more we open ourselves up to their transforming power.

O God, help me be open to your transforming power, and enable me to be a good storyteller so that my children also may be open to the transforming power of Jesus' stories.

NOVEMBER 12

One of the greatest challenges of motherhood is knowing when and how to respond to our children when they tease one another. Allison knows exactly which of Sam's buttons to push to cause him to scream at the top of his lungs. She does it quite deliberately, for it gives her a sense of power when she can cause such an immediate and intense reaction. Sam is quickly catching on to the art of teasing, and it won't be long before he'll be able to hold his own against his sister. But what is a mother to do?

A more sophisticated form of teasing constantly surrounds us as Christians. Every time we open the pages of our favorite magazine, we are teased by someone dangling a beauty product in front of our noses, saying, "Buy this. You'll look and feel years younger." Each time we turn on the television, we are teased by some fictional ideal family living out the American dream that few of us will ever achieve. Many of the times we read a self-help book, we are teased into believing that all our problems will be solved if we follow a few easy steps.

Perhaps the best way to avoid being teased is to ignore the teaser and do something else, something meaningful and constructive. Read the Bible. Volunteer at the community center. Teach a Sunday school class. The possibilities are endless.

The next time Allison teases Sam, I'll tell Sam, "Ignore her and she'll stop." Maybe we, too, should ignore those who tease us and concentrate on doing what God wants us to do.

Dear God, help me resist the teasers of the world.

NOVEMBER 13

Sam has always been a climber and a jumper. One of his favorite jumping spots is a steep set of stairs at our church. He mastered jumping off the lowest step about the same time he learned to walk. The second step was conquered not long after that. The third step now seems to be his favorite jumping spot. Not long ago, however, he stood on the fourth step and contemplated a jump. I was waiting for him at the bottom of the steps and instructed him quite firmly that he was not to jump from the fourth step because it was too high and he would most certainly hurt himself in the landing.

"But, Mommy, you can catch me," he said. And before I had the chance to respond, he jumped from the step and was about to land on his nose. I reached out and caught him just in time to prevent a nosebleed. "See, Mommy, I told you that you would catch me," he said with a confident smile. Sam's faith in me was unwavering. I did catch him, and he knew I would.

An unwavering faith in God is what many of us need to develop in our spiritual lives. Having unwavering confidence in God's presence enables us to take risks, to reach out, and to leap at challenging opportunities that come before us. An unwavering confidence in God's presence does not mean that we will never fail in the challenges of life. But it does mean that we can continue to live confidently and fully in spite of our failures, knowing that God will be there to catch us when we fall and to challenge us to take further risks with our lives.

God, thank you for a child's example of trust. Help me to trust you with my whole being and soul.

NOVEMBER 14

Competition comes naturally to my children, and I must admit that I use it to my advantage. In order to get Sam to pick up his toys, I make him race with himself by challenging him to put everything away by the time I count to twenty. At bedtime, Allison and Sam get their pajamas on without delay when I ask, "Who can get ready for bed first tonight?"

It's easy to encourage competition because it comes so naturally to children. It's harder, however, to encourage Jesus' teaching that "the last will be first and the first last" because it seems to go against human nature. Indeed, much of Jesus' teachings and actions seem to go against natural human instincts—turn the other cheek, give away all that you own, offer to go the extra mile.

As mothers, we must somehow encourage our children to value cooperation over competition, to think of others first and themselves later, to be selfless rather than selfish, to be last rather than first. For me, this is a tremendous challenge.

Yet I must accept the challenge if I am to show my children what it means to be a follower of Christ in today's world.

God, help me teach and live out your lessons of love.

NOVEMBER 15

"I'm thirsty, Mommy."

Whenever I hear those words, I know that my children have spotted a drinking fountain. There is something about drinking fountains that attracts children like flowers attract bees. My children don't mind that most of the water—usually lukewarm—runs down their cheeks and chins and gets their clothes soaking wet. They don't mind standing on their tiptoes and sticking out their tongues just so they can get a drop or two of water. Somehow, the stream of water that comes from a drinking fountain quenches their thirst much better than water from the faucet.

Many of us are thirsty, too—thirsty for the "living water" that will satisfy all who are seeking to know God in a deeply personal way. Jesus offered "living water" to a woman at the well, and she, like many of us today, did not fully understand the gift of life that was offered.

When I see my children scramble to a drinking fountain, I am reminded that I need to seek out the "living waters" offered by God—waters that will quench my soul's thirst for God, waters that are a basic necessity to my spiritual life. Just as my children cannot ignore a drinking fountain, so also I cannot afford to ignore opportunities that will lead me to the "living water" that will satisfy me in my spiritual journey—opportunities to serve, to share, to lead, and to love.

O God, help me continue to thirst after you.

NOVEMBER 16

We had just moved to a new town, and Allison, who was almost three, and I were making our first visit to the grocery store. I was selecting apples when I spotted some nice-looking melons in the next bin. As I took my hand off the grocery cart to examine the melons, Allison, who was riding in the cart, cried out, "Don't leave me, Mommy! I might get lonely!"

Most people, when faced with new or unfamiliar situations, experience some degree of loneliness. I feel lonely at large social gatherings where I know very few people. Those who are single may feel lonely at events oriented toward couples. Those who are new Christians and are trying to fit into a church family may feel lonely on Sunday mornings.

It is during times when we are feeling lonely that we need to seek God's assurance. If we ask, God will remain close beside us, embracing us, guiding us, giving us confidence and direction. All we need to do is recognize and confess our feelings of loneliness and say, "Don't leave me, God. I might get lonely." How reassuring it is to know that just as a concerned mother will respond to her child's request, so also God will respond to us.

Assuring God, stay by my side today.

NOVEMBER 17

It was almost time for lunch, and Sam, who was barely two years old at the time, was clinging to my legs as I tried to hustle about the kitchen making sandwiches. In order to avoid stepping on my son, I gave him an empty milk jug and the instruction to put it in the "recycle box," which is located near our back door. About five minutes later it was time to eat lunch, and Sam was nowhere to be found. When he didn't respond to my calls, I began a room-to-room search and asked my husband to search the neighborhood.

We tried to ignore the terrifying thoughts that kept popping into our heads as we called out Sam's name throughout the house and the neighborhood. After twenty minutes of frantic searching, we found our son! He had gone to the community recycling bins two and half blocks away to deposit the milk jug!

Every mother experiences at one time or another the feelings I had as I took Sam into my shaking arms—feelings of overwhelming relief, joy, concern, and, most of all, love. My experience helped me to understand God's love and concern for each of us. I would have searched for Sam for as long as it took to find him, but God searches even more diligently for the lost children of the world— children lost to selfishness and greed, children lost to poverty and oppression, children lost to abuse and addiction. For twenty frightening minutes, all of my limited energy was focused on finding my son, but God's unlimited energy goes on forever as God seeks out the lost.

As difficult as it is for me to comprehend, I know from the depth of my being that God's love and concern for me—and for all of God's children—is greater even than my love for my own children. That's some kind of love!

Dear God, thank you for loving me.

NOVEMBER 18

It was a dismal November day. The drizzling rain darkened the sky, and at 9:00 A.M. it was still dark outside. Although I had a long list of errands to run, the rain seemed to stop all my energy. My errands would have to wait until tomorrow. As I was lamenting the weather, Allison tried to lift my spirits. "I like rainy days," she insisted, "because I get to paint!"

Allison was right. On sunny autumn days, outdoor activities seem to occupy much of our time. We play at the park, walk to the library, feed the ducks, or run errands. We are on the go much of the time. But on rainy days, as Allison reminded me, we have the luxury of staying home and doing things that we don't often give ourselves the time to do.

Allison painted pictures of rainbows all morning long, and I curled up with a good book. It was a beautiful day after all.

Regardless of our situation, we mothers know that sometimes things don't turn out as we'd like them to. But may we always remember to look for the opportunities and blessings that new or unexpected situations bring.

Thank you, God, for rainy days and unforeseen opportunities.

NOVEMBER 19

My husband and I spent many hours preparing for the birth of our third child. We reviewed the relaxation and breathing techniques. We re-read books on pregnancy and childbirth. We lovingly prepared the nursery. Although we could not predict the exact day or hour that our baby would arrive, we waited with joyous anticipation, for we knew that we were well prepared.

In spite of all our preparations, my labor didn't proceed as we had expected. My contractions were much longer and more painful than I had anticipated, and I began to panic when I thought of experiencing hours of such intense pain. Fortunately—and again unexpectedly—Jonathan arrived at the end of the first hour of hard labor. The unbearable pain I had experienced just moments ago was almost forgotten as feelings of indescribable joy came over me when I held my nine-pound miracle for the first time.

Those of us who have given birth may be able to understand more fully Jesus' teachings about the kingdom of heaven. We have prepared ourselves well, yet the actual event of childbirth comes as a surprise and goes beyond our wildest expectations. We have experienced pain, but the joy of giving birth far surpasses the intensity of that pain.

Isn't that part of what the kingdom of heaven is about? Although Jesus did not use the image of childbirth in his teachings about the kingdom of heaven, he did teach that those who are prepared for the kingdom can wait in eager anticipation, knowing that although there may be pain along the way, they will experience surprise beyond belief, joy beyond expectation, and life beyond life.

Almighty God, thank you for the miracle of life.

NOVEMBER 20

As I rock Jonathan to sleep each evening, a sense of awe overcomes me. I count each of his tiny fingers and toes. I study the expressions on his face. I listen to his breathing. I touch his soft skin. And I thank God for the miracle that I am holding—the miracle of life.

I am relaxed with Jonathan, perhaps because he is my third child and experience has taught me not to jump at every cough or to worry excessively if he fusses. I savor every moment with him, knowing that he will be tiny for only a short time. He is, indeed, a miracle.

Tonight as I rock Jonathan to sleep, I pray this prayer:

God, help me maintain my sense of awe when Jonathan breaks something irreplaceable. Help me stay relaxed as I scrub his red crayon marks off the wall. Help me thank you for the miracle of Jonathan as I mop orange juice off the floor for the third time in a day.

As I place Jonathan into his crib, he snuggles into the blanket and softly sighs. I know that he will sleep peacefully for several hours. Yes, he is a miracle.

God, thank you for the miracle of children. As my children grow, may I continue to appreciate the miracles that they are.

NOVEMBER 21

With three young children, it is very difficult for me to find time to be alone. One evening, I desperately needed some time to myself, so I drew a hot bath and instructed my children to go to their father if they needed anything. As I was about to lock myself in the bathroom, Allison volunteered, "Mommy, I'll stay right by the door so you won't be lonely." How could I refuse such an unselfish offer? For the next twenty minutes I was serenaded through the bathroom door—and, believe me, I was *not* lonely!

Time to be alone is a luxury that too few mothers indulge in. On second thought, time to be alone is not a luxury but a necessity that we need to schedule into our lives just as we schedule doctor appointments, meetings, and play time with our children. Whether we allow our husbands or someone else to take total responsibility for our children for fifteen minutes or several hours, once a week or once a month, we need time to be alone—alone not to plan tomorrow's activities or to organize our day, alone not to meditate (although we need private time with God, too), but alone simply to relax, to enjoy, and to appreciate a rare moment of solitude. It's a gift that only we can give ourselves.

Gracious God, help me take the time to be alone—but not be lonely.

NOVEMBER 22

The other day I sent Allison to the bathroom to wash her face. Allison trotted toward the bathroom to carry out her task—or so I thought. Five minutes later she came to me with a pencil and paper asking me to help her write a letter to her grandmother. Seeing that her face had not been touched, I refocused her attention and sent her back to the bathroom. Five more minutes passed, and I heard her singing in the bathroom. When I saw her with a still dirty face, I reminded her that her current job was not to sing but to clean. Yet another five minutes passed, and I found my dirty-faced daughter in her room hosting a tea party for her doll. As I led her to the bathroom she explained, "There are so many things to do that I keep on forgetting what I'm supposed to do."

Many of us have the attention span of a five-year-old when it comes to praying. The other day as I sat down to pray, I was distracted by the thought that I needed to defrost the chicken we were having for dinner. Then I remembered that tomorrow it is my turn to provide preschool snacks. By the time I got back to my prayer, the baby was demanding to be fed.

It takes discipline and practice to develop a rich prayer life. I have found that having a prayer partner helps me to be more disciplined in my prayers. Some of my friends say that praying out loud or praying in the shower helps them stay focused on their task. Another busy mother keeps a pad and pen handy as she prays and simply jots down the distracting thoughts that invade her prayers, promising to attend to them at a more appropriate time.

The methods we employ to help us deal with our distractions are not important. What is important is that we find ways to spend quality time in developing a closer relationship with God.

O God, be patient with me as I try to find ways to overcome the distractions that interrupt my time alone with you.

NOVEMBER 23

"Please, can I have just *one more* cookie?" Sam pleaded, holding up his index finger to emphasize his desire. "I promise

I'll eat all my dinner and take a bath and go to bed all by myself tonight. Just one more cookie."

Sam is a real bargainer. He knows what to say to try to get me to see things his way. He would promise me the moon if he thought it would help him get what he wants. Sometimes the bargain he strikes with me works. Most of the time it doesn't.

How many times have we bargained with God? How many times have we, from sick beds, promised to attend church more regularly if God will make us well? How may times have we told God that we'll increase our giving if God blesses us with a raise at work? How many times have we told God that we'll spend more time with our children if only God will help us find and finance our dream home?

Bargaining must be an integral part of human nature. God doesn't love us any less for trying to strike a bargain, but God probably takes our calculated pleas as seriously as we take our children's! Rather than trying to strike a bargain with God to get what *we* want, wouldn't it be better to listen, through prayer, to what God wants for and from us?

Gracious God, help me listen for your will in my life.

NOVEMBER 24

Allison takes pride in her ability to say "adult prayers" at the dinner table. Her prayers usually begin like a formal invocation given during Sunday worship. Then she slips in a few phrases from the Lord's Prayer. But her favorite part of her prayer is when she begins her "thank you's." She always thanks God for healthy food and for her family. But she thanks God for other things too—for anything that catches her eye or pops into her head—clocks, houses, trees, grass, refrigerators, lights, flowers, forks, toasters, and so forth. When we encourage her to say "Amen" before her dinner gets cold, she protests until she is able to finish her prayer on her own terms.

Thanksgiving is a time when many of us pause to give thanks for our many blessings. Often we give our prayers of thanks in generalities rather than specifics. We thank God for our families, but we don't name individuals. We thank God for our material blessings, but we don't identify them. We thank God for the ways that God has worked in our lives, but we don't mention specific events.

This Thanksgiving I'm going to take a lesson I learned from Allison and include as many specific blessings in my prayers as I can think of. By naming each blessing, I will become more aware of the many gifts I have received and of how truly blessed I am. And who cares if my dinner gets a little cold!

Almighty God, help me appreciate the many gifts you have bestowed upon me—especially the gift of my children.

NOVEMBER 25

When we think of *family,* we naturally think of our immediate and extended family members; but there is another family that is extremely important to us—and to our children.

Several years ago, my husband and I offered to host our family's Thanksgiving dinner. My husband worked very hard to figure out ways to accommodate all of our out-of-town guests while I spent most of the month in various stages of preparing a traditional Thanksgiving feast. I wanted this Thanksgiving to be perfect.

Two days before Thanksgiving, we experienced a snowstorm that closed down the roads leading to our town, and all of our Thanksgiving plans were ruined. I was in tears. Not only would I miss seeing my family, but I also had a refrigerator filled with food that my husband and I could not possibly eat before it spoiled. As we were wallowing in self-pity, it occurred to us that others must be experiencing similar disappointment. We began making phone calls, and within a matter of hours we had organized a Thanksgiving celebration with our church family.

A Thanksgiving that could have been cold and lonely was transformed into a day of warmth and happiness as sisters and brothers in Christ shared in the ample food, fun, and fellowship that the day had to offer. How thankful I am for my church family!

Generous God, thank you for my brothers and sisters in Christ, who enrich my life and the lives of my children.

NOVEMBER 26

At 2:30 every morning, Jonathan is hungry. His soft cries awaken me and I pick him up, settle into a rocking chair, and offer him my milk. Jonathan is totally dependent on me and his father to meet his needs. When he is hungry, I feed him. When he is tired, we rock him. When he is lonely, we comfort him. Jonathan trusts us to take care of all his needs. He doesn't question his dependence upon us. To him, dependence is literally a necessity of life.

Dependence was also a necessity of life to the people of Israel as they wandered through the wilderness under the leadership of Moses. God took care of them just as a mother takes care of her infant child. God fed them, comforted them, watched over them, and protected them. As long as they trusted in God and did not question their dependence upon their Deliverer, they were cared for.

We, too, must allow ourselves to be dependent upon God. We must realize that by trusting totally in God alone, we will be truly fed, truly comforted, and truly secure. We need somehow to capture the gifts that an infant seems to have naturally—the gift of being dependent without feeling threatened, the gift of trusting without question. If we can reclaim those gifts within us, we will be one step closer to full communion with God.

Comforting God, help me surrender myself to you.

NOVEMBER 27

Not long ago I was helping Allison dress for a social event. I pulled several dresses out of the closet and asked her to choose the one she wanted to wear. She looked at each dress carefully and then announced, "I think I'll wear pants today."

"But all the other girls will be wearing nice dresses," I explained, trying to convince her to see things my way.

"I don't care, Mommy," she responded. "It's good to be different."

As I reflected on our short conversation, I remembered that Jesus, too, was different. He was not afraid to go against the status quo with his actions and words. Everywhere he went, he challenged the thinking of his day. He healed on the Sabbath. He associated with those shunned by society. He taught that the last shall be first. And everywhere he went, people recognized that he was, indeed, different.

I have never been one to challenge the status quo in radical ways, although there are times that I wish I had the courage to be different. Allison reminded me, in her own simple way, that I, as a Christian, am called to be different. While others sleep in on Sunday morning, I need to go to church. While others build their material assets, I need to make decisions to limit my material possessions. While others turn their backs to the injustice in their communities, I need to respond to the many needs that I see. While others rely strictly on themselves, I need to rely more on God, following the One who was never afraid to be different.

God, give me and my children the courage to be different.

NOVEMBER 28

Not long ago, Sam was given his first dollar bill. That evening we went out to eat, and Sam was determined to treat us to dinner with his money. The moment we stepped into the restaurant, Sam tried to give the cashier his money. When she refused to accept it, Sam waved his bill and offered it to the waitress. She didn't notice him as she hustled by. Not to be discouraged, Sam followed the waitress around the dining room until he caught her attention. "Here," he said, as he held up his dollar. "This is for you."

The waitress looked quite surprised by his offer. After all, she hadn't done anything, so why was this little boy offering her all that he had? She looked to my husband and me for guidance. When we motioned that it was okay for her to accept the money, she stooped down, took the dollar bill, and thanked him. She continued to thank him—and us—by offering the best table service we had ever received.

Sam's exchange with the waitress helped me to understand God's grace more fully. Just as Sam was persistent in finding someone who would accept what he had to offer, so also God is continually offering grace to anyone who will accept it. Just as the waitress had done nothing to deserve Sam's dollar, so also nothing that we can do will ever earn God's grace, for it cannot be bought. Just as the waitress looked to us to help her know how to respond to Sam, so also we ought to look to Christ to guide us in our decisions.

God's gift of grace is always offered. All we need to do is accept it and say "thank you" through our words and service.

O God, thank you for your unconditional gift of grace.

NOVEMBER 29

Sam had a pair of shoes that he refused to give up. They were comfortable, easy for him to put on by himself, and best of all, they had turtles on them! Throughout the hot summer, he refused to wear sandals or light-weight canvas shoes, opting instead for his heavy black "turtle shoes" and socks that had to be pulled up to his knees. As the summer progressed, it became obvious that his shoes were getting too small, yet Sam still insisted on cramming his feet into them, ignoring the new summer play shoes we had purchased for him.

It wasn't until we gave him a pair of leather high-top shoes with fluorescent laces that he finally admitted that his turtle shoes were hurting his feet. The moment he tried on his new shoes, he totally lost interest in his old ones and enthusiastically showed off his new ones to everyone he saw.

The scribes and Pharisees of Jesus' day refused to give up their "old shoes" even when they were offered something new and better. Their rigid interpretation of the law was like a pair of old shoes that was comfortable but didn't have enough space to allow further growth. Jesus offered something new, and those who accepted what Jesus had to offer abandoned their old ways and, like Sam with a new pair of shoes, enthusiastically told others about their new way of life.

The apostle Paul was well aware of the stark contrast between old and new when he reminded his Christian friends in Corinth that "if anyone is in Christ, there is a new creation: everything old has passed away; see, everything has become new" (II Corinthians 5:17). Although it is sometimes difficult to give up old and comfortable ways of life, Christ offers something new and better.

O God, enable me to be open to the new ways you reveal yourself to me. And as my children grow and change, enable me to embrace the new and unfamiliar with joy and enthusiasm.

NOVEMBER 30

I don't remember exactly when Allison began to talk. All I know is that over a period of about two years her coos became babbles, her babbles became syllables, her syllables became words, and her words became sentences. By the time she was two years old, her speech was fluent and complex. .

On the other hand, Sam's speech developed in a totally different manner. When he was two and a half years old, his speech was so limited that the pediatrician referred him to a speech therapist for further evaluation. Then one day Sam suddenly spoke in full sentences, and he hasn't stopped talking since!

Faith development is as varied and individual as speech development. Beacuse I was born into a Christian home and attended church every Sunday, my faith journey has been gradual and fairly steady. I can identify several important milestones in the development of my faith, but I cannot pinpoint the exact time and place that I first believed in God through Christ. In contrast, a friend of mine had a dramatic conversion experience several years ago, and she is able to point to the precise moment that her faith was born.

It matters not how or when our faith journey began. The important thing is that we allow our faith in God through Christ to guide us through life's journey, to give us strength when we are troubled, to challenge us when we stray, and to remind us of God's constant presence in our lives.

Gracious God, guide me as I continue to grow in faith and to nurture the faith development of my children.

DECEMBER

A Mother's Conversations

PATRICIA D. BROWN

DECEMBER 1

'm talking to my friend as I move the phone to glance at the clock.

"I don't think I can make it. He's cutting another tooth—and I'm losing sleep!"

She tells me that a person we both know just received her second mammogram reading. It's positive, and she is scheduled for a lumpectomy.

"Great," I say. "So I'm not supposed to complain; I'm supposed to feel better because I should remember things could be worse?" It's a tactic that only seems to work in theory.

"You know what might help you?" she asks.

"What?"

"Get your mind off teething. You know this won't last forever. Start thinking about good things. What do you enjoy doing most?" she asks with a hopeful tone.

"I like eating Ben and Jerry's cookie dough ice cream."

"That's a good start."

"But even Ben and Jerry probably don't appreciate fat women, so that's out." I won't be consoled.

"You still have your sense of humor. That's a plus in your life—especially now," she says encouragingly.

"Look," I say, "I appreciate what you're trying to do. But could you stop giving me advice and just be there for me?" I stop to listen. I think I hear my son crying again.

"I'm here," she says.

We hang up. I go to my son's room, pick him up, and move to the familiar rocking chair in the corner. We rock back and forth together in the dark.

The next day I leave a message on my friend's machine.

"Hello. Thanks for being there. Call me when you have time."

Gracious God, thank you for being present through the people in my life. I am grateful for understanding friends who help me make it through the difficult challenges of life and motherhood.

DECEMBER 2

I call to tell my friend that I've really had it.

"Four years old," I say, "and Stephen still hasn't given up his pacifier. I've tried everything. Nothing works."

"Yes," my friend says—she's heard me say this before—"it can really get annoying."

"It's not just the poofer" (the word we've adopted for that slimy plastic thing that protrudes from my son's mouth), "it's that I feel like a failure. People look at me disgustedly as if I'm the worst mother in the world."

"Remember when you couldn't potty train him?" she sympathetically reminds me. "Remember that in his own good time he learned?"

"True," I say hesitantly, not really wanting to be consoled. I recall that quizzical day when my son, under his own volition, climbed right up to the "throne" when I wasn't even paying attention.

"I can't believe we are having this conversation," I continue. "I have a major conference and two papers due in the coming days, and I'm talking about pacifiers and toilet training!"

"Stay cool," my friend says. "It will be the same way this time. Kids are like that. Only worry if he still has the pacifier in his mouth when it's time to start kindergarten. They have their own timetable, known only to them and, perhaps, to God."

After we hang up, I think about what my friend has said, and I wonder if God ever loses patience with us when we follow our own timetables. Then I remind myself that despite our hesitance—and sometimes our fear—God's constant love is ever present, reassuring and encouraging us to take the next step in faith.

Dear God, thank you for having patience with me as I grow in grace. And help me to have patience with my growing child.

DECEMBER 3

"How do you do, Ms. Bear? It's so good to meet you, Mr. Raccoon." I shake the paws of our guests as I sit down at the low table for the tea party, hiding the kitchen sponge out of sight.

"Would you like some tea?" my four-year-old asks.

"Yes, thank you," I say as I note the napkin, plate, cup, and saucer at each place. My son pours juice from the miniature teapot.

"Would you like some sugar or milk in your tea?" he asks with a touch of a British accent. He's quite proper.

"No, thank you."

"I baked these delicious cookies myself this morning," he informs me. "Would you care for one?"

"Yes, I believe I will have one."

He places a graham cracker on each plate, including that of Ms. Bear and Mr. Raccoon, who soon confess they are simply too full to eat them. So we eat the crackers to save our guests the embarrassment of leaving their plates untouched.

Dear God, thank you for the special moments I share with my children in play. These moments become cherished memories that bring me joy again and again.

DECEMBER 4

"My husband's hand is the one Stephen seeks to hold when taking a stroll," I say to my friend. "His dad's lap is the one he crawls up on to relate the highs and lows of his day. His dad's opinion is the one he appears to value more. Truth be told— all mothering notions aside—my husband is the parent who is the anchor in my son's life."

"And how do you feel about that?" my friend and confidante asks. I hate being asked such a rhetorical question, and yet I find relief in finally putting my thoughts into words.

"I certainly don't feel guilty," I answer. And, as an afterthought, I ask, "Should I feel guilty about not feeling guilty?"

"I don't think so," she says.

"What I really feel is relief—relief that his whole life doesn't hinge on me."

My longtime friend and I both lived through the weighty years of single motherhood. With our husbands absent, hers through divorce and mine through death, we remember the tiring years of doing it alone. We've both remarried now, and I have since had a child with my second husband.

"I feel the same way," she says, thinking of her almost four-year-old. "With Jim now part of the family, it's really freed me to be a mother in the ways I know how and feel comfortable. I don't have to be the be-all-and-do-all parent . . . and I suspect it has freed our kids, too."

I smile knowingly. The trials of the past lend perspective and wisdom to the present.

Dear God, it feels good to be a part of my child's world, but not all of it. Help me always to remember that I cannot and should not be "everything" to my child.

DECEMBER 5

My friend calls to tell me that "it's really over."

"Two years now, and we can't get her out of our bed!" she says. I know she's not talking about another woman but about her toddler.

"She starts out in her bed but eventually climbs into ours," she continues. "I saw a TV show yesterday about sex and marriage. I wanted to call in and say, 'Sex life? Who has a sex life?'"

"Sex lives are nice," I say.

"I told my husband that if we don't get her out of our bed soon, I'm moving to another room. They can have the bed!" She sobs and tells me how she misses being held a certain way.

"Tell him you need him to hold you that way," I suggest.

"I've been telling him that," she says, "but I'll tell him again."

As I come in from work the next day, the answering machine is blinking.

"Hello, friend. We're going away for the weekend—without the 'other woman'—to see if there is sex after babies after all!"

Dear God, you understand a mother's mixed emotions for her child. We love our children so much, and yet there are moments when we long for uninterrupted "private time"—with ourselves, our husbands, or others. Help us through this difficult and yet joyful transition in our lives, and thank you for understanding.

DECEMBER 6

"Mommy, today I got four stars and a certificate for being the best boy in class."

"That's great, honey," I say to my five-year-old on the other end of the line.

"And Jeffrey hit Jennifer again. He's really bad. And the teacher made him sit in the corner."

"I'll bet Jennifer cried," I add to the story line.

"Yeah," he acknowledges and then scurries on to other stories. "Dad says we can go and get a movie video tonight, because it's Friday and I don't have to go to school tomorrow. Did you know that?" He continues telling me the details of his day.

It's not that I feel guilty traveling away from my son on nights like tonight. It's just that I miss living in the constancy and ordinary parts of his day.

"Mom?"

"Yes?"

"I have to go now. Do you want to talk to Dad?" He hands the phone off before I can respond.

My being away is a normal part of life for my son. It's all he's ever known. I doubt if it will ever feel "normal" to me. Although being apart from him for even a short time is not easy, at least I am able to reassure him of my love and concern by talking with him on the phone. Daily communication is so important to a parent-child relationship.

Daily communication is also important to our relationship with God. Knowing that God is only a prayer away can help us make it through even the most difficult of days.

Dear God, keep my child safe in my absence, and help me to show my love even when I am away from home. As I face each day, may I remember that you are only a prayer away.

DECEMBER 7

My friend calls me in tears.

"You're going to get through this," I say.

"I'm fat," she sniffs, "and I'm old."

"I'm fatter and older than you," I respond. "You can't complain about being fat and old to someone who is fatter and older."

"I'm starving," she says. "It's all this fat left over from having the baby. I haven't eaten all week, and the scale went up one pound! I just can't diet any more!"

"What's *really* wrong?" I ask.

"I asked him if he still loves me, and he said yes."

"That's good," I say.

"But when I ask him why, he can't tell me. Maybe he doesn't love me anymore. Maybe I don't love him, either."

I tell her of the years of change my marriage has weathered before offering a final piece of advice.

"The thing about marriage is that it keeps changing. It never stays the same. What I mean is that it's okay to have different feelings for your husband. It doesn't mean that he doesn't love you or that you don't love him."

There's a long silence on the line.

"I guess I'll stay on my diet," she says, "at least for today. Tomorrow I'll decide again."

God, change is never easy, and sometimes it's even frightening. Motherhood has brought so many changes into every realm of my life. Help me face the changes and grow through them, one day at a time.

DECEMBER 8

I think about my family as I lie still on the queen-size bed we bought after my youngest son was born so that I could nurse him beside me and then fall back to sleep. It was the only way I could get the rest needed to maintain a hectic work schedule. Life wasn't always like this, I think to myself.

The next day I am having a cup of coffee and talking to my friend on the phone. "Family life is a roller coaster," I say.

She tells me of the years she hated, adored, championed, and commiserated with her family.

"One morning you wake up and see them lying beside you, their bed clothes scattered," she says, "and you think, 'How vulnerable and sweet they are. I must be the most blessed woman alive.' Another day you see this guy in bed beside you and a baby as well and think, 'Who are these people in my life? What happened to simpler times?' And you dream of getting up and walking out the front door, never to return."

"So what do you do when you're thinking of running away?" I ask.

"I just picture what life would be like without them. I imagine going to a museum alone one day, my newspaper tucked under my arm, and as I ascend the steps, there they are in their jeans and T-shirts—and they've found a new wife and mother who is standing with them. I don't like it. I want to be the one laughing through their escapades."

The next morning I sit on the edge of the bed and count my blessings.

God, I'm so thankful for my family, even though sometimes I think life would be simpler without them.

DECEMBER 9

Stephen comes home with Sunday school papers on the creation story as well as a plastic margarine tub containing soil and seeds.

"My teacher said I have to water these seeds until the green leaves appear."

"Seeds need water to grow," I agree.

"Then she said I have to put the plant in the window so it can get light."

"Sunshine will make it green," I say. With the container now on the windowsill, he runs from the room and returns with an alarm clock.

"What are you doing with that?" I ask.

"I'm putting it with my plant. My teacher said my plant will need light, water, and time to grow."

Dear God, as I strive to teach my child, remind me again and again that some of life's lessons can be learned only with time.

DECEMBER 10

My friend calls me one afternoon.

"I'm thinking of having an affair," she says matter-of-factly.

"Really?" I ask, my attention piqued.

"Sure. Why not? My family would never notice. They treat me like a piece of furniture. They take me so much for granted."

"With whom?" I ask exploringly, knowing that she's only half serious. She's serious about the take-me-for-granted-like-a-piece-of-furniture part.

"Perhaps with the milkman—if we had one," she says with a stifled laugh.

"You sound bored," I say, knowing she's nearing the end of her two-month maternity leave. "Perhaps you'll feel more appreciated and valued once you're back to work."

"It's true; I need to get out. I never thought I'd be so eager to get back to the job. It's not that I don't love spending time with the new baby, but . . ." She pauses.

"But you don't expect the baby or your family to fulfill all your life's expectations," I say. "That sounds healthy to me."

I hear her deep sigh on the other end. From one mother to another, her sigh says more than words ever could.

Dear God, it's not easy deciding whether to stay at home or return to work. Most of us don't even have a choice, and that's not easy, either. Be with each of us as we prayerfully consider the needs of our children and families as well as our own needs, and, regardless of our choice, help us to be the best mothers we can be.

DECEMBER 11

"Of course you're feeling bewildered," my friend says as she assures me of my sanity. "No one knows how to do it. We're making this up as we go."

"It seems like I have to do it all, and do it excellently," I say. "I feel like everyone's watching me to see if I can have a career, two kids, a husband, and still keep my sanity. I want to be a good Christian and a good example of a contemporary woman, but, to be honest, it just gets to be too much sometimes."

"I think you're confused," my friend says. "You're talking about trying to be a super woman, not a contemporary woman."

I don't feel comforted to think that I am not only insane but also confused.

"I feel lied to," I explain. "I thought I could do it all. And I feel like I'm deceiving others. I don't want to live one life and espouse another. It's hypocritical. I don't want to send the message, 'You can do it all; look at me.' "

She lets me ramble on, and then she says, "For a long time my husband and I were confused about what our roles were. They certainly were not the roles our parents followed, but neither were they the roles from the 'feminist handbook.' We tried to live in prescribed ideals. We concealed our feelings and beliefs about each other. It was during a time when you were either a feminist or a sexist. The demands were rigid."

My friend continues with words of wisdom. "You love your husband and sons. You just want them to be people who care about equality and justice as much as you do."

There's silence on the line as we both consider this.

"It's the 'human factor,' " I lament. "You aim for the ideals and live in the reality of who you are. So where does that leave us today?" I ask.

"It leave us to make it up as we go."

Dear God, each day we wake up and clutch onto our integrity as we wonder what we must choose to compromise of ourselves. Despite what some might have us believe, we can't do it all. Help us to remember that you don't expect us to be "super women," but just to do the best we can. And help us to make wise decisions as we are faced with the reality of many choices.

DECEMBER 12

"Yeah, I suffered a momentary stab of 'daddy envy' the first time my little one crawled into his dad's side of the bed one lazy Saturday morning," I confide to my friend.

"It's no wonder they love their dads so much," she says. "I mean, who else takes them for fast food whenever they want it and lets them stay in their pajamas until noon? I think it's the Peter Pan/father-son syndrome."

She pauses and then continues, "Sometimes it's hard not feeling like number one in your kids' lives. Do you think we're betraying our long lineage of female matriarchy?"

"No," I reply. "I think we're just living the mommy role differently. When my youngest needs a bandage or a lap to sit on, he finds his dad. But when he wants to dance to his favorite record or play a game, he finds me. I guess it all became clear the day my youngest asked me, 'Mom, who do you love best?' I gave him the standard—that I love them both. It was at that moment that I realized that I really do love both of my children not more or less, just differently."

Dear God, thank you for children who don't love one parent more or less, just differently. And thank you for giving us hearts that have room enough for every family member—regardless of how many there may be.

DECEMBER 13

I sit at the kitchen table as I write and talk to my husband.

"I remember the times my father would cut my bangs when I was a child," I say. "He would pick me up, set me on the countertop, and, with scissors in hand, carefully clip away."

It was a rare moment in a family of five children—rare in its touch and its single concern. It was also one of the few times that I can recall direct contact with my father.

"Fathers had it rough then," I continue in my reflection. "So much responsibility dictated by society—to be the sole supporters of their families, with everyone's happiness seeming to depend on them."

My husband is busy chopping lettuce for the evening's meal. As a registered nurse and one of two equal wage earners in the family, he has more freedom to change jobs, care for skinned knees, play in the treehouse, or cook the macaroni and cheese. So many more choices.

"Most important," my husband adds, "I have the opportunity to really be there for my kids. I wouldn't want to miss the day-to-day caring that my father missed."

He must be remembering what it was like to be one of six children, I think to myself.

"I think we all were cheated," I say. "I needed him so, but he just couldn't be there for me. I wish he had been." Sadness sweeps over me like a silent rain.

"I know you do," he says as he sets aside his task and hugs me.

Dear God, many of us grieve for lost time or lost relationships with our fathers. Help us to recognize the important role fathers

*and adult male relatives or friends play in the lives of our chil-
dren, and enable us to make time for our children to enjoy these
special relationships.*

DECEMBER 14

"The Sunday school superintendent still thinks Ward and
June Cleaver live next door," my friend says over coffee. "If I
get one more permission letter asking for a 'parent's signature,' I'll scream!"

My neighbor, a grandmother, is rearing one of the nation's
61 percent of children who will live in a single adult household at some time in their lives.

"They should just have a line for the 'primary caregiver,' "
she continues. "At least in this neighborhood, blood relations
don't cut it anymore. And how do they think Annie feels—
with a letter addressed 'To the parents of . . .'? If she hands it
to me, does that make her disloyal to her mother, who simply
cannot rear her?"

I imagine Ward and June growing pale.

"Let's face it," I reply. "You're not alone. The dad-at-the-
office and mom-at-home family is no longer the standard. For
most families, it's a financial necessity for all able adults to
work."

"Yeah, for us the Cleaver family is as unrealistic as the super-
heroes on the Saturday-morning cartoons."

"So," I ask hesitantly, "what are you going to do about the
letter?"

"Well, of course I plan to let Annie participate in the Christmas pageant. But I think I'll make it a point to talk to the
superintendent after church on Sunday."

*Dear God, in these shifting times, help us to be sensitive to the life
situations of others. And thank you for the many loving caregivers who joyfully and willingly assume the role of parent.*

DECEMBER 15

I walk down the street to invite my friend and her toddler to dinner. As we sit at her kitchen table, she bursts into tears. I wait for a pause in what has now turned to sobs, and then I ask, "Now tell me what's wrong. What's the matter?"

My friend glances up from her coffee cup, tears running down her face. "I don't know," she says, continuing to cry.

"I have time," I say. "Why don't you just tell me, one thing at a time."

"Well," she answers, "it just seems that since I lost my job, I've felt so useless. I'd put so much of my life into my work."

"Being laid off like that really wasn't fair," I reply. My neighbor has been out of work for six months. The company simply closed its doors and left town.

"Now we're looking at food stamps—maybe even welfare," she says sadly.

We avoid meeting eyes. I tell her that after our first baby was born, my husband became ill and had a long hospital stay, and we had to go on welfare and food stamps.

"It was embarrassing," I say. "Social workers patronized us. The grocery store clerk checking out my purchases judged each item I bought. My husband couldn't work, and my part-time job paid $2.85 an hour. It was the only time in my life I didn't have to worry about my weight! The Women Infants Children [WIC] program enrollment was filled, and I dropped twenty pounds nursing the baby."

It feels strange sharing these details of my life. I am surprised at the grief and embarrassment that creep into my voice, even this many years later.

"So what did you do?" she asks.

We pour another cup of coffee, and I hand her another tissue.

"It was not what I did," I say. "It was what an older couple from the church neighborhood did. They told me to bring my

318

baby down and they would feed him. In reality, they fed all three of us; they got us through the winter."

We sit, quietly sipping our coffee, each in her own thoughts.

"We'll be eating around six," I say, drinking the final drops of a now-empty cup. "See you then?"

Our eyes meet in a smile. We understand.

God, thank you for all the experiences of life, even the hard ones. When hard times do come, give us the courage to allow others to help, for it is through others that you reach out to us and our children with loving arms.

DECEMBER 16

I tell my husband about my accident.

"When I stepped off the curb, I didn't see through the slush and snow to the drainage grill beneath that caught my heel, causing me to fall," I explain. "I must have looked really silly falling like a heap with my arms waving. I thought I was a goner."

I'm in fairly good physical shape, and I'm not prone to break my stride. So the fall came as a big surprise to me.

"Well, thank goodness you're all right," he said reassuringly. "The cuts on your knee will heal."

A young woman dressed in sweats had stopped on the busy street to ask if I was all right. "Sure, I'm fine," I'd said, getting up quickly. She had helped me gather my papers and shoulder bag, which were scattered about me. "I can't believe I fell. Thank you," I'd said to her, still dazed. She had smiled—what looked like a smirk at the time—and walked on.

I wish I could consider the incident humorous, but I don't. Instead I feel like a punch line to a bad joke. I now understand why my youngest son was so angry last week when he tripped over the edge of the seesaw and fell onto the mats. He had tumbled in such a floundering fashion that I'd laughed. "It's not funny!" he had yelled. "Don't be so touchy," I had replied. Now I see how "unfunny" it was. "Don't be so touchy"? What a stupid thing to say.

Even a mother doesn't have the right to tell her son where the tender spots of life are. He must learn this for himself. But a mother does have the responsibility to consider her son's feelings and perspective before offering advice or judgment. I'm grateful for the reminder.

Dear God, thank you for reminding me to view life from the eyes of my child.

DECEMBER 17

"She has so much to look forward to," I say half jokingly to my associate who has joined me for a coffee break at work. We're talking about a mutual friend who just gave birth to her first child.

"Did you see that nursery she put together?" my friend asks. "Everything was so picture-perfect. I tried to tell her to enjoy it while she could—that after the baby came, all the romantic idealism would go out the window." She shares a knowing smile with me.

"Then reality hits you!" I interject. "I remember my pregnancy was so much fun—with all the showers and cute little baby things. Except for those grueling last weeks, pregnancy was certainly idyllic compared with the reality of how a baby affects your life."

"And as much as you think you're ready, there's just no way you can ever really be prepared," she adds.

"Yeah, it's just one of those things in life you have to live through to understand," I say. "There's no substitute for being there." With relief, I remember that my youngest is finally in preschool.

"You know what I don't miss about those early years?" she asks. "I don't miss the lost pacifiers that made us drive around at 2:00 A.M. in search of an open drugstore. I also don't miss cutting out diaper coupons or the combination of drool and silk blouses. And how can we forget the 3:00 A.M. wake-up calls? There were nights I'd have given anything for a full night's sleep. Mine never did sleep through the night until he was three."

"What about the mystery-colored poop, the low-grade fevers after DPT shots, and the appearing-disappearing rashes? I never knew if or when to call the doctor. We were sure someone would turn us in for child neglect!" I say, carrying the conversation to the most outrageous scenario.

The coffee break is over, and we both need to get back to more immediate concerns.

"The one thing I miss least," I say, "is the unsolicited advice from all those 'I've-been-there' experts. It's not that I didn't appreciate hearing others' harrowing tales. I mean, the stories helped me to know I wasn't going crazy. But advice is another thing. Somehow other people's experiences just didn't make mine less trying."

Again we look at each other knowingly, and we part with these words of remembrance between us.

Dear God, thank you for friends who understand, but, most of all, thank you for enabling us to "make it through" new experiences with little or no preparation. Memories may fade, but we keep the lessons of life.

DECEMBER 18

"Mom, I want a GI Joe."

"Oh, you want a male doll?"

"No, Mom. Girls have dolls. Guys have action figures," my son informs me. He hesitates and then continues. "Mom, I want one of those games where the frogs hop, hop, hop all over."

"They don't really hop. The commercial just makes them look like they do," I tell him.

"Mom, I want a car with a motor, you know, the kind I could really ride in!"

I don't answer. It's clear that the "I wants" have broken out like a bad rash. It's the first year that our youngest has been bitten by the Christmas consumer bug.

"I think we should practice a bit of 'creative deprivation' this year," my husband says.

"He certainly has a bad case of the 'gimmies,'" I say.

We agree that our son can ask for two items that we all can "live with," but no more. We are not bad parents because we won't "buy Christmas" for our children. During this holy season, there are too many things on our own "want list" for our children to jeopardize the true gifts of the season.

We want them to enjoy the gift of reflective moments: lighting the Advent candles, attending the Christmas Eve service, and seeing the tree lit for the first time this year. We want to give them the gift of seasonal sounds—of their own voices singing manger lullabies, of someone playing "Silent Night" on the piano, and of old records playing on the phonograph. We want time together with family and friends, old and new, as we tell again the story of a babe born in Bethlehem who instills in us the most precious gift of all: *love*.

Dear God, help us to teach our children the real meaning of Christmas so that, most of all, they may want the gift of your Son, Jesus Christ.

DECEMBER 19

"Honey? Could you just go watch TV for a bit? Mommy is really tired and wants to rest a few minutes," I say to my five-year-old. It was an exhausting day at work, and the commute home in the last-minute Christmas shopping rush doubled my usual travel time. Now I simply want to sit and stare.

"But you said we could bake Christmas cookies tonight when you got home," he whines.

"Oh Stephen, why don't we wait until tomorrow night?"

"That's what you said last night," he reminds me. "And I really wanted to take some to my teacher for the Christmas party." Then he lowers the boom, adding the clincher to his argument: "Besides, *you promised!*"

"Okay! At least let me go change my clothes first," I snap as I get up off the chair and head up the stairs.

"Then forget it!" he retaliates. "I don't even want to make the dumb old cookies with you!" He stomps from the room.

As I sit on the edge of the bed, I sigh deeply and take off my heels. I catch sight of the reflected woman in the dresser mirror. I'm not pleased with the scene between my son and me, nor with myself. I think I'll go apologize to my son—and bake cookies.

Dear God, sometimes the parent is the one in most need of forgiveness. Help me to be patient and sensitive as I interact with my child after a long and trying day; and remind me to make the most of our time together, for childhood does not last forever.

DECEMBER 20

It was an early-morning conversation several months ago.

"Stephen, what did you learn in Sunday school this week?" I ask. Reviewing the Bible story he learned in Sunday school is part of our weekly ritual.

"I learned about Moses," Stephen responds and turns to his coloring.

"What did you learn about Moses?" I coax. It's a bit like pulling teeth to get him started, but then the story spills forth in a rendition only a child could tell.

"When Moses was a little child, his mother pushed him down the river in a basket, and then he got found by a princess. When he got a little bigger, he killed somebody. Then he took his people away from the pharaoh, and they caught food because of the birds and the bread. Today he climbed up his mountain and prayed to God. On two stones God made ten rules."

I sit on the edge of my seat waiting to hear his rendition of the Ten Commandments, and I'm not disappointed. Stephen begins:

"You shouldn't kill.

You shouldn't steal.

You shouldn't blame somebody else when they didn't do anything.

You should trust some people and don't trust others.

Everyone should have freedom.

You should have faith.

You should listen to your mom and dad.

You should be nice to your friends.

You're supposed to pray to God."

Stephen pauses, his forehead furrowed, pondering deeply.

"That's only nine rules, Stephen," I remind him. "You said there were ten."

"Oh yeah. The last one is 'be careful.' "

Dear God, I thank you for my child's lesson that calls me back to the basics of practicing my faith in concrete ways. With childlike faith, help us to place your rules for living in our hearts.

DECEMBER 21

The constant banter of the TV set sitting in our family room has simply become a part of our everyday lives. Amid the constant blare of the comedy shows, the music videos, and the news broadcasts, we carry on with our day-to-day lives. It has become like the background music played over the intercom in the mall—heard but not paid attention to.

"Let's face it; our kids spend more time listening to sitcom moms and dads than to us," I lament to my husband.

"Yeah, and now Stephen insists we call him by the names of his latest cartoon heroes, or he won't respond," Dale says.

"And Christian may not be able to name the twelve apostles, but he sure knows the names of the music video 'veejays,'" I add.

"Maybe this statistic in the morning paper is correct, but *twenty-eight hours* of viewing each week? That's a lot of commercials!" he says.

"But I'll bet that if we kept a record of our children's TV time for a week, it would come pretty close to that," I say. "I hate to admit it, but perhaps it's time we 'tame the tube.'"

We make the announcement to our two sons. It's not received with warm affirmations.

"But, Mom, I always watch my favorite re-run at 6:30!" Stephen protests.

"Yes, but now I want us to do more things together instead," I say calmly.

"Like what?" he asks skeptically.

I am prepared for this question.

"Like playing a game of checkers. Or you could exercise with me as I watch my workout video. Or we could read a good book."

It's clear we share different interests.

"There are a lot of things we could do!" I say, pushing on. I'm beginning to sound falsely enthusiastic, even to myself. His frown is growing.

"Or we could go outside and play football," I add in a last-ditch effort.

Where did *that* come from? It's cold outside, and I don't even know how to play football! Suddenly images of tackles and blocks flash through my mind. I visualize someone getting hurt—probably me.

"Okay," he says. He's smiling now as he switches off the set. The room suddenly takes on an eerie silence. "Now that sounds like fun," he continues. "Let's go!"

We pick up the football and walk outdoors into the great unknown.

Dear God, we do want quality family time, but we also know we are the ones who must make it a priority in our daily schedules in order for it to happen. I want my children to see me as a friend and companion as well as a parent. As we spend time together as a family, may we reinforce the values and strengthen the beliefs we hold dear.

DECEMBER 22

I've just come in from my daily commute only to hear the crash at the other end of the house. I walk quickly to the living room to find my husband and five-year-old son on the floor with pieces of the nativity set scattered around them. It is clear to see that in the fall, the wise man has lost his head and the shepherd is shattered into tiny glass fragments beyond repair.

"We were just playing hide and seek," my husband explains as he peers up at me sheepishly.

"I was hiding. Daddy was seeking," my son adds as he rubs his head to indicate how this accident happened.

"I can't believe you two did this!" I say angrily. "What were you romping in the living room for in the first place?" As I pick up the angel's wing, my eyes meet those of my bewildered son.

"Look, Mom, Mary and Baby Jesus are all right," he points out. Sure enough, the crèche filled with straw buffered the fall of the figurines so that they are still intact.

"And we can glue the wise man's head back on," my husband adds with a warning look in his eye and an edge to his voice.

He clearly sees the impending conversational disaster that could leave not only the nativity set but also us in pieces for the evening.

Dear God, replace my temper with forgiving love, and my impatience with understanding. And as I encounter trying situations with my children and loved ones, may I always seek your wisdom.

DECEMBER 23

The Christmas after my first husband's death was unbearable. Throughout the day I lived in fear of the sobs that began in the empty part of my stomach, worked their way up into my throat, and then lodged there. When the sorrow welled up past the point of endurance, I retired to the only place of privacy, the family bathroom. There I fought off the screams of fear and sadness that threatened to swallow me up. When and where others of the family cried, no one said. The grief remained unexpressed.

My then three-year-old son, Christian, wasn't as aware of his father's absence but only of my untouchable sorrow. He broke the unspoken rule.

"Mom, don't feel sad today," he said as he wrapped his arms around my leg. He led me to the rocking chair, sat me down, and crawled up into my lap. Then we began the slow, methodical swaying rhythm I had used to calm him as a baby. With his small hands he stroked my head as finally I allowed tears to quietly flow. He cried too—for me. We sat rocking for a long spell.

"It'll be all right. You'll see," he reassured me. "You still have me."

Dear God, there are no easy explanations to the "Why?" of death and suffering. But you give us new relationships—not to replace the lost ones but to help mend our broken hearts. Thank you for the healing power of a child's love.

DECEMBER 24

There is a knock at the front door to which all four of us respond. It is Christmas Eve, and we are eager to see who it might be.

"Good evening, Sir," a middle-aged man peers at us through the cracked door. We take the chain off, inviting him to step in out of the cold.

"Good evening, John. What can I do for you?" Dale greets him.

John is our "can man." Each Monday he makes his usual rounds to our curbside recycling bins, rummaging for the aluminum and glass that bring him a few cents per pound. I also give my greetings and then, along with my older son, Christian, exit to busy myself elsewhere. We know why he's come, and we are sensitive to his embarrassment. I leave Stephen and Dale to continue the conversation.

"I went to the recycling center to cash in my cans but found it wasn't open," John says. "I guess I forgot they would close early tonight, it being Christmas and all."

"Yeah, it's amazing that even in our big city things still close up pretty tight tonight," Dale agrees.

They continue with some small talk as Dale asks about his wife and kids. John is a recovering drug addict and father of two. This past summer John confided to Dale that he and his wife were both diagnosed with AIDS. Even though we know the statistics for AIDS and HIV infections in the metropolitan area, we were still stunned by the death of our neighbor at Thanksgiving and now by the diagnosis of John and his wife.

Stephen continues to stand intently by his dad's side, gazing at the two men in conversation.

"Well, I've stashed the cart of cans for the night, but now I don't have any money to take the bus home," John says.

"Here," Dale says as he slips him a five.

"Thanks, I really do appreciate this," he responds.

Dale and Stephen come to the kitchen to pack groceries from the shelf, an act performed numerous times each month. Stephen takes the bag back to the front door and hands it to John. The three talk a few more minutes, and then I hear Stephen ask, "Where's your coat, John?"

"I don't have one," John replies.

My husband reaches into the hall closet and hands John a coat.

"Thanks. I'll return it," John promises.

"If you want to, okay. But if you need the coat, keep it. Merry Christmas, John."

"Merry Christmas, Dale."

Smiling, John shakes Stephen's hand and runs for the bus.

Dear God, thank you for the opportunities we have to give the gift of love and to teach our children the importance of this gift.

DECEMBER 25

It was a Christmas evening several years ago.

"What a day!" I say with a deep sigh. The kids have gone up to bed with the promise that we'll be up to read a book and tuck them in. At the end of this Christmas Day, we sit on the sofa in the light of the tinseled tree. In this romantic moment, we're entwined in one another's arms.

"I think the kids had a great day. I know I did!" my husband says.

"I like our quiet Christmases together. I always feel like we are wrapped in a cocoon filled with so many good times and special traditions," I respond. Our traditions are a combination of those we inherited from our families and others that we've simply made up on our own.

I think about how special this Christmas Day has been, because one or both of us are usually scheduled to work during the holiday and because we live so far from family that we are not able to celebrate with them.

"I really cherish this day," I say aloud. "Maybe it sounds self-ish, but I'm glad we have this time that is just ours as a family. I like the quietness of it after so much hustle and bustle."

We soak in the silence, enjoying the luxury of the moment.

"Mom? Dad? When are you coming up? I'm ready to read my book!" our youngest son says, breaking in on the moment. My husband and I look at each other and smile.

"We are so blessed," I say, rising to pull the plug on the tree.

"We certainly are," he agrees.

Dear God, thank you for all the blessings of Christmases past, present, and those yet to come.

DECEMBER 26

"Our son just trooped through the kitchen with five other kids in tow," I say to my husband with the wall-phone tucked under my chin as I fold clothes.

He's at work; I'm at home taking vacation days during the Christmas holiday school break. It's rare that we can take the same days off. Instead, we stagger vacation days to meet child-care needs.

"I'd better let you go, then, so you can do what you need to," he says. "Besides, my break is almost over."

I hang up the phone and walk into the living room. My son Stephen and the neighborhood kids have just shed their coats and are oohing and ahhing over our Christmas tree.

"Mom, I thought we could have some of those chocolate cookies—and Monique, Latiqua, and Cedric want some milk, too," Stephen says, acting the part of the grown-up host. I go to the kitchen to prepare a tray.

Rearing my children in a big city is certainly different from the way my parents reared me. I grew up in a comparatively small community where my friends had names like Betty, Joe, and Dave. Because I grew up in an all-white European-American neighborhood, I was unaware of the rich diversity I had missed. Now, because we are one of two white families on the block, I am slowly overcoming the "dis-ease" the transition has evoked. The children have found new friends, and so we have we. These people are part of our everyday lives, and we are part of theirs.

My son runs into the kitchen. "Come on, Mom. Here, let me help," he says as he picks up the carton of milk cautiously. I carry in the cookies and glasses and thankfully deliver them to the lovely miracles under my Christmas tree.

God, thanks for all the miracles of Christmas, especially the miracle of children. May we adults embrace the unconditional love and acceptance that come so naturally to our children.

DECEMBER 27

My friend and I compare notes over coffee and bagels—light on the cream cheese.

"I know it's the Christmas season, but you seem to stay in good spirits all year," she says. "What keeps you going?"

"If only you knew!" I say with a laugh, stalling my response. I want to give her an answer worthy of the question. "Politics," I say.

She smiles, half stunned. She knows my political views.

"Yeah," I continue, "anytime I'm beginning to feel compla cent, some government invades another country, cuts another human right, or makes some questionable political appoint-ment, and I'm awakened from my creeping apathy. [I'm on a roll now.] I'd also have to say my faith and spiritual life—and other friends who share my journey."

She gives me that look that says she expected me to say this. She urges me on in the exercise.

"But I think a major reason I keep on are my children," I tell her. "At night when I tuck them into bed, they give me a hope that is deep and enduring. They hold the promise of the future and give me the courage to do God's work so that things don't remain as they are. Children are God's agents of hope."

We agree in parting that these answers are not carved in stone but are open to God's refinement.

Dear God, thank you for the gift of hope you give me every day through my children.

DECEMBER 28

It is a brisk, sunny day, and I am taking a walk with my son, Stephen. It is nice to be home for the holidays this year, and I relish the soft, sweet feel of his hand in mine. After a while, I notice that our pace has slowed. We've begun to climb an incline—a small effort to me but a steep climb to my small son. And then I overhear him mumbling, repeating something under his breath. I listen more closely and hear this:

"With God, nothing is impossible. With God, nothing is impossible. With God, nothing is impossible. . . . "

At that moment I am flooded with a strange refreshment of spirit. I recognize it as a joy that touches a mother when her children delight her. My child has not asked for support or rest; he has simply energized himself up the hill by drawing on the angel's words to Mary in a familiar Bible story: "For nothing will be impossible with God" (Luke 1:37).

That walk stays with me, reminding me that the Bible stories we tell our children are so much more than old tales of people who lived long ago. For children and for us, these stories are also keys to the Christian life. They are lessons about how to live and be in God's world.

It tickles me to know that someday I will have the pleasure

of telling my once-little boy about the time a Bible story helped him, and me, overcome a hill.

Dear God, may stories of courageous people in the Bible continue to prepare us and our children for the challenging obstacles to come.

DECEMBER 29

Christian and I sort through boxes of old toys as we clean out the attic and prepare to put away the Christmas decorations. On top of the pile are a stack of old 45 LPs.

"It's a shame to get rid of these records," Christian says with a touch of sadness. "Remember 'Curious George'? And here's 'Sleeping Beauty.' Maybe we should keep them."

"And use what to play them? The old record player just doesn't turn anymore," I say.

"Yeah, and now Stephen has a tape player," he says, referring to one of his brother's favorite toys. "And you and Dad have the CD player."

"CDs didn't even exist when you were born," I say.

"What else has changed during the years between when I and Stephen were born?" he asks, continuing to sort through the records.

"Well," I say, "when you were a baby, I used cloth diapers." I enjoy reminiscing. "Paper ones were seen as a luxury, and we used them only when traveling on vacation or going to church."

"TV hasn't changed much. It's pretty much the same," Christian notes. "We both watched 'Sesame Street.'"

"Yes, but now Stephen has the option of watching commercial-free videos, whereas you had only commercial-filled television programs. I think he has better choices, and I like being able to control his viewing to a greater extent. That's one change for the better," I reflect.

The telephone rings, breaking in on our conversation.

"I think we should keep the 45s, Mom. You never know

when the old record player might start working again," he says.

My teenage son slides the pile of records from his lap to get up from the floor and run for the phone.

Dear God, some things in our world have changed—many for the better. But the basics remain the same. We still believe that Christian values must be taught, that our children must get and give respect, and that laughter should always be encouraged. As our children grow and things change even more, continue to remind us of "the basics."

DECEMBER 30

"Mom, are you writing about me again?" my young son asks as he peers over my shoulder.

"Yes. I'm busy," I reply. I've been struggling with the last few meditations, and Stephen knows how frequently he shows up in my manuscripts. You can't live with a six-year-old boy and not have him impinge in whatever project you undertake!

"What's the title of the story?" he asks, inserting himself into my world again.

"It doesn't have a title," I answer impatiently.

I begin to record our conversation—a technique he's seen me use before. The other piece I'm working on just isn't coming together. I'll do anything to divert from my work. It's called procrastination. He notices.

"You mean you're writing this down?" Stephen asks.

"Yes, I'm writing this down," I say.

"Mom? Mom, stop. *Stop!*"

I continue writing.

"I want to talk to you! *Now!*" he says as he grabs at my hand, causing my pen to slide sideways off the paper.

"Okay, Stephen, talk!" I say, pretending to sound irritated. He sees through the pretense.

"Now, Mom, write this: 'Stephen has one turtle and two cats.' You got that?"

"Yes," I assure him. He sees me writing steadily, and so he presses on.

"Good. Now write 'He plays with his friends a lot.' Gee, that's a fancy way of writing, Mom." He notes my hurriedly scribbled script.

"It's called cursive writing," I inform him. "You'll learn it in a couple of years." I poise my pen for more input, and I'm not disappointed.

"Write 'My mom and dad and brother love me very, very much.' And say 'God is a wonderful person who makes some of our dreams come true, and God loves everybody' . . . and that's it. I'm done now. No, no wait. Tell them 'Stephen is a very good boy.' Now I'm done. But remember to write 'The End.'" He sits down contentedly in the chair beside me, watching me type his words into the computer.

"What should I title it, Stephen?" I ask before he flys off to yet another household adventure.

"Call it 'Stephen Asks His Mom Questions and Tells Stuff About God and Himself and His Mom and Dad and Brother. Amen.'"

Dear God, thank you for the interruptions in my work that call me back to the basic love of my family and of you.

DECEMBER 31

My computer screen is blank—not one dot or letter, only that slow-flashing square begging me to type someting, *anything*. Mercifully, the telephone rings.

"This is me," the familiar voice says. "I knew today was your deadline to complete your meditations. I called to congratulate you! Come over for tea and we'll celebrate."

"Don't move too fast," I say reproachfully. "I'm trying to

write my last one, and it just won't come. Believe me, it's really hard writing Christmas in July!"

"What is it you want to say in the end?" she coaxes.

"I guess I simply want to talk about children and grace. I want to say that we rear them the best we can, taking each day and each year as it comes. Some of our decisions we're pleased with, and others we're not. But we do the best we can for who we are in the moment, we forgive or celebrate, and we move on."

"That seems pretty clear to me," she says. "So why don't you just say that?"

"I think we just did," I say.

"Happy new year, friend."

"God's blessings to you, too."

Dear God, thank you for the blessed opportunity to be a mother. As I strive to be the best mother I can be in each moment, help me to learn from my mistakes and remind me to celebrate the joys. May I always see the blessings in each.